Medieval Imaginaries in ' Heritage and the Media

CW00760523

This book examines the pervading influence of medieval culture, through an exploration of the intersections between tourism, heritage, and imaginaries of the medieval in the media.

Drawing on examples from tourist destinations, heritage sites, fictional literature, television and cinema, the book illustrates how the medieval period has consistently captured the imagination of audiences and has been reinvented for contemporary tastes. Chapters present a range of international examples, from nineteenth-century Victorian notions of chivalry, knights in shining armour exemplified by King Arthur, and damsels in distress, to the imagining of the Japanese samurai as medieval knights. Other topics explored include the changing representations of medieval women, the Crusades and the Vikings, and the challenges faced by medieval cathedrals to survive economically and socially.

This book offers multidisciplinary perspectives and will appeal to scholars and students across a variety of disciplines such as cultural studies, history, tourism, heritage studies, historical geography and sociology.

Jennifer Frost is Associate Professor in the Department of Management, Sport and Tourism at La Trobe University, Australia. She is Co-editor-in-Chief of the *Journal of Heritage Tourism* and her research interests include travel narratives, heritage tourism and rural tourism and events.

Warwick Frost is Professor of Heritage, Tourism and the Media in the Department of Management, Sport and Tourism at La Trobe University, Australia. He is Co-editor-in-Chief of the *Journal of Heritage Tourism* and his research interests include heritage tourism and tourism and the media.

Routledge Cultural Heritage and Tourism Series

Series editor: Dallen J. Timothy,
Arizona State University, USA

The Routledge Cultural Heritage and Tourism Series offers an interdisciplinary social science forum for original, innovative and cutting-edge research about all aspects of cultural heritage-based tourism. This series encourages new and theoretical perspectives and showcases ground-breaking work that reflects the dynamism and vibrancy of heritage, tourism and cultural studies. It aims to foster discussions about both tangible and intangible heritages, and all of their management, conservation, interpretation, political, conflict, consumption and identity challenges, opportunities and implications. This series interprets heritage broadly and caters to the needs of upper-level students, academic researchers, and policy makers.

Deconstructing Eurocentric Tourism and Heritage Narratives in Mexican American Communities
Juan de Oñate as a West Texas Icon
Frank G. Perez and Carlos F. Ortega

Creating Heritage
Unrecognised Pasts and Rejected Futures
Edited by Thomas Carter, David C. Harvey, Roy Jones, and Iain J.M. Robertson

The Economics and Finance of Cultural Heritage
How to Make Tourist Attractions a Regional Economic Resource
Vincenzo Pacelli and Edgardo Sica

Urban Recovery
Intersecting Displacement with Post War Reconstruction
Edited by Howayda Al-Harithy

Resilience, Authenticity and Digital Heritage Tourism
Deepak Chhabra

Cultural Heritage and Tourism in Japan
Takamitsu Jimura

Medieval Imaginaries in Tourism, Heritage and the Media
Jennifer Frost and Warwick Frost

For more information about this series, please visit : https://www.routledge.com/Routledge-Cultural-Heritage-and-Tourism-Series/book-series/RCHT

Medieval Imaginaries in Tourism, Heritage and the Media

Jennifer Frost and Warwick Frost

Routledge
Taylor & Francis Group

LONDON AND NEW YORK

First published 2022
by Routledge
2 Park Square, Milton Park, Abingdon, Oxon OX14 4RN

and by Routledge
605 Third Avenue, New York, NY 10158

Routledge is an imprint of the Taylor & Francis Group, an informa business

British Library Cataloguing-in-Publication Data
A catalogue record for this book is available from the British Library

Library of Congress Cataloging-in-Publication Data
A catalog record has been requested for this book

ISBN: 978-0-367-13277-4 (hbk)
ISBN: 978-1-032-05391-2 (pbk)
ISBN: 978-0-429-02561-7 (ebk)

Typeset in Times New Roman
by Straive, India

Contents

Figures

Table

Acknowledgements

We would like to thank Professor Jonathan Wooding, Sir Warwick Fairfax Professor of Celtic Studies at the University of Sydney, for his kind assistance and advice on Chapter 7 of the book. Our grateful thanks also go to our families, who, like us, have a fascination with the medieval world and have enjoyed many of the media productions and tourism attractions that we discuss throughout this work.

1 The continuing fascination for the medieval

Introduction: Dubrovnik and *Game of Thrones*

For many of us, Dubrovnik conjures up vivid images of the siege in 1991, when the breakup of Yugoslavia saw the medieval walled city hit by sustained bombing by the Serbian army for three months. It had been designated a World Heritage site by UNESCO just 12 years earlier and was a popular destination for tourists. Sandwiched between Split and Kotor on the Dalmatian Coast, Dubrovnik was the most well-known of the three medieval masterpieces. The majority of the visitors had fled, and international television news broadcasts were filled with searing images of crumbling buildings, sniper attacks and the death of civilians, in what was described by the International War Crimes Tribunal in The Hague as, 'wanton destruction' with, 'devastation not justified by military necessity' (Wood, 2001). It had survived an earthquake in 1667, but this level of damage was crippling. The Old Town was placed on UNESCO's list of endangered sites and removed only in 1998. Its medieval heritage was subsequently restored, and today, it is difficult to find remnants of the war. The restoration work has been sensitively carried out; avoiding a Disney version of the city that looks like it has been newly built, while at the same time not aiming for fake antiquity. The wounds to the physical fabric essentially look like the result of the passage of time and add to the ambience of what is again a premier drawcard for tourists.

Nowadays, visitors pour off cruise boats and head to the walls and streets of the Old Town, whose shops, bars and restaurants largely depend on the constant foot traffic (Figure 1.1). The large number of cruise boats that dock in Dubrovnik's harbour has been criticised for leading to *over-tourism*, 'the excessive growth of visitors leading to overcrowding in areas where residents suffer the consequences of temporary and seasonal tourism peaks, which have caused permanent changes to their lifestyles, denied access to amenities and damaged their general well-being' (Milano, Novelli and Cheer, 2019: 354). Dubrovnik is often cited as one of the worst examples of this along with other medieval cities such as Venice, Granada, Barcelona and Malta (Milano *et al.*, 2019). The appeal of these hotspots is partly an attractive medieval core such as the winding streets of Barcelona's Old Town (Ciutat Vella) and Gothic District (Barri Gòtic), and partly iconic medieval architecture like St Mark's Basilica in Venice and Granada's Alhambra Royal Palace. The high level of visitation of these destinations reflects a widespread fascination with the heritage of the medieval period.

Figure 1.1 Tourists in the Old Town of Dubrovnik.
Source: Jennifer Frost.

Dubrovnik, however, has one further string to its bow. It has been used as the setting for a number of film and television productions in recent years, including *Star Wars: The Last Jedi* (2017) and *Robin Hood* (2018), but is best known as the location for King's Landing, the capital of the imaginary medieval kingdom of Westeros in *Game of Thrones* (2011–2019). Based on the book series *A Song of Ice and Fire* (1996–2011) by George R. R. Martin and set in the fictional world of Westeros and Essos, *Game of Thrones* is not only a fantasy where knights fight with swords and joust in tournaments and dragons really exist, but additionally, Martin has adapted many historical incidents and themes from medieval history (Larrington, 2016). For a television series, *Game of Thrones* was distinguished by very high production values, spearheading the modern trend for television productions to aim for a look and feel comparable to cinematic blockbusters. This was in part achieved by the exceptional use of attractive locations in Croatia, Iceland, Northern Ireland and Iceland, all places that have consequently attracted increased tourism flows as a result (Waysdorf and Reijnders, 2017). In the first season, the scenes of King's Landing were shot in Malta, but after that, production was shifted to Dubrovnik to take advantage of better financial and logistical inducements. In tourism terms, Dubrovnik benefited from a 38% increase in tourist arrivals between 2011 and 2015, a period in which a financial recession meant that most competing destinations were experiencing a decline in visitation (Tkalec, Zilic and Recher, 2017). For fans, the appeal of Dubrovnik as King's Landing was that:

Most of the characters are linked to this city, and because it is the capital, it is a place of political plots, intrigues and secrets. The medieval-like context of the series highlights Dubrovnik's most attractive tourist assets such as the rich and preserved historic town center.

(Tkalec *et al.*, 2017: 707)

We conducted our fieldwork in 2019, following on from visits to other *Game of Thrones* locations in Girona and Seville in Spain. The series had just concluded, and in entering the city, we were immediately struck that we had seen the Stradun (Main Street) completely destroyed only weeks before in the penultimate episode 'The Bells'. Such devastation, we would later learn, was achieved through an elaborate CGI representation of King's Landing comprised of multiple shots of Dubrovnik. Even so, it was a somewhat disconcerting juxtaposition, following on from the interpretive panels next to the city walls regarding the 1991 bombardment that we had only read minutes before.

We participated in a commercial all-day *Game of Thrones* tour (Figure 1.2). In the morning, we walked around the city with a group of about 20 fellow fans, listening to a guide explain how certain sites had been used in the series. A major undertaking was climbing the steep stairs up to Fort Lovrjeniac (Fort St Lawrence), which stands in for the Red Keep, the main citadel of King's Landing. Here, the guide produced a series of laminated A4 stills from the series, matching them to our various stopping points. Returning to the city, the tour followed a

Figure 1.2 Tourists on the *Game of Thrones* Tour.
Source: Jennifer Frost.

similar pattern, with the guide stopping every few minutes and explaining key scenes at various spots. In many cases, we had walked past these in the preceding days without grasping their significance in terms of the show. In the afternoon, we took a ferry to the island of Lokrum to see the Iron Throne set from the series and then a 24 km bus trip to Arboretum Trsteno, which stood in for the palace gardens of King's Landing on-screen.

As fans of the show, we found the tour stimulating and revealing, providing us with deep insights into a production with which we were highly engaged. We found our experience to be similar to Waysdorf and Reijnders's observation of a similar tour in Dubrovnik, 'rather than a complete immersion in fantasy, the key places instead function as ways to grasp the narrative in greater detail and precision' (2017: 179). As the tour took place in the crowded public spaces of Dubrovnik, complete immersion was difficult, and it was notable that none of our fellow tour members dressed in costume or attempted to re-enact scenes – as has been recorded for other film tours. Even though our primary interest was in the television series, the tour contained a great deal of historical explanation, particularly in relation to the form and usage of medieval structures utilised in filming the show. A fascinating element of our tour was the emphasis on the artifice of film-making, particularly how set-design and camera angles were used to make the real Dubrovnik look like a much larger fantasy city. Such themes generated a feeling that we had been privileged to go 'behind the scenes' and better understand how the show was made (this aspect was also recorded by Waysdorf and Reijnders and other researchers on film-tourism tours around the world).

The association with *Game of Thrones* arguably adds another intriguing layer to medieval Dubrovnik for many visitors, forming a *palimpsest* of narratives that warrant discovery. The origins of this word relate to the re-use of old manuscripts, which have been 'over-written with more recent text, but the older text can be seen showing through' (Marvell and Simm, 2016: 126). It can be applied as a metaphor to the idea of place, where 'layers of meaning … can include attributes such as geography, history, culture, socio-economics, arts, architecture and language' (p. 126). Another way of conceptualising this is to refer to places as a *cultural landscape*, which is not just a collection of heritage buildings to be conserved but also includes *associative landscapes* where there are, 'religious, cultural or artistic associations with the natural environment rather than any significant or present material culture' (Jewell and McKinnon, 2008: 153). For many medieval places, like Dubrovnik, the overlay of media such as literature, films, television and now video games contributes to the cultural landscape but also *relies* on the continued existence of these medieval urbanscapes, in a form of symbiotic relationship.

Medievalism and the media

The medieval period has consistently captured popular imagination, but not just in current times. As Eco (1986) noted, 'The Middle Ages have always been messed up in order to meet the vital requirements of different periods' (p. 68). This is an example of *medievalism*, which Pugh and Weisl defined as:

The art, literature, scholarship, avocational pastimes, and sundry forms of entertainment and culture that turn to the Middle Ages for their subject matter or inspiration, and in doing so, explicitly or implicitly, by comparison or by contrast, comment on the artist's contemporary sociocultural milieu.

(2013: 1)

The medieval is represented across a range of modern media, including film, television, literature and art. Those representations – and how they affect how we imagine the medieval – will be discussed more deeply throughout the book, but some exemplars are introduced here.

Novels: Sir Walter Scott started the fashion for 'historical romances' set in the medieval period with *Ivanhoe* (1819). More recent novels have tended to take a darker and grittier view of the period, as in *The Name of the Rose* (Eco, 1980) and Bernard Cornwell's 13-book *Last Kingdom* series (2004–2019). Many fantasy works are set in fictional worlds that are essentially medieval, but with magical elements and mythical creatures. These include *The Lord of the Rings* trilogy by J. R. R. Tolkien and Martin's *Game of Thrones* series. There are also medieval works aimed at children and young adults, again often with fantasy elements. Examples include *The Sword in the Stone* (White, 1939) and *The Letter for the King* (Dragt, 1962). It is notable that all of these works have been adapted for cinema and/or television.

Cinema: The incidence of films specifically associated with the key medieval figures of Robin Hood and King Arthur spans over a century. Examples include: *Robin Hood* (1922) with Douglas Fairbanks, *The Adventures of Robin Hood* (1938) which made Errol Flynn a star, *The Knights of the Round Table* (1953) and, more recently, *King Arthur: Legend of the Sword* (2017) and *Robin Hood* (2018). Other more broadly medieval-themed films include *The Vikings* (1958), *Braveheart* (1995) and *A Knight's Tale* (2001). Whilst many Hollywood productions have been criticised as formulaic and low-brow, there are critically acclaimed examples of medieval-themed cinema from non-English sources, such as Russia's *Alexander Nevsky* (1938), the Japanese *Seven Samurai* (1954) and Sweden's *The Seventh Seal* (1957) (Aberth, 2003). The cinematic predilection for medievalism has also led to films that spoof the period like *Monty Python and the Holy Grail* (1975) and *The Princess Bride* (1987).

Television: Early television representations of the medieval tended to be English and limited by their budgets. These include various iterations of *Robin Hood* (1953, 1955–1960, 1984–1986), while *Doctor Who* (1963–2020) has time-travelled to the medieval period on at least six occasions. In recent years, television has become more highly focussed on the medieval, recognising a strong public appetite for high-quality productions with complex plots and characters. Examples of these include *Merlin* (2008–2013), *Game of Thrones* (2011–2019), *Vikings* (2013–2021) and *Knightfall* (2017–2019).

Heritage tourism

The medieval period underpins a range of successful heritage tourist experiences and attractions. Tourists flock to medieval old towns with historic streetscapes, historic gems where economic change has preserved areas from modern development such as York (England), Girona (Spain), Dubrovnik (Croatia), Bergamo and San Gimignano (Italy), Sighişoara (Romania) and Bruges (Belgium); castles such as Chinon and Chateau d'Angers in France and Alnwick, Warwick and Windsor in England; cathedrals like Notre Dame in Paris, St Marks in Venice, Monreale in Sicily, Cologne in Germany, Hagia Sophia in Istanbul and the Mosque-Cathedral of Córdoba in Spain; and collections of preserved medieval buildings, sometimes marketed as a precinct, with examples including the Old St Elizabeth Beguinage in Ghent, Belgium, and Spon Street in Coventry, England. Medieval-themed visitor attractions include theme parks like Puy du Fou in France, Medieval Times in Florida, United States, combining dinner theatre and a mock tournament, and Disneyland's Fantasyland, a fairy-tale evocation of the medieval complete with its iconic castle (Bayless, 2012). A number of museums are based around medieval exhibits or collections – notably the Richard III Visitor Centre in Leicester, England, built to house the discovery of his body buried under a nearby carpark after years of searching (Buckley *et al.*, 2013), the Book of Kells exhibition in Dublin and the Medieval Museum in Waterford, Ireland; while there are medieval-themed exhibitions touring the globe, such as *Vikings: Life and Legend* (which we saw at the British Museum in 2014). Some tourists attend historical re-enactments based on important moments in medieval history, such as English Heritage's annual restaging of the Battle of Hastings in Battle, southern England (Figure 1.3), or Renaissance fairs and banquets. Tourism may also be centred on faux medieval reconstructions, such as Castello di Amorosa, the mock thirteenth-century Tuscan castle built as a winery in the Napa Valley of California and opened to the public in 2007 (Figure 1.4), and Kryal Castle in Ballarat, Australia, opened in 1974 and operating as a theme park, function venue and accommodation provider. This broad range of medieval-themed tourist products and experiences, located in many countries around the world, reflects Lowenthal's pithy observation that if the past is a foreign country, then it's 'a foreign country with a booming tourist trade' (1985: xvii).

The medieval world

While there is not space to provide an extensive overview of medieval history, it is important in this introduction to explain some key ideas from the period, as well as major historical events, to frame the discussion of modern imaginings of the medieval world. The medieval period is widely accepted to apply to Europe and span the period from 500 to 1500, roughly from the fall of the Roman Empire to the Reformation (Wickham, 2017). We have adopted this definition as a logical way to structure and bound the discussion, but also because it is generally used as the broad parameters of what we think of today as 'medieval'. Whilst generally applied to Western Europe, the medieval is also applicable to Eastern Europe, Scandinavia and the Iberian Peninsula.

Figure 1.3 Re-enacting the Battle of Hastings, 2011.
Source: Warwick Frost.

Figure 1.4 Castello di Amorosa.
Source: Warwick Frost.

The term 'medieval' itself is curious in that it was originally created to distinguish it from the time of the ancient or classical world – which was understood as an apotheosis of learning and creativity – and the modern period. That time period in between accordingly became known as the *medium aevum* or 'middle age', which was later turned into the phrase *medieval* (Wickham, 2017). Today, it is sometimes used as a derogatory term for something which is outdated and dysfunctional, even as we mythologise aspects of the period such as chivalry and courtly love. This is just one of the paradoxes that we will explore in this book.

The medieval period accordingly includes the *Dark Ages*, from approximately 500 to 1000. Like 'medieval', the term is pejorative, being utilised to 'portray the time as one of violence and chaos' (Wells, 2008: xiv). Its use has contributed to the erroneous perception that Western civilisation and culture regressed after the great flourishing of knowledge during classical antiquity, leading to a time of ignorance and prejudice. Though some writing flourished in pockets of learning, often centred on monasteries, the lack of written sources of the period meant that there is a greater reliance on archaeology to understand the period. Recent scholarship now disputes this bleak view, arguing that it was a time when culture continued to move forward (Wells, 2008). Examples often given to support this shift in understanding include the sophistication of the burial treasures found at Sutton Hoo, most of which are exhibited in the British Museum, and the glorious Byzantine mosaics at Ravenna. It was a period of technological advances in areas such as agriculture and metallurgy, while architecture also flourished, notably in the form of churches and fostered by the spread of Christianity throughout most of Europe after 500 (Wickham, 2017).

In this book, we refer to a number of major historical events of the period. A timeline shown in Figure 1.5 depicts these events, and also shows how they coincided with major events outside a Western context. This period covers the histories of diverse groups or societies such as the Vikings in Scandinavia, the Moors in Spain (Andalusia) and the Samurai in Japan, which are discussed in this book alongside more classical Western European histories, such as those of England, France, Germany and Italy. The timeline therefore shows useful corollaries such as the fact that around the time that Viking chief Ivar the Boneless captured York in 866, the Great Mosque in Córdoba was being built and Byzantium was on the rise again under the rule of the Emperor Basil I.

Whilst there is a reasonable consensus amongst historians as to what constitutes the medieval, we are conscious that not all laypeople may view this period in this way. Sturtevant (2012) conducted an interesting research study to investigate this. He asked young British adults (aged 18 to 26) to discuss their concept of the medieval. From this, he concluded that amongst non-historians, there was 'a similar vocabulary of settings and icons that have come to denote this period' and these 'powerful indicators of "medievalness"' included 'queens, knights, peasants, castles, horses and swords' (Sturtevant, 2012: 83). Geographically, they saw the medieval in quite narrow terms, applying it to Britain and France, while the story of Aladdin was excluded as it did not feature 'England, forest and that sort of setting … [it's] got a completely different setting' (Sturtevant, 2012: 84).

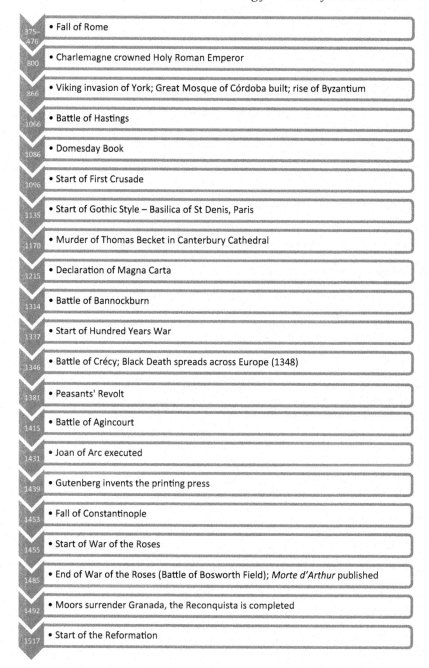

- 375–476 • Fall of Rome
- 800 • Charlemagne crowned Holy Roman Emperor
- 866 • Viking invasion of York; Great Mosque of Córdoba built; rise of Byzantium
- 1066 • Battle of Hastings
- 1086 • Domesday Book
- 1096 • Start of First Crusade
- 1135 • Start of Gothic Style – Basilica of St Denis, Paris
- 1170 • Murder of Thomas Becket in Canterbury Cathedral
- 1215 • Declaration of Magna Carta
- 1314 • Battle of Bannockburn
- 1337 • Start of Hundred Years War
- 1346 • Battle of Crécy; Black Death spreads across Europe (1348)
- 1381 • Peasants' Revolt
- 1415 • Battle of Agincourt
- 1431 • Joan of Arc executed
- 1439 • Gutenberg invents the printing press
- 1453 • Fall of Constantinople
- 1455 • Start of War of the Roses
- 1485 • End of War of the Roses (Battle of Bosworth Field); *Morte d'Arthur* published
- 1492 • Moors surrender Granada, the Reconquista is completed
- 1517 • Start of the Reformation

Figure 1.5 Timeline.

Such views suggest narrower definitions of the medieval, but also open up that stories set in later periods or fantasies may still be seen as medieval, as long as they contain these key markers.

Theoretical frameworks

In this book, we use several theoretical frameworks to shape the discussion. In this section, we will briefly introduce, review and justify the utility of six different theoretical frames, all of which collectively may shed light on the continued interest in the medieval period within tourism and popular culture.

The medieval as a shared heritage

Heritage is generally viewed as 'some sort of inheritance to be passed down to current and future generations', though it 'is not simply the past [or history], but the modern day use of elements of the past' (Timothy and Boyd, 2003: 2, 4). This modern-day use and interpretation often involves imaginaries of how we connect to the past. At a national level, the imagining of a *shared heritage* based on historical events, stories, myths and legends is one of the institutions that have developed to define identity and bind the citizens of countries together (Anderson, 1983). For modern-day European polities, the medieval has become an integral component of their national heritage.

Heritage is often contested, with multiple, dissonant – even irreconcilable – viewpoints and claims to ownership (Lowenthal, 1998; Timothy and Boyd, 2003; Tunbridge and Ashworth, 1996). This is because history is rarely absolute. Historians have no problems with this, but it is often confusing for government agencies and destination marketing organisations involved in developing heritage tourism attractions, who prefer to have certainty and clarity and are often over-worried about causing offence. Unfortunately, it is often little appreciated within the tourism industry that it is these differences and arguments that often make heritage engaging and compelling for many tourists (Frost, 2006).

In the competitive global tourism market, many European destinations have what marketing calls a 'unique selling proposition' in their medieval cultural heritage. As the medieval refers to a specific historical time and geographical region, only European destinations can claim that authenticity. Others outside of Europe can copy, with faux castles and renaissance fairs, but these are just a simulacrum, as most tourists generally know and accept. In monopolising medieval heritage tourism, Europe gains huge tourism flows through individual sites (such as castles) and more general urbanscapes (for example, Dubrovnik). Heritage is sometimes seen as arising from a personal connection, usually through ethnicity or family history (Timothy and Boyd, 2003). However, it is notable that many of the tourists who flock to Europe's medieval attractions have little or no direct connections. Many come from cultures outside of Europe. Others might claim European ancestry, but there is no living memory connection to the medieval, and most would struggle to push family histories back this far. For those who travel to Europe to experience the medieval, what do they see as valuable, worth preserving and relevant to the present and future? Our argument, as developed throughout this book, is that there is a global shared connection to the medieval which is mediated by film, books, myths and stories.

Authenticity and anachronism

If our view of history is shaped by the media, this raises the question of how accurate are these media representations. Indeed, it is often held that media versions of history, such as films and historical novels, are prone to inauthenticity (Frost, 2006). Such issues arise from the need to shape history to the form of the medium. Dutifully copying historical texts and evidence may result in productions that are too boring for commercial success (Rosenstone, 1995). Novelist Bernard Cornwell noted how necessary it was to make changes, as, 'history is rarely kind to historical novelists by providing a neat plot with great characters who act within a defined time period, so we are forced to manipulate history to make our own plots work' (2015: 8). Film studies researcher Paul Seydor was even blunter, commenting that:

> People who want history should read histories and biographies or watch documentaries. Novels, plays and films will always invent, distort or falsify because their priorities consist not in fidelity to facts but in telling good stories … adapting history to fiction, drama, or film always involves more elimination than inclusion, more reduction than expansion; composite characters have to be created; events discarded, changed, reordered, or invented for purposes of structure and plot.
>
> (2015: 278)

History provides constraints, and the challenge is how far these can be bent for narrative purposes. Much depends on the level of historical knowledge that is held by the potential audience (Frost, 2006). In terms of the medieval, 'this is why the overwhelming majority of medieval films deal with legendary material – King Arthur, Robin Hood – or with openly fictional characters, such as William Thatcher of *A Knight's Tale*' (Lindley, 2007: 19). A common approach is to mix fictional and historical characters. This was popularised in the novel *Ivanhoe* (1819), by Sir Walter Scott. The two main protagonists were rivals Wilfred of Ivanhoe and Brian de Bois-Guilbert. They were completely fictional, but interacted with historical figures in King Richard, Prince John and Robin Hood. This allowed Scott to:

> create secondary characters as heroes, so that he did not have to distort the historical material, but was still able to include adventures, love interests, triumph of good over evil and so on, which it would not have been possible to do with historical characters whose fate was too well documented.
>
> (Ortenberg, 2006: 48)

Film-makers often overly focus on the right historical imagery, reasoning that, 'as long as you get the look right you may freely invent characters and incidents and do whatever you want to the past to make it more interesting' (Rosenstone, 1995: 60). For the medieval, the right look usually includes the defining markers of castles and knights in armour. There is also a common approach of claiming historical accuracy and highlighting the research that was undertaken by film-makers. As Lowenthal comments, 'both the public and producers alike require a *semblance* of accuracy: historical films must be touted as "based on a true story"' (1998: 166). Such claims need to be treated cautiously, for 'filmmakers talk up historical research, as research is what directors and screenwriters have to say they have done because an illusion of factuality validates whatever lesson or parable they have in mind' (Lindley, 2007: 19).

Representing history comes with the risk of including anachronisms. For the medieval, the two most well-known are fourteenth-century armour and castles in Arthurian stories and Vikings with horned helmets. Neither are recent inventions, but rather come from earlier versions. With the surge of interest in Arthur during the late medieval period, it became commonplace to represent him and his knights in the fashion of the day. Accordingly, we still usually see him imagined that way rather than as an early medieval Romano-Briton. The horned helmet comes from nineteenth-century opera and book illustrations, and there is no material evidence for its existence (Williams, 2017). The other source of anachronisms is *multitemporality*, in which the media representation is like a mirror held up to the present and the medieval story is used to produce a commentary about current issues and concerns, even resulting in modern-style dialogue. An example of this is the *Chivalric Cycle* of the 1950s, which dealt with Cold War fears of covert infiltrators subverting the state for the benefit of a foreign power (Richards, 2008). Another is how the plague in *The Seventh Seal* suggests a nuclear apocalypse (Lindley, 2007). Whilst *The Adventures of Robin Hood* (1938) commented on Nazism and the New Deal, *Robin Hood* (2018) can be interpreted as pro-Brexit.

Eco's medieval typology

To better understand the modern fascination with the medieval, we utilise a framework developed by the Italian philosopher and novelist Umberto Eco. He reasoned that the continuing interest in the medieval was logical, given that many of the big issues that concern us today had their origins in the medieval world, such as banking, modern armies and capitalist economies, arguing that, 'our return to the Middle Ages is a quest for our roots' (Eco, 1986: 65). To understand how and why contemporary people were so interested in their medieval heritage, he identified ten main ways that the medieval was represented and interpreted. Each was a form of *medievalism*; where the meaning we make of the Middle Ages is based on or framed by our own cultural understanding and carries with it 'a sense of nostalgia for a lost past' (Pugh and Weisl, 2013: 2).

We discuss next eight of the ten of Eco's medievalisms. We do not cover two that stem from his background in the philosophy of language and have little relevance for our discussion of heritage and the media. These are his Middle Ages of the *philosophic perennis* and his Middle Ages of *philological reconstruction* (Eco, 1986).

Pretext/context for a narrative

Eco began by observing that the Middle Ages could be used as a *pretext* or context for a narrative, so that the historical background is merely a foil for the story. Examples are video games like *Assassin's Creed* or *The Legend of Zelda*, some of which have subsequently been made into films. Their storylines are not based on actual historical events; instead, the period is a device to give the characters a romanticised quest to complete, with castles to storm or hide out in and armour for defence, providing a novel and engaging background.

In television or cinema, setting a story in the medieval period may facilitate commentary on issues in the modern world. The television adaptation of *Merlin* (2008–2013) features strong female characters who are not the damsels in distress of storybooks. Guinevere (played by bi-racial actress Angel Coulby) is feisty and practical. This often puts her at odds with Arthur (Bradley James), who is surprised at her lack of deference but finds her honesty appealing. Morgana (Katie McGrath) chafes at the restrictions on an upper-class woman of the times and is forced to hide her talents (in her case, magical powers) from those around her. Her frustration boils over into vengeance on those who have thwarted her. Both these women are far from conventional romantic heroines. A further example of an emancipated female character depicted in medieval times is Lagertha (Katheryn Winnick), wife of Ragnar Lothbrok (Travis Fimmel) in the TV series *Vikings* (2013–2021). She is a shield-maiden and fights as savagely and athletically as the men around her but is also shown as a wise and pragmatic ruler and mentor to younger characters, notably her son Björn Ironside (Alexander Ludwig) and his first wife Torvi (Georgia Hirst). She is a modern counterpoint to the generally male-dominated culture and power structures that usually characterise stories regarding Vikings.

Ironical revisitation

The medieval may be used as the setting for an *ironical revisitation* or parody. It has been a rich source of material for comedians, notably in *Monty Python and the Holy Grail* (1975). This comic retelling of Arthur and the Knights of the Round Table was used to present Monty Python's, 'anti-authoritarian [satire] … relentlessly ridiculing the assumptive power of kings, texts and history' (Massey and Cogan, 2017). In 2005, Eric Idle created a stage musical version called *Spamalot!*, featuring 'singing knights in gaudy tights' and with its roots in English pantomime. The comedy was less biting and more whimsical, befitting ageing comedians who no longer wanted – or needed – to push such a political agenda (Massey and Cogan, 2017).

Medieval satire has an older history than the Python productions. An example from the nineteenth century is Mark Twain's novel *A Connecticut Yankee in King Arthur's Court* (1889), where an American is taken back in time to medieval Camelot. The book may be viewed as Twain's criticism to the romanticisation of medieval chivalry in the nineteenth century. *The Court Jester* (1956) was Hollywood's attempt to parody the popular medieval films of that decade. More recent attempts to mine the period for comedy were *Blackadder* (1982) and *Robin Hood: Men in Tights* (1993).

Barbaric age

Another way of viewing the Middle Ages is to see it as a *barbaric age* – 'a land of elementary and outlaw feelings' (Eco, 1986: 69). This emphasises the violence of the period, notably the cruel or harsh punishment for crimes and the visceral nature of medieval warfare. The *Game of Thrones* (2011–2019) television series exemplifies this, with stomach-churning scenes such as those showing eyes being gouged out during combat or swords being thrust through the mouths of unwitting victims. In *Braveheart* (1995), William Wallace (Mel Gibson) is hung, drawn and quartered for treason against the English king. In *Vikings* (2013–2021), ritual execution known as the *bloodeagle* is depicted (though whether this was a real punishment or a misinterpretation is the subject of debate, see Williams, 2017). It involved ribs being detached from the spine and the lungs pulled through the gap to create a pair of 'wings'. The graphic nature of these scenes is often difficult, yet compelling, to watch. The common medieval narrative of outlaws rebelling against cruel and oppressive lords is another example of interpreting this as a barbaric or violent period and allows for comparisons with similar settings in the action genre, particularly the Wild West of the nineteenth-century USA.

The Romantic Middle Ages

The ideal of a *Romantic* Middle Ages is often centred on the period being an age of damsels in distress, chivalrous knights, tournaments and courtly love. This longing for escapism and spectacle is partly nostalgia for a perceived Golden Age, 'when society, customs and morals were far better than in the modern world' (Laing and Frost, 2012: 71), notably the ideal of chivalry, which gave a sense of certainty or order to transactions and lives. This view sharply contrasts with the preceding interpretation of the medieval as an age of barbarism.

The legend of King Arthur is the most obvious example of this romanticism. Even in medieval times, Arthurian romances were widely popular. The Pre-Raphaelite movement of the nineteenth century, epitomised by the paintings of Dante Gabriel Rossetti and John William Waterhouse, popularised an ethereal form of female beauty with lissom heroines dressed (*sans* corset) in flowing robes with long waved or curled tresses cascading down their backs, often in languorous poses (Bryden, 2011; Mitchell, 2010).

Fashion designers have often taken inspiration from the ideal of this romanticised medieval woman. Queen Elizabeth, the Queen Mother, then Lady Elizabeth

Bowes-Lyon, wore a drop-waisted ivory chiffon silk moire dress at her wedding to the Duke of York in 1923. It was worn complete with a lace veil worn low on her forehead and secured with a chaplet of leaves, reminiscent of the way that Maid Marian is often depicted on screen. The *Toledo News-Bee* newspaper in the United States sported the headline, 'Medieval Gown for Lady Betty' (Bronner, 1923). *British Vogue* at the time more decorously described it as, 'suggesting a medieval Italian robe' (Bowles, 2011). This was a remarkably simple style for a royal wedding dress, but it was shown to great effect by the Gothic backdrop to the ceremony of Westminster Abbey.

National identities

The Middle Ages can be linked to *national identities*, where the period is used to signify a time of 'political utopia' (Eco, 1986: 70). There is a similarity between this view and the romanticism discussed in the previous section, in the sense of a Golden Age of a country's history, which forms the backdrop of how we see ourselves today. Modern nations are often represented as 'imagined communities', where coherence and functionality required those within a country to see themselves as connected through national institutions, histories, stories and myths (Anderson, 1983). For many European countries, the medieval is the source of this national identity. One common trope is of the individual who arises when the country seems destined to be completely subjugated by oppressive outsiders and leads the resistance. Examples include El Cid in eleventh-century Spain, William Wallace in thirteenth-century Scotland and Joan of Arc in fifteenth-century France. It is notable that all three are not royal but rally support for the threatened king, sacrifice their lives for their cause and have remained highly popular national heroes, inspiring a range of media productions including highly successful films (Aberth, 2003). Another variation of this trope is the 'sleeping hero' such as Arthur and William Tell, who will return in times of national emergency. The reincarnation of Arthur is the subject of the steam-punk novel *Morlock Night* (Jeter, 1979) and the film *The Kid Who Would Be King* (2019).

Decadence

The Middle Ages is commonly associated with *decadence*. Eco (1986) uses the example of the Pre-Raphaelite Brotherhood, who saw 'the value to be gained both from experience of all sorts and from indulgence in a life of sensation' (Goldfarb, 1962: 373). Decadence for *fin de siècle* Victorians was linked to *aestheticism*, based on the idea of 'art for art's sake', a 'motto, generally credited to the French writer and critic Théophile Gautier' (Isaac, 2014: 560). This quest for beauty and its links to medievalism was lampooned by Gilbert and Sullivan in their comic opera *Patience*, with lines such as 'Though the Philistines may jostle, you will rank as an apostle in the high aesthetic band, If you walk down Piccadilly with a poppy or a lily in your mediaeval hand'. This is generally construed as a joke at the expense of the likes of Oscar Wilde, who often wore ostentatious flowers in his lapel, though Wilde's tour to America in 1882 was in fact financed by impresario D'Oyly Carte, on the proviso that his arrival in various cities was to coincide with the scheduling of *Patience* (Isaac, 2014).

The decadent interpretation of the Middle Ages concentrates on its debauchery, lechery, sensuality and luxury, epitomised by the wearing of jewels, fur, especially ermine, and velvets; banquets and feasts that feature whole animals on spits; and a promiscuous lifestyle. This is of course a trope which can apply only to the very top echelons of society – the average peasant at the time was not living a life of ease, let alone over-indulgence. The Borgias spring to mind, a noble Italian family in the late fifteenth century whose history is littered with allegations of incest, priests who maintained mistresses and sired bastards, orgies and murder; all while being dedicated patrons of the arts. Lucrezia Borgia, in particular, is a fascinating figure – variously painted as a murderous femme fatale or an innocent pawn (Bradford, 2005).

Another decadent aspect is the sumptuous medieval banquet. This is often re-created by theatre restaurants, accompanied by bawdy humour, which links to the use of the medieval for its comic potential. Dirty Dick's Theatre Restaurant in Australia was established in 1970 and uses the slogan 'Come and Enjoy a Brilliant Night of Medieval Fun and Feasting!' with 'a delicious 3 course meal of Friar Tuck proportions' (Dirty Dick's, 2020). In the United States, Medieval Times offers a dinner and tournament in ten different locations, with a '"hands-on" feast' (Medieval Times, 2020). The 'food is served by 'wenches' to 'Lords and ladies' decked in paper crowns who eat with their hands' (Emery, 2017). The foodservice experience of attendees at the Abbey Medieval Festival in Queensland, Australia, was considered by Robinson and Clifford (2012), who focussed on the medieval banquet with its multiple courses. Featured dishes included whole roast pig and venison, and the spectacle incorporated 'ritual hand washing and service protocol of bowing to High Table' (p. 584), as well as 'entertainment both serious and slapstick' (p. 583). Food which was eaten by peasants, such as Norway's traditional Sheep's-head meal, is now a 'modern consumer product' favoured by tourists (Mykletun and Gyimóthy, 2010: 436) who are both fascinated and repelled by the combination of its size and appearance and the thrill of consuming part of an animal that is not an everyday experience for modern diners.

So-called tradition

The Middle Ages of '*so-called tradition*' (Eco, 1986) is a medievalism that focusses on supernatural forces, such as alchemy, witchcraft and wizardry. The period is often represented as one of superstition and magical forces, usually found deep in dark forests. Certainly, pagan beliefs continued to be widespread throughout the medieval period, often co-existing with Christian practices. It was only with the Reformation and the rise of Puritanism in the seventeenth century that they diminished (Thomas, 1971). Nonetheless, the concept continued of another magical world lying just below the surface of normality and is often used in modern fiction through representations of witches and sorcerers, elves, fairies and spirits. For example, in *The Book of Dust*, Lyra lives in twentieth-century Oxford but gradually becomes aware of a 'secret commonwealth' that only becomes apparent at times. Giorgio Brabandt, an old boatman, first mentions it to her, stating that, 'young people don't believe in the secret commonwealth … they got an explanation for everything and they're all wrong'. He defines it as, 'the world of fairies, and the ghosts' (Pullman, 2019: 223–224). She asks an old priest, Farder Goram, about this, and he explains it in animistic terms that would have made perfect sense in medieval times:

> When I was young there wasn't a single bush, not a single flower nor a stone, that didn't have its own proper spirit. You had to have a mind to your manners around them, to ask for pardon, or for permission, or give thanks … They en't bad nor wicked, not really, nor partic'ly good neither. They're just there, and they deserve good manners.
>
> (Pullman, 2019: 287)

Further examples of this secret medieval world overlapping with the present through magic occur in films such as *The Navigator* (1988), *Les Visiteurs* (1995) and *Merlin: The Return* (2000). There is also a trope of sinister medieval secret societies continuing to be active in the present, as in *National Treasure* (2004), *The Da Vinci Code* (2006) and *Assassin's Creed* (2016). This view of the medieval is often manifested through the use of *magical realism*, the combination of 'realism and the fantastic so that the marvellous seems to grow organically within the ordinary, blurring the distinction between them' (Faris, 2004: 1).

Many medieval narratives naturally combine the magical and the prosaic. The King Arthur story involves the sorcerer Merlin and a sword that only the true King can pull from a stone, and there are encounters with characters such as the Green Knight and the Lady of the Lake who have otherworldly origins. Tolkien's *Lord of the Rings* trilogy is set in the fictional Middle Earth, complete with magic rings, trolls and elves, dragons and invisible cloaks, yet with recognisable elements of our world. Tolkien modelled the Shire on English rural village life, complete with a village green and a local pub. The juxtaposition between the familiar and the extraordinary is complicated by the fact that even the simple life in the Shire is a fantasy for many of us. It represents an attractive and bucolic idyll of rural life, a refuge from stress and busyness, where a welcoming community awaits. It also harks back to a much earlier era, associated with the medieval for many modern readers, given the lack of technology and the mostly agrarian economy. This pre-industrial age with its villages is seductive in its simplicity, promising a connection to rurality and a life lived in harmony with the natural world (Ortenberg, 2016). Paradoxically, there is sometimes a dark side to the rural village narrative, with the village keeping secrets or becoming claustrophobic for its residents. This lifestyle may also be fragile or unsustainable in the face of internal or external threats (Frost and Laing, 2014).

The expectation of the millennium

The final medievalism drawn from Eco (1986) is the *Expectation of the Millennium*, otherwise known as the doomsday warning of the end of the world. In the highly religious medieval world, the likelihood of the apocalypse was ubiquitous, particularly through its widespread visual depiction in churches, often with quite literal renditions of the dead rising from their graves and demons tormenting sinners. At times, the end of days seemed quite imminent. The fourteenth century was one such time. Coming after centuries of steady progress, Europe was thrown into chaos, 'plague, war, taxes, brigandage, bad government, insurrection, and schism in the Church ... a violent, tormented, bewildered, suffering and disintegrating age, a time, as many thought, of Satan triumphant' (Tuchman, 1978: xv). In fictional media, this focus is often on the Black Death, as in *The Seventh Seal* (1957), *The Navigator* (1988) and *World Without End* (Follett, 2007). Eco took a different path in his novel *The Name of the Rose* (1980), focussing more on religious wars and the collapse of society, which, while downplayed in the 1986 film version, were highlighted in the 2019 television series.

Tourism imaginaries

Much of this book is concerned with the way that our understanding and fantasies of the medieval period are framed through tourism, which makes the theoretical framework of *tourism imaginaries* highly pertinent. Salazar defines imaginaries as, 'meaning-making and world-shaping devices' (2012: 864) and notes that they can be studied only by examining channels through which they become tangible, such as film, television or books. In previous work, we have explored imaginings about travel through the aegis of reading books (Laing and Frost, 2012) and watching films (Frost and Laing, 2015) and made the point that these channels can be powerful sources of myths around travel and the places that we would like to visit.

Salazar (2012) conceptualises this process using the model of the *Circuit of Culture*; the idea that there is a circular process of cultural production. This is akin to Jenkins's *Circle of Representation*, based on a study of tourist photographs, where she observes that, 'particular visual images circulate within a culture and become imbued with particular meanings, associations and values' (2003: 307). In contrast, the work of Forsey and Low (2014) suggests a more nuanced understanding of cultural production. Their study of American student travellers in Australia found that the circle of representation can be disrupted by actual travel experiences, which can alter or challenge previously held ideas and images, including those shaped by the media.

Tourism imaginings lead to the creation of *Places of the Imagination*; involving a 'search for physical references to a phenomenon that actually takes place in their mind' (Reijnders, 2011: 233–234); where tourists seek out Dracula's Transylvania or Sherlock Holmes's London. The medieval equivalent is the search for King Arthur's Camelot in places like Tintagel, as well as places connected to medieval-influenced fantasies of *Lord of the Rings* and *Game of Thrones*. Another way to look at these places is to see them as cultural landscapes; a palimpsest of 'layers of meaning'. In this way, the landscape contains traces of various narratives or meanings from and of the past, beyond the physical form, which contribute to the experience for the tourist. Visiting Sherwood Forest, the Robin Hood legend is all pervasive for most visitors and makes us see the otherwise ordinary natural landscape in a different light.

These tourism imaginings may be co-constructed between tourists and tourism operators, with the tourist often bringing their own views, values and background to a travel experience, rather than simply being a passive recipient. They may also elicit deep feelings. Chronis therefore defines a tourism imaginary as 'a value-laden, emotion-conferring collective narrative construction that is associated with and enacted in a particular place through tourism' (2012: 1809). As tourism imaginaries evolve over time, multiple and conflicting narratives may be circulating, which makes their study challenging. These imaginaries may be based on romanticised stories of an earlier era (Salazar, 2012). The discourse of medieval chivalry is such an example that will be discussed in this book.

Mediatisation and intertextuality

Månsson argued that the boundaries 'between imaginary, symbolic and material spaces' (2011: 169) have been dissolved in contemporary society through *mediatisation*, which acknowledges the increasing importance of the media in our lives, including its links with tourism. The *Game of Thrones* tour in Dubrovnik is an example of mediatisation, with a tourism industry created to take advantage of interest in a narrative that has been disseminated through both a book series and television show. It also shapes tourist behaviour, with visitors taking photos of places that were used as settings for the filmed narrative, which frames their gaze (Urry, 2002). The convergence of media (Månsson, 2011), where a narrative is circulated across different platforms or channels, potentially helps keep interest in the medieval period alive for a younger generation, but may also increase its familiarity. For example, the story of the Knights Templar has spanned multiple platforms in recent years, including the video game *Assassin's Creed*, a film version in 2016 and the television series *Knightfall* (2017–2019).

An allied idea with mediatisation is *intertextuality*, which refers to an 'interrelationship [between texts] through either hidden or open references' (Månsson, 2011: 1637). We see intertextuality at play where cultural productions take a story linked to the medieval period and reshape it to appeal to contemporary audiences, although drawing upon the tropes and archetypes of earlier works. Two cogent examples are this are the variety of versions of films about Robin Hood and King Arthur, which focus on different elements of the story or present the narrative through the lens of different characters.

Aims and objectives of this book

This book follows on from *Imagining the American West Through Film and Tourism* (Frost and Laing, 2015), in terms of an understanding of how imaginings of a historical era, mediatised through film, fashion and television, can influence tourist behaviour. It is not so firmly geographically bounded, however, with coverage in this book including the UK, France, Spain, Belgium, Italy, Germany and Japan. It is a largely Western-centric analysis of the phenomenon and our geographical focus is on Britain, France, Spain, Italy, Germany, Croatia and Scandinavia. This approach reflects that the concept of the medieval time period originated in the West to specifically cover historical events in Europe and is arguably not applicable to other parts of the world. We have, however, made one exception in considering Japan (Chapter 11), where the samurai era is sometimes equated with the medieval in Europe. Apart from that chapter on Japan, our discussion is ordered along thematic rather than geographic lines. Some of the areas we particularly wanted to highlight were those focussing on voices that we felt deserved prominence (women, the Other and outlaws); selected non-Western cultures (Japan and Muslims in Spain, Sicily and the Middle East); the Victorian era's fascination with the medieval; and those topics that one would expect to see covered in a book on the medieval, including knights and chivalry, castles, kings and kingship, princesses, and the construction and modern-day usage of great cathedrals. In the last chapter, we discuss areas of future research and some of the topics that warrant future analysis.

References

Aberth, J. (2003) *A knight at the movies: Medieval history on film*, New York and London: Routledge.

Anderson, B. (1983) *Imagined communities: Reflections on the origins and spread of nationalism*, London and New York: Verso, 2006 reprint.

Bayless, M. (2012) 'Disney's castles and the work of the medieval in the Magic Kingdom', in T. Pugh and S. Aronstein (Eds.), *The Disney Middle Ages: A fairy-tale and fantasy past*, New York: Palgrave Macmillan.

Bowles, H. (2011) 'A *Vogue* history of royal wedding dresses', *Vogue*, April 25, https://www.vogue.com/article/hamishsphere-a-vogue-history-of-royal-wedding-dresses (accessed May 1, 2020).

Bradford, S. (2005) *Lucrezia Borgia: Life, love, and death in Renaissance Italy*, London: Penguin.

Bronner, M. (1923) 'Medieval gown for Lady Betty', *Toledo News-Bee*, April 24, p. 2, https://news.google.com/newspapers?id=HPRXAAAAIBAJ&sjid=FkUNAAAAIBAJ&dq=wedding%20dress&pg=2165%2C4832492 (accessed May 1, 2020).

Bryden, I. (2011) 'All dressed up: Revivalism and the fashion for Arthur in Victorian culture', *Arthuriana*, *21*(2), 28–41.

Buckley, R., Morris, M., Appleby, J., King, T., O'Sullivan, D. and Foxhall, L. (2013) ''The King in the Car Park': New light on the death and burial of Richard III in the Grey Friars Church, Leicester, in 1485', *Antiquity*, *87*(336), 519–538.

Chronis, A. (2012) 'Between place and story: Gettysburg as tourism imaginary', *Annals of Tourism Research*, *39*(4), 1797–1816.

Cornwell, B. (2015) *Waterloo*, London: William Collins.

Dirty Dick's Theatre Restaurant (2020) http://www.dirtydicks.com.au/home.htm (accessed August 15, 2020).

Dragt, T. (1962) *The letter for the king*, London: Pushkin, 2020 reprint.

Eco, U. (1980) *The name of the rose*, London: Vintage, 2004 reprint.

Eco, U. (1986) *Faith in fakes*, London: Seeker & Warburg.

Emery, E. (2017) '*Medieval Times*: Tournaments and jousting in twenty-first-century north America', in G. Ashton (Ed.), *Medieval afterlives in contemporary culture*, London: Bloomsbury.

Faris, W. (2004) *Ordinary enchantments: Magical realism and the remystification of narrative*, Nashville: Vanderbilt University Press.

Follett, K. (2007) *World without end*, London: Pan.

Forsey, M. and Low, M. (2014) 'Beyond the production of tourism imaginaries: Student-travellers in Australia and their reception of media representations of their host nation', *Annals of Tourism Research*, 44, 156–170.

Frost, W. (2006) '*Braveheart*-ed *Ned Kelly*: historic films, heritage tourism and destination image', *Tourism Management*, 27(2), 247–254.

Frost, W. and Laing, J. (2014) 'Fictional media and imagining escape to rural villages', *Tourism Geographies*, 16(2), 207–220.

Frost, W. and Laing, J. (2015) *Imagining the American West through film and tourism*, London and New York: Routledge.

Goldfarb, R. (1962) 'Late Victorian decadence', *The Journal of Aesthetics and Art Criticism*, 20(4), 369–373.

Isaac, V. (2014) '*Poppies, lilies, poets and potatoes: An initial exploration of aestheticism and its impact on the operettas of Gilbert & Sullivan*', *Proceedings of fashioning opera and musical theatre: Stage costumes from the late Renaissance to 1900*, Venice: Giorgio Cini Foundation, 560–576.

Jenkins, O. (2003) 'Photography and travel brochures: The circle of representation', *Tourism Geographies*, 5(3), 305–328.

Jeter, K.W. (1979) *Morlock night*, London: Watkins, 2018 reprint.

Jewell, B. and McKinnon, S. (2008) 'Movie tourism – a new form of cultural landscape?' *Journal of Travel & Tourism Marketing*, 24(2–3), 153–162.

Laing, J. and Frost, W. (2012) *Books and travel: Inspiration, quests and transformation*, Bristol: Channel View.

Larrington, C. (2016) *Winter is coming: The medieval world of Game of Thrones*, New York: IB Tauris.

Lindley, A. (2007) 'Once, present and future kings: Kingdom of heaven and the multitemporality of medieval film,' in L. Ramey and T. Pugh (Eds.), *Race, class and gender in "medieval" cinema* (pp. 15–29), New York and Basingstoke: Palgrave Macmillan.

Lowenthal, D. (1985) *The past is a foreign country*, Cambridge: Cambridge University Press.

Lowenthal, D. (1998) *The heritage crusade and the spoils of history*, Cambridge: Cambridge University Press.

Månsson, M. (2011) 'Mediatized tourism', *Annals of Tourism Research* 38(4), 1634–1652.

Marvell, A. and Simm, D. (2016) 'Unravelling the geographical palimpsest through fieldwork: Discovering a sense of place', *Geography 101*(3), 125–136.

Massey, J. and Cogan, B. (2017) '*Spamalot*: Lovingly ripping off/ripping on the establishment', in G. Ashton (Ed.), *Medieval afterlives in contemporary culture*, London: Bloomsbury.

Medieval Times (2020) *About the Show*, https://www.medievaltimes.com/about-the-show/index.html (accessed May 1, 2020).

Milano, C., Novelli, M., and Cheer, J.M. (2019) 'Overtourism and tourismphobia: A journey through four decades of tourism development, planning and local concerns', *Tourism Planning and Development, 16*, 353–357.

Mitchell, R. N. (2010) 'Acute Chinamania: Pathologizing aesthetic dress', *Fashion Theory, 14*(1), 45–64.

Mykletun, R.J. and Gyimóthy, S. (2010) 'Beyond the Renaissance of the Traditional Voss Sheep's-head Meal: Tradition, culinary art, scariness and entrepreneurship', *Tourism Management, 31*(3), 434–446.

Ortenberg, V. (2006) *In search of the Holy Grail*, London and New York: Hambledon Continuum.

Pugh, T. and Weisl, A. (2013) *Medievalisms: Making the past in the present*, London and New York: Routledge.

Pullman, P. (2019) *The book of dust: Volume 2, The secret commonwealth*, London: Pickling.

Reijnders, S. (2011) 'Stalking the count: Dracula, fandom and tourism', *Annals of Tourism Research, 38*(1), 231–248.

Richards, J. (2008) 'Robin Hood, King Arthur and Cold War chivalry', in H. Phillips (Ed.), *Bandit territories: British outlaws and their traditions* (pp. 167–195), Cardiff: University of Wales Press.

Robinson, R.N. and Clifford, C. (2012) 'Authenticity and festival foodservice experiences', *Annals of Tourism Research, 39*(2), 571–600.

Rosenstone, R. (1995) *Visions of the past: The challenge of film to our idea of history*, Cambridge, MA: Harvard University Press.

Salazar, N. (2012) 'Tourism imaginaries: A conceptual approach', *Annals of Tourism Research, 39*(2), 863–882.

Scott, W. (1819) *Ivanhoe*, London: Dent, 1965 reprint.

Seydor, P. (2015) *The authentic death and contentious afterlife of Pat Garrett and Billy the Kid: The untold story of Peckinpah's last western film*, Evanston, IL: Northwestern University Press.

Sturtevant, P. (2012) '"You don't learn it deliberately, but you just know it from what you've seen": British understandings of the medieval past gleaned from Disney's fairy tales', in T. Pugh and S. Aronstein (Eds.), *The Disney Middle Ages: A fairy-tale and fantasy past* (pp. 77–96), New York: Palgrave Macmillan.

Thomas, K. (1971) *Religion and the decline of magic*, London: Penguin, 1988 reprint.

Timothy, D. and Boyd, S. (2003) *Heritage tourism*, Harlow: Pearson.

Tkalec, M., Zilic, I. and Recher, V. (2017) 'The effect of film industry on tourism: *Game of Thrones* and Dubrovnik', *International Journal of Tourism Research, 19*(6), 705–714.

Tuchman, B. (1978) *A distant mirror: The calamitous 14th century*, London: Papermac, 1992 reprint.

Tunbridge, J.E. and Ashworth, G.J. (1996) *Dissonant heritage: The management of the past as a resource in conflict*, Chichester: Wiley.

Twain, M. (1889) *A Connecticut Yankee in King Arthur's court*, 1994 reprint in *Mark Twain Historical Romances* omnibus, New York: The Library of America.

Urry, J. (2002) *The tourist gaze*, London: Sage, 2nd ed., 1st pub. 1990.

Waysdorf, A. and Reijnders, S. (2017) 'The role of imagination in the film tourist experience: The case of *Game of Thrones*', *Participations, 14*(1), 170–191.

Wells, P. S. (2008) *Barbarians to angels: The Dark Ages reconsidered*, New York and London: Norton.

Wickham, C. (2017) *Medieval Europe: From the breakup of the Western Roman Empire to the Reformation*, New Haven and London: Yale University Press.

Williams, T. (2017) *Viking Britain: A history*, London: William Collins.

White, T.H. (1939) *The sword in the stone*, London: Harper Voyager, published in *The Once and Future King* omnibus 2015.

Wood, P. (2001) 'Charges over Dubrovnik bombing', *BBC News*, March 2, http://news.bbc.co.uk/2/hi/europe/1196879.stm (accessed September 8, 2019).

2   Gazing at the Gothic

Medievalism and tourism in the nineteenth and early twentieth centuries

'In terms of our popular culture, we still live in the shadow of the Victorians'.
(Sandbrook, 2016: xxxi)

Introduction: the Eglinton Tournament

The modern interest in the medieval has its roots in the Victorian era, as Sandbrook's quote attests to. An example of this fascination with the medieval was the Eglinton Tournament. In the summer of 1839, Archibald Montgomerie, Earl of Eglinton, staged a three-day medieval tournament at his estate just south of Glasgow. The public were invited, and Eglinton initially expected that he may have to cater for 1,500 spectators. Instead, he received tens of thousands of visitors, conveyed by special excursion trains and a dozen steamships. In addition to a tournament between mounted armoured knights, the event was planned to open with a lavish costumed procession, and each evening there were to be banquets and medieval costume balls. Authenticity was seen as paramount by the organisers, who went as far as finding a set of tournament rules created for Edward IV in 1465 (Pionke, 2008). Unfortunately, the first day of the tournament was ruined by heavy summer rain. Though the later days were better for weather, it is the image of sodden and muddy re-enactors that is most associated with this event.

The impetus for the tournament was dissatisfaction with the lack of pageantry at two recent coronations (Anstruther, 1963; Pionke, 2008). Whereas George IV's coronation in 1821 was extravagantly theatrical with medieval and Elizabethan themes, those of William IV (1831) and Victoria (1838) were cheaper and more restrained (Laing and Frost, 2018). Indeed, the latter earned the derogatory nickname of the 'Penny Coronation' (Anstruther, 1963). These cutbacks were not only an attempt to deflect criticism of excessive expenditure, but they reflected changing societal attitudes that saw the coronation rituals that were cut as 'antiquated and now pointless ceremonies' (Anstruther, 1963: 5) and 'an unnecessary and meaningless display of vanity which sought to mask deficiencies in true national strength' (Williams, 1997: 234). Chief among those omissions were those rituals that stretched back to the medieval period. For example, the coronation of William IV had included the ancient ceremony of having the King's Champion ride on horseback into Westminster Hall in full armour and then throw down his gauntlet and challenge anyone who disputed the king's right to the throne to step forward.

Lord Eglinton – like many of the conservative nobility – was annoyed at missing out on the chance to participate in the customary traditions of the coronation. Sometime just after the coronation, he was dining with a friend who suggested that he stage some medieval games as part of a horse-racing meeting he was conducting on his estate. When the press picked up the idea, Eglinton was flooded with letters of support and finally agreed that he would undertake a medieval tournament. Initially, about 150 young nobles were interested in competing. A meeting was held at the London premises of Samuel Pratt, who was a dealer in medieval arms and armour. Pratt's business was booming, for there was a strong fashion for decorating manor houses with suits of armour – whether original or high-quality copies. With adjustments, such suits could be worn by the participants, though they were expensive. It wasn't just the men who were prepared to pay handsomely to look the part. According to an entry in Queen Victoria's journal, Lord Melbourne told her of a woman who was reputed to have paid £1,000 for three dresses to wear at the tournament. A series of rehearsals were held outside a tavern in Regent's Park, allowing the potential competitors to practice riding and jousting in full armour. Due to the cost and effort involved, the number of knights had shrunk to only 19, but they were cheered on by crowds of approximately 2,000 supporters (Anstruther, 1963).

It quickly became apparent that demand for tickets was outstripping Lord Eglinton's organisational capacity. Spectators flooded into Ayrshire and 'The ideals of chivalry came to seem terribly modern. Thus, to take a steam train to a Gothic tournament was to enter fully into the spirit of this particular age' (Hill, 2007: 214). From London, they caught the new steam train to Liverpool and then a steamship; while from Glasgow there was a direct train service, whose owners took the opportunity to put on special services and double the prices. The regional town of Ayr was packed, with all accommodation booked out. Lord Eglinton constructed a special Gothic-themed grandstand with a capacity of 4,000. Tens of thousands watched from nearby slopes, and there may have been as many as 100,000 in attendance (Anstruther, 1963).

As the crowd poured in, a series of cascading logistical disasters caused havoc. The procession contained a wide variety of participants. None had taken part in anything similar before, and there had been no rehearsals. Ironically, this was one of the criticisms of Queen Victoria's coronation. Consequently, it took three hours longer than planned just to assemble them in order. As they set off, torrential rain began. If they had been on time, the initial proceedings would have been completed in dry weather. As it was, the combination of lateness and rain led to the cancellation of a number of segments, including the important ritual introductions that would have explained to the crowd what was happening. The jousting field quickly became a quagmire, making it almost impossible for the competitors to score hits as practised. Instead, the increasingly restless crowd simply witnessed the competitors riding slowly past each other, with no clash of shields and lances. As the rain continued, the grandstand began to leak, so that its elite occupants – most of whom were in medieval fancy dress – were quickly saturated.

After a few hours, it was announced that the evening ball and banquet were can-celled. Two days later, the tournament was successfully restaged in dry condi-tions, but it was the disaster in the rain that was publicised throughout Britain by the press (Anstruther, 1963; Pionke, 2008).

Whilst the lack of pageantry at Victoria's coronation was a catalyst for the Eglinton Tournament, the widespread interest in medievalism that it demon-strated arose from much deeper-seated social issues. Britain was rapidly chang-ing, and this pushed some to look backwards to the medieval period as some sort of *Golden Age*. Modernity was threatening, seemingly out of control:

> Their world, like ours, was one of industry, cities, mass media and mass com-munications, a landscape transformed by innovation, entrepreneurship and globalization. Like us, they felt that time had somehow speeded up.
>
> (Sandbrook, 2016: xxxii)

The 1830s were dominated by concerns about growing urbanisation, the decline of traditional rural societies and the increasing numbers of people who were poverty-stricken. Such problems fuelled reform, leading to political debate focus-sing on electoral reform and the removal of tariffs on grain imports. Many groups in society felt threatened by these changes and turned longingly towards earlier times that they romantically reimagined as better and more stable. The medieval period was particularly attractive in its reimagined form, for it was constructed as an ordered agrarian society in which people knew their place and were protected and sustained by established institutions. Feudalism, for example, was reinter-preted as a positive social safety net administered by a benevolent aristocracy (Hill, 2007; Pionke, 2008). Throughout the nineteenth century, the media played a major part in stimulating these imaginaries regarding the superiority and desir-ability of the medieval world. Such views – born of the nineteenth century – have continued to hold sway into the current time.

Literary foundations

The resurgence of interest in medievalism was stimulated by romanticised media imaginaries. Their dissemination was aided by changes in improved technology, which allowed access to cheaper publications by the growing literate middle class. The publishing of books and magazines boomed, with the latter featuring illustrations that increased interest in the works of artists. Alfred, Lord Tennyson, Queen Victoria's Poet Laureate, referred to King Arthur as 'the greatest of all poetical subjects' (quoted in Rosenberg, 1987: 147) and was introduced to the legend of Camelot when reading Malory's *Le Morte d'Arthur* as a boy. His *Idylls of the King* (1859–1885), a collection of poems about King Arthur and *The Lady of Shalott* (1832), were influential on the work of the artists known as the Pre-Raphaelite Brotherhood and helped to popularise Arthuriana more generally (see Chapter 3). Another person at the forefront of this trend was Sir Walter Scott and his novel *Ivanhoe* (1819). At that time, Scott was an established poet and novelist, being particularly well known for work that focussed on Scotland in the eighteenth century. For *Ivanhoe*, Scott shifted his gaze to twelfth-century England. Tapping into the growing interest in the medieval, it was a great success and established a template for many historical romances set in that period.

Ivanhoe (Sir Walter Scott, 1819)

In 1194, Saxon noble Wilfred of Ivanhoe returns home to England from the crusades. He finds that the country is divided, with the rapacious Normans under Prince John oppressing the Saxons. Prince John has been acting as regent while his brother King Richard the Lionheart is away at the crusades, and John hopes that Richard will never return. To curry favour with the Norman knights, John allows them to exploit the conquered Saxons. This division is represented by the ongoing rivalry between Ivanhoe and the cruel Norman knight Brian de Bois-Guilbert. Aiding Ivanhoe is Robin of Locksley (Robin Hood), and Scott's utilisation of the outlaw revived interest in this legendary figure, who would feature heavily in the print media for the rest of the nineteenth century. As the country descends into chaos, the only resolution is for the Saxons Ivanhoe and Robin to work together with the Norman Richard – who has returned secretly – and forge a new identity for all as being English rather than Saxon or Norman.

In reality, the distinction between Normans and Saxons had ended by this date. However, for Scott, it was useful to utilise this anachronism as he was constructing a story of national reconciliation, particularly relevant in the period of social unrest just after the French Revolution and the Napoleonic Wars. The odious Prince John and his Norman henchmen are portrayed as tyrannical and cruel, whereas Ivanhoe is loyal and tolerant. Interestingly, Richard's return to power comes with a caveat. While the Lionheart is brave and heroic, he tends towards being impetuous and foolhardy. For the new, unified England to work, King Richard's enthusiasm must be tempered by the wisdom of loyal advisers such as Ivanhoe and Robin. The ideal – as presented by Scott – is a constitutional monarchy.

Romanticising the medieval through events

The paucity of pageantry at Victoria's coronation stimulated interest in re-enacting the medieval and bringing to life the increasingly popular tales of knights and chivalry. Even the young queen herself was swept up in this wave of enthusiasm. In 1840, she married Prince Albert, and he was interested in reviving the medieval. It was at his instigation that they staged a grand costume ball in 1842 (recreated in the episode 'Warp and Weft' of the television series *Victoria* in 2018). The theme was medieval. Some of the guests wore armour, referencing the Eglinton Tournament three years earlier. The royal couple were in costume as the fourteenth-century King Edward III and his wife Queen Philippa. The symbolism was strongly apparent, linking the couple with a past period romanticised for chivalry and military power. Edward was an appropriate choice in that he had been obsessed with Arthurian romance, as the Victorians would continue to be (see Chapter 3). Victoria's third son would be named Arthur; a name which is still in royal vogue, as Arthur is the third of Prince Charles's names and the second of Prince William's names. An interesting element of ritual inversion was that the nineteenth-century couple swapped roles with their medieval predecessors. Albert was controversially only a prince and had never fought in battle, but appeared costumed as a king, complete with crown and jewelled sword. Victoria played the medieval consort, who was foreign-born, just like Albert. The event was a huge success and was reported in positive terms throughout the rapidly expanding mass media (Laing and Frost, 2018). Prince Albert was also heavily involved in promoting the medieval through the rebuilding of the Houses of Parliament at Westminster (see the section on Gothic architecture in this chapter) and the inclusion of a Medieval Court at the 1851 Great Exhibition in London.

Interest in the medieval period grew as the pace of change increased throughout the Victorian Age. Rapid urbanisation and industrialisation drew population out of rural areas. Those who shifted from the countryside tended to be younger, leaving behind ageing communities. In East Anglia, it was recorded that, '"Only boys, girls and old folks are left" is a general complaint of the farmers ... The best and most intelligent labourers are the first to leave' (Graham, 1892: 20, 26). The novelist Henry Rider Haggard was also a farmer in Norfolk, and he similarly noted that, 'the population of our village is waning' and, 'all my best hands, those who can be trusted to plough or thatch, are over fifty years of age. The pick of the young men crowd to the towns' (Rider Haggard, 1899: 338). The issue of the decline of rural villages was seen as important throughout the century and went hand in hand with the tendency towards romanticising rural villages as a lost idyllic world (Frost and Laing, 2014). The desire to reclaim the idealised past was sometimes manifested through events and festivals, which were often imagined as reviving pre-modern traditions such as those from the medieval period.

In the nineteenth century, a number of English villages revived well-dressing festivals, reinforcing community identity and even attracting tourists from nearby towns. Well-dressing involved the elaborate decoration of wells with designs constructed from flower petals and was associated with May Day and other spring festivals. At Tissington in Derby, the ritual of well-dressing is claimed to have begun in the fourteenth century as a thanksgiving for the passing of the Black Death, but it was not recorded until 1818 (Shirley, 2017). Such an absence of documentary evidence might suggest a nineteenth-century invention of tradition, though it is likely that there was some oral tradition that was drawn upon in its revival. More importantly, the nineteenth-century inhabitants were keen to revive what they viewed as an authentic medieval custom.

The reinvention of rural customs and pastimes was well illustrated in the changes that occurred with cricket. Up until the eighteenth century, it was one of a wide number of village sports. During Georgian times, it became popular amongst the gentry as an opportunity for gambling – a similar process occurred with horse racing. In the early to mid-nineteenth century, there was a growth of professional touring teams. Assisted by the expansion of railways, they travelled to towns and cities as professional entertainers, playing matches against odds, and some even travelled to Canada, the USA and Australia (Frost, 2002). In the second half of the nineteenth century, this all changed as this traditional sport became gentrified. Cricket became popular in schools as a means of instilling discipline and encouraging teamwork. Higher-level competitions were organised by social elites, with the peculiar convention that batsmen were generally gentlemen and amateurs, whereas bowlers were professionals. In a very short time, the game became distinguished by a series of strict social conventions linked to a Victorian view of chivalry. Players were expected to be gracious, fair and honourable, and previous characteristics of betting and match-fixing were prohibited (Allen, 2012).

Gothic architecture

The interest in medievalism was physically manifested by the revival of Gothic architecture. This fashion was popular amongst the wealthy owners of manorial estates, where:

> Castles were built and rebuilt because they were Romantic, picturesque, suggested ancient lineage and authority, drew attention to the owner's generous display of hospitality in the baronial hall, and recollected knights and damsels. Following Scott's example, landowners exhibited heraldry and weapons in great halls and on grand staircases ... It became all the rage as more and more dealers in London, such as Samuel Grose, began to trade in arms.
>
> (Ortenberg, 2006: 55)

As the century progressed, demand for armour increased. Members of the wealthy elite became avid collectors, sometimes buying large blocks of hundreds of pieces and seeking out complete suits of armour as the capstones of their collections (Figure 2.1). While renovated castles with medieval collections were strongly in fashion, perfect authenticity was not being striven for. This was fantasy architecture. As Ortenberg argued, 'what the landowners built was of course a modern house, with all the convenience and comfort expected, to which were added various turrets, crenellations and battlements' (2006: 57). The ultimate exemplar was Neuschwanstein in Bavaria, built by King Ludwig II between 1869 and 1886. Inspired by the operatic works of his friend, composer Richard Wagner, it was a romanticised vision of a fairy-tale castle. It also became a byword for excessive expenditure, sending the king bankrupt. Ironically, it attracts over a million visitors a year to Bavaria and is famous as the model for Sleeping Beauty's Castle in Disneyland (Bayless, 2012).

Restoring medieval buildings had its difficulties. Constructing the right sort of romantic ruin sometimes meant the razing of existing structures (Hill, 2007). In some cases, even restoration with the best intentions had destructive consequences. In 1831, repair work at Coventry's Holy Trinity Church uncovered a large 'Doom' painting, representing the Day of Judgement. This was most likely painted between 1430 and 1440 and may have been covered up to save it from Puritans in the seventeenth century. Excited by the find, the church authorities decided to restore the painting. A local artist was employed to remove the protective limewash, touch up the painting as needed and then apply a varnish coating

Figure 2.1 Suits of Armour, Collected in the Nineteenth Century to Grace Grand Houses.

Source: Jennifer Frost.

to protect it. Unfortunately, the varnish contained bitumen, which over time darkened, so that by the beginning of the twentieth century the painting was virtually invisible. It was not until 2004 that the medieval painting was again restored and visible (McGrory and Gill, 2010).

As the fashion for medieval architecture took hold, it was increasingly applied to the construction of new buildings. Designated as Neo-Gothic or Gothic Revival, it became ubiquitous in the Victorian Age. Most influential was the decision to rebuild the Houses of Parliament in the Gothic style after they burnt down in 1834. The rebuilding took decades and was often a subject of much controversy due to cost overruns, but the interiors and exterior were crafted as the high point of the Gothic style (Alexander, 2007; Hill, 2007). Architect Augustus Pugin, who designed much of the building, was instrumental in this revival of the Gothic, which he saw as reflecting the values of medieval society that were 'rooted in a rigid social order that did not question the legitimacy of clerical or aristocratic power' and 'a catalyst for moral betterment' (Mackechnie and Urban, 2015: 174). Furthermore, building projects elsewhere looked to it for inspiration, most notably the Hungarian Parliament Building (1885–1904) and the Woolworth Building in New York (see the section on this building later in the chapter). Over time, the application of the Gothic style broadened well beyond grand public buildings. Whether profane or secular, monumental or vernacular, architects saw advantages in utilising the style for a wide variety of different uses. Adopted for railway stations, banks, universities and other commercial buildings, the medieval architectural revival was 'seen as an indispensible component of contemporary Victorian culture' and, throughout Britain and even its colonies, was a way for organisations and businesses to claim cultural superiority and a pedigree dating back deep in history (Ortenberg, 2006: 51). Major examples of the use of the Gothic style in commercial construction in London include St Pancras Station (1873) and Tower Bridge (1894).

The Pre-Raphaelites and the reimagining of medieval art

The year 1848 was the Year of Revolutions, when all across Europe it seemed that the old regimes would be swept away in the fervour for change. In England, 150,000 Chartist protesters called for parliamentary reform, Karl Marx and Friedrich Engels published *The Communist Manifesto* and the Pre-Raphaelite Brotherhood took on the artistic establishment. The Brotherhood started with three young artists: Dante Gabriel Rossetti, William Holman Hunt and John Everett Millais (dramatised in the television series *Desperate Romantics*, 2009). Studying at the Royal Academy of Arts in London, they had become frustrated at the stale conventions of that institution, particularly the emphasis on following the style of painters such as Raphael in Renaissance Italy. The new group argued that the time had come to return to a style of painting that was simpler, a period before Raphael. They promoted symbolism and narrative complexity, the use of vibrant colours and the importance of detail (particularly in backgrounds). The new style became particularly associated with the medieval, drawing on the art of that period and featuring subjects such as Arthurian legends and the ideals of chivalry and courtly love (Alexander, 2007).

The Pre-Raphaelites were distinguished by their representation of beautiful women, often symbolising the unattainable; a common motif in the romanticised versions of medieval courtly love. Dante Rossetti recorded how the group sought out female models who they described by using the new term 'stunners' (Alexander, 2007: 141). One of these was the statuesque Jane Morris, the wife of the designer William Morris, another member of the Pre-Raphaelite Brotherhood. These ethereal and erotic representations of women became strongly associated with the movement and also entered the popular imagination of how aristocratic medieval women looked. When the Pre-Raphaelites were founded, English painting had mainly focussed on portraits and landscapes, but the revolutionary new style introduced the public to complex narrative compositions with a heavy emphasis on symbolism and allegory. As the English middle-class expanded, these new ideas were further disseminated by illustrated magazines and the trend towards public art galleries (Alexander, 2007).

Whilst the Pre-Raphaelites functioned as a group for only a few years, Hunt and Millais carved out long careers in the new style. They also influenced painters such as Ford Madox Brown and decorative artists like William Morris and Edward Burne-Jones. The style of eroticised – often nude – medieval women was continued by John Collier. His *Godiva* (1898) represented a Victorian romanticisation of the medieval legend of the noblewoman who, having asked her husband to reduce taxes, receives the blunt response that he will do this if she rides naked through the streets of Coventry. Accordingly, she does this, but out of respect, none of the inhabitants look (except for peeping Tom). In *Tannhäuser at Venusberg* (1901), Collier represents the legend of Tannhäuser, a thirteenth-century Germanic knight who had become popular through the opera *Tannhäuser* (1845) written by Richard Wagner. Tannhäuser is a worthy knight who is enticed into the fairy-like underground realm of the pagan goddess Venus. There he is trapped, captivated by a magical spell. Collier's painting juxtaposes the chivalrous armoured knight with the naked Venus and her nymphs. Such works by Collier and others may be thought of as examples of *authorised transgression*, whereby Victorian voyeurs were allowed to view erotic images within the genteel confines of art galleries.

The critic John Ruskin, also associated with the Pre-Raphaelite Brotherhood, argued for the superior merits of medieval decorative arts and architecture in comparison to those of the industrial age, in his book *The Stones of Venice* (1851). His support for the Gothic revival style was founded on a belief that contemporary society could benefit from looking back to a utopian past (Cosgrove, 1982). It was associated with a romantic view of the honest toiler, where physical labour and intellectual input are the province of all, rather than diametrically opposed concepts. This was a 'dictum that good art could only come from a good person in a good society' (Stankiewicz, 1992: 169). This flowed through to his views on the widespread passion for grand houses in the medieval style, with Ruskin pithily observing that he was 'probably much happier to live in a small house, and have Warwick Castle to be astonished at, than live in Warwick Castle, and have nothing to be astonished at' (quoted in Frost, 2014: 20).

Ruskin's distaste with modern industrialism led him in 1871 to create the Guild of St George. His goal was to establish small agricultural and artisanal communities, which would use and preserve old crafts. To achieve this, Ruskin used the model of a medieval order for which he recruited 'companions':

> Every Companion, Ruskin conceived, would work to return to a neo-medieval social ideal ... and pledge themselves to self-sacrificing reformation of the nation. Forming a military-monastic order of 'delivering knights' inspired by the Master [Ruskin] and the medieval example of St George, they would combat the steam-fuelled dragon of unrestrained capitalism, and create an ascetic self-sacrificing society, that would reject unnecessary mechanisation.
>
> (Frost, 2014: 4)

William Morris shared Ruskin's passion for medieval craftsmanship and was responsible for the Arts and Crafts movement, which rejected Victorian industrialisation in favour of artisan-led production of items such as textiles, furnishings, stained glass and books (MacCarthy, 2015). His company, Morris, Marshall, Faulkner and Company, was set up in 1861 and later became William Morris and Co. in 1875. The company not only created hand-crafted items to beautify the home, such as rugs, wallpaper and embroidered wall-hangings, but took on commissions such as the creation of stained glass for churches and the decoration of interiors including the South Kensington (now the Victoria and Albert) Museum and many aristocratic homes. It revived a variety of artisanal techniques ranging from tapestry making and carpet weaving to the hand woodblock printing of textiles and printing on handmade paper. Morris also founded the Kelmscott Press, producing books that were exquisitely illustrated, sometimes on vellum, often with medieval themes such as their collection of the works of Chaucer, illustrated by Burne-Jones. His fabric designs like Acanthus (1875) and Pimpernel (1876) endure to this day on the likes of bedlinen, cushions and wallpaper, having been acquired by Sanderson in 1940 after the financial demise of William Morris & Co. Suggestions that his work has lost its popularity appear to have been premature. Indeed, in the middle of the coronavirus epidemic of 2020, the authors purchased face masks that were made from Morris's iconic Strawberry Thief design (Figure 2.2). In a time of chaotic change, wearing something nostalgic and reminiscent of a gentler time seemed appropriate.

The Vikings revived

The Victorians were fascinated by the Vikings, and 'in many ways, the Victorians invented the Vikings' (Wawn, 2000: 3). Up to the 1830s, they were hardly discussed, and the term was virtually unknown. Then, on the strength of work by Scandinavian scholars, interest in the Vikings grew, and this led to a flood of plays, poems and books (Wawn, 2000). Two examples of how Viking culture and stories entered popular culture are worth noting. The first is the novel *Journey to the Centre of the Earth* (Verne, 1864). The story commences when Professor Liedenbrock buys a medieval manuscript from a second-hand shop. An avid

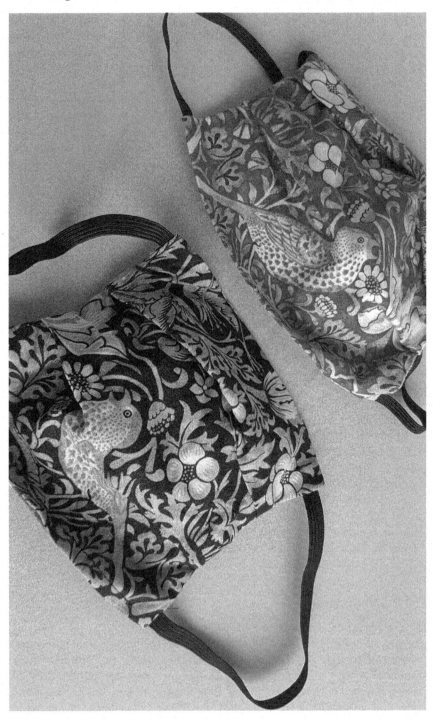

Figure 2.2 William Morris Print Face Masks.

Source: Jennifer Frost.

antiquarian, he is overjoyed to find that it is a chronicle of the Norwegian rulers of Iceland by the thirteenth-century Icelandic writer Snorri Sturluson, who was very popular amongst Viking enthusiasts in the nineteenth century. The professor excitedly tells his less-than-impressed nephew that this is a 'priceless treasure', handwritten in Icelandic on parchment. When they discover a mysterious runic inscription, the Viking book becomes a treasure map – a common device in Verne's stories – which sets them upon an adventurous quest (Verne, 1864: 5).

The second is the novel *King Solomon's Mines* (Rider Haggard, 1885). Allan Quatermain (the narrator) meets Sir Henry Curtis, an English aristocrat visiting South Africa. He describes Sir Henry as:

> one of the biggest-chested and longest-armed men I ever saw. He had yellow hair, a big yellow beard ... I never saw a finer-looking man, and somehow he reminded me of an ancient Dane ... I remember once seeing a picture of some of those gentry, who, I take it, were a kind of white Zulus. They were drinking out of big horns, and ... I thought that if one only let his hair grow a bit, put one of those chain shirts on those great shoulders of his, and gave him a battle-axe and a horn mug, he might have sat as a model for that picture.
>
> (Rider Haggard, 1885: 11)

Sir Henry hires Quatermain to be his guide on an expedition to the interior, where they find the lost civilization of Kukuanaland and become involved in a civil war. In the final battle, Sir Henry is the *Boy's Own* hero and is again described as a modern Viking, being 'like his Beserkir [*sic*] forefathers'. At the front of the rebel army, 'there he stood, the great Dane, for he was nothing else, his hands, his axe, and his armour, all red with blood, and none could live before his stroke' (Rider Haggard, 1885: 226).

The passionate interest in all things Viking led to a range of strange theories based on interpretations of legends and ancient texts. Most striking was the claim that Queen Victoria herself was descended from Ragnar Lodbrok, the legendary Viking war chief who invaded England in the ninth century (and features so heavily in modern representations; see Chapter 9). With the benefit of hindsight, such a claim seems impossible to sustain, but it was believed, even by such noteworthy a person as the decorative artist William Morris (Wawn, 2000). Another royal connection that caught the public imagination concerned the Danish-born Alexandra, wife of Edward VII, who was Princess of Wales from 1863 to 1901 and Queen from 1901 to 1910. As she was a member of the Danish royal family, it was held that she was descended from King Harald Bluetooth, who united all Denmark in the tenth century (Wawn, 2000). This claim was at least plausible.

In the Shetland Islands of northern Scotland, the historical connections with the Vikings were celebrated through an event. In 1878, Up Helly Aa was invented as a medieval festival. Prior to then, the townspeople of Lerwick in the Shetland Islands had celebrated New Year's Eve with rolling a burning tar-barrel through the streets. Such a festivity had high potential for damage to property, and there was also growing concern with the associated drunkenness and rowdyism. Accordingly, a new tradition was developed that featured the burning of a traditional Shetland boat. Moving the fire from the narrow town streets to an open space reduced the likelihood of the flames getting out of control. Making a traditional craft the centre of attention highlighted the Viking heritage of the Shetland Islands, and the Viking elements quickly became the focus of this popular event (Finkel, 2010).

Medieval imaginaries outside Europe

While Europeans were rediscovering the medieval throughout the nineteenth century, their cousins who had migrated outside of Europe were having similar experiences. Regions of recent European settlement, including the USA, Canada, Australia and New Zealand, were just as passionate about medieval imaginaries. As diaspora societies, they shared a common culture with their homeland and looked to Europe for both heritage and the latest trends. In common with many diaspora societies, there was also a tendency to romanticise and even invent traditions in regard to the lands and societies they – or their forbears – had migrated from.

In the second half of the nineteenth century, these regions of recent European settlement went through a period of tremendous economic development. Even though these economic booms were underpinned by agriculture and mining, these societies all experienced intensive urbanisation. The new cities – some dating only to early in the nineteenth century – were characterised by the latest technology, including electricity, tall buildings (with the growth of skyscrapers just starting to take off), sanitation systems and mass transit networks. Amongst all of this modernity, however, the New World also turned to the Gothic as a widely recognised indicator of the latest fashionable taste, status, legitimacy and substance.

Imitating the trends of Europe, monumental public buildings were constructed in the Gothic style. Cathedrals were the most prominent, dominating skylines with their spires. In Australia, the major cities all built cathedrals in the neo-Gothic style. This trend was also followed in secular buildings throughout the New World. To illustrate how the Gothic was utilised in commercial architecture, we consider the example of the Woolworth Building in New York (Figure 2.3).

The Woolworth Building, New York

The Woolworth Building was designed as an office building in the heart of lower Manhattan and was for nearly twenty years the tallest building in the world. Technically, this is neither Victorian nor nineteenth century, for it was constructed between 1910 and 1913. However, it is a fascinating example of the peak of the Gothic style. Furthermore, it illustrates the complexities of this architectural movement, particularly the issues involved with marrying romanticised imaginaries with modern needs, technologies and economics. As Fenske argued:

> The Woolworth Building's contradictory architectural hybrid of fanciful Gothic ornamental features – tracery, tourelles, gables, gargoyles, and finials – and technologically audacious steel-framed engineering calls attention to the jarring discontinuities, startling proximities, and unpredictability of the modern urban experience.
>
> (2008: 4)

Figure 2.3 Woolworth Building, New York.
Source: Jennifer Frost.

For owner Frank Woolworth, a retailer from humble origins, it 'functioned primarily as a conspicuous form of elite, high-style consumption' (Fenske, 2008: 6). It was designed to be seen and appreciated, strategically placed bordering the open space of City Hall Park, where pedestrian flows were at their highest as traffic from the Brooklyn Bridge met Broadway. The building was a majestic 55 storeys high, even though Woolworth needed only one of the floors to accommodate his headquarters staff. For architect Cass Gilbert, it was his artistic masterpiece, the epitome of Gothic Revival rendered in the Beaux-Arts style.

Many of the Gothic elements in its design were borrowed from buildings in Europe. Both Woolworth and Gilbert travelled extensively throughout Europe, picking up ideas as they went. We can regard both of them as examples of elite tourists on a version of the Grand Tour; seeing the sights and building a stock of cultural capital that would increase their status when they returned home. Woolworth was attracted to symbols of power and was particularly fascinated by Napoleon. However, what he focussed upon as his preferred model for his building was the Victoria Tower of the Houses of Parliament in London (Fenske, 2008). This was itself Neo-Gothic rather than medieval, being constructed between 1843 and 1860 and having a cast iron framework. Starting in 1890, Woolworth made annual trips to Europe, combining business with sightseeing. He was accordingly quite familiar with this famous English landmark. In 1910, Woolworth and Gilbert met in London and toured the Houses of Parliament, discussing which design features they wanted to incorporate into their building.

Cass Gilbert was a university-educated member of the cultural elite. His regular travels to Europe followed the conventions of a sophisticated gentleman of the time. Whereas businessman Woolworth called his travels 'buying trips', the scholarly Gilbert engaged in what he termed 'sketching holidays' (Fenske, 2008: 34, 84). Through regular trips to Europe, Gilbert built a portfolio of sketches, notes and ideas that he used for the Woolworth Building. In many cases, its architectural features were duplicated from the medieval sites that Gilbert had visited and sketched. As Gilbert wrote,

> the Palace of Jacques Coeur at Bourges, the Hotel de Cluny in Paris, the Town Hall at Middelburg, Hotel de Ville, Compiègne, the towers of Reims, Antwerp, and Malines [Cathedrals], and many others all contributed their quota of precedent and suggestion to the development of the detail.
>
> (quoted in Fenske, 2008: 155–158)

Recognising that the Gothic style would make the elevator lobby too dark, Gilbert copied the fifth-century domed mosaic ceilings of the Mausoleum of Galla Placida in Ravenna, Italy, which he had visited in 1912 (Fenske, 2008).

Drawing heavily on the tourist attractions of Europe for its architecture, the Woolworth Building was designed to be a major tourist attraction within New York. Apart from its advantageous location, it offered the unique tourist experience of a public observatory on top of the world's tallest building. At a cost of 50 cents, visitors could take the elevator to the 58th floor and take in unrestricted panoramic views. The inspiration for such a feature came from

Woolworth's experiences at the Eiffel Tower in Paris. The price was deliberately set relatively high to make the observatory a premium experience and restrict visitors who did not accord with the building's high-status image. Visitation was in the order of 300,000 people a year and the operation was highly profitable (Fenske, 2008). Indeed, when the Empire State Building was designed to surpass the Woolworth Building in height, it also included an observatory intended to attract tourists.

With its widespread use of medieval design features, the Woolworth Building attracted comparisons with the nineteenth-century fashion for Neo-Gothic Cathedrals. The alliterative epithet 'Cathedral of Commerce' was applied to it at its foundation ceremony and was further reinforced through a promotional booklet of that name. This booklet, with Gothic lettering on its cover and designed to suggest a prayer-book, was freely distributed to attract potential tenants (Fenske, 2008). Further reinforcement of this paradoxical connection came from the comments of former British Prime Minister Arthur Balfour, who visited New York in 1917. According to the interpretive panel outside the building which we observed in 2018, Balfour famously stated, 'what shall I say of a city that builds the most beautiful cathedral in the world and calls it an office building'. A cute aphorism, it can be interpreted as either passionate admiration or veiled criticism.

Medieval literature and legends in the New World

The diaspora societies of the New World were also avid consumers of the literary trends in refashioning medieval stories and concepts. Two examples illustrate how medieval imaginaries penetrated American society in the nineteenth century. The first concerns Lord Byron's poem *Childe Harold's Pilgrimage* (*childe* being a term for a young man who is seeking to become a knight) and its most famous line in 'There is pleasure in the pathless woods' (Byron, 1818: Canto the Fourth, Stanza CLXXVIII). Such a sentiment epitomised the Romanticist view of nature, and it seemed especially written for those travelling westwards. Accordingly, it comes as little surprise to find nineteenth-century travel accounts referencing Byron's work. In 1870, a small expedition ventured into the Yellowstone area of Montana. They were following up reports of spectacular mountains, gorges and geysers. On returning home, this group became heavily involved in a campaign that led to Yellowstone becoming designated in 1872 as the world's first national park. In Nathaniel Langford's account of the expedition, he recorded that in skirting Yellowstone Lake, they became frustrated in spending days slowly struggling through dense fallen pines and scrub:

> our tempers had been sorely tried and we were in a most unsocial of humours, speaking only in half angry expletives, I recalled that beautiful line in Byron's 'Childe Harold,' 'There is pleasure in the pathless woods,' which I recited with all the 'ore rotundo' [full voice] I could command, which struck the ludicrous vein of the company and produced an instantaneous response of uproarious laughter, which … had the effect to restore harmony and sociability.

(Langford: 1905: 69)

Langford's joking recitation of Byron's medieval imaginary went down well with the expedition members because they were mainly young, college-educated professionals familiar with Byron's work, the concepts of Romanticism and its application to the appreciation of nature. Furthermore, Langford was confident that most of his readers shared the same cultural capital and could understand and appreciate the incident.

The second example comes from almost exactly the same time period and concerns the notorious outlaw Jesse James. In the 1870s, James and his gang engaged in a series of violent robberies across the Midwest. During this period, James and his media supporters engaged in what we would now term a public relations campaign to justify these robberies. As former Confederate soldiers, they framed their outlawry as a response to what they saw as the corruption of the federal government under President Ulysses Grant. In a series of newspaper reports, they presented their case, relying heavily on romanticised medieval imagery, which they knew would appeal to readers.

This use of this medieval imagery was initiated by journalist John Newman Edwards. During the American Civil War, Edwards was a Confederate officer with General Jo Shelby, had refused to surrender after the Battle of Appomattox and had fled to Mexico. Later returning to the USA, he became a journalist and founded the pro-Confederate *Kansas City Times*. In 1872, Edwards wrote an editorial titled 'The Chivalry of Crime'. In this piece, Edwards wrote that recent robberies in the border states of Kansas and Missouri were 'a feat of stupendous nerve and fearlessness that makes one's hair rise to think of it' and they were 'chivalric; poetic; superb'. In regard to the qualities of the outlaws, he commented:

> The nineteenth century with its Sybaric [Sybaritic] civilization is not the social soil for men who might have sat with ARTHUR at the Round Table, ridden at tourney with Sir LAUNCELOT or worn the colours of GUINEVERE.
>
> (capitalisation in original, quoted in Stiles, 2002: 224)

From being equated with Arthurian romances, the next step was to position James and his gang as modern-day Robin Hoods. Later in 1872, Edwards's newspaper published a letter from one of the outlaws – most probably Jesse James – stating, 'we are not thieves – we are bold robbers ... we rob the rich and give to the poor' (quoted in Stiles, 2002: 224–225). These words were later repeated almost verbatim by the outlaws when conducting a train robbery in Iowa the next year (Stiles, 2002).

These sentiments were picked up by other pro-Confederate writers. The most striking of these came in 1874, from Peter Donan, the editor of the Missouri newspaper, the *Lexington Caucasian*. Following a recent bank robbery in Lexington, Donan began his editorial by commenting that 'In all the history of medieval night-errantry and modern brigandage, there is nothing that equals the wild romance of the past few years' career' of the James-Younger gang. Taking a completely contrary view of the robbery to what one might expect from a newspaper, Donan enthused that 'Lexington has just had the honor of one of their

Robin-Hood-like, rattling visits ... the whole proceeding was conducted in the coolest and most gentlemanly manner possible' (quoted in Stiles, 2002: 267).

Such enthusiastic application of medieval heroes and chivalry to contemporary American culture was bound to lead to a reaction. It came through the most prominent humourist of the day in Mark Twain. Born and raised in Missouri, Twain was disgusted in how the Confederates had appropriated for themselves the rhetoric of chivalry, honour and knighthood. In a reworking of the Arthurian legend, he set out to lampoon such conceits.

A Connecticut Yankee in King Arthur's Court (Mark Twain, 1889)

The story starts with the common literary device of the narrator Twain having a chance meeting with a mysterious stranger who tells him a fantastic tale. Their encounter occurs at Warwick Castle, one of England's best-preserved medieval castles. Since the 1970s, Warwick Castle has operated as a major tourist attraction, first under the ownership of Tussauds and more recently Merlin Entertainments (see Chapter 6). Even when it was still in private hands in the nineteenth century, it hosted a steady stream of tourists, and Twain was aware that many of his readers would have known of it. Twain and the stranger are taking part in a guided tour, where, 'we fell together, as modest people will, in the tail of the herd that was being shown through, and he at once began to say things which interested me'. The stranger is much more engaging than the 'droning voice of the salaried cicerone' conducting the tour (Twain, 1889: 219). Later, he catches up with the stranger at the Warwick Arms Hotel (which still operates) and over whiskeys, the full story is told.

The stranger is from Hartford, Connecticut. He was a skilled mechanic for a weapons manufacturer and rose to be a foreman. One day he was hit on the head and woke up to find himself inexplicably transported back to sixth-century England. Trapped in Arthurian times, the stranger applies both his technical knowledge and his Yankee pragmatism to engage in improving works. He acquires the epithet 'Sir Boss', recognising his technological superiority. His adventures are episodic and typically involve subverting and ridiculing the characters of the Arthurian legends. Merlin, for instance, is a pompous and vindictive windbag, who hates Sir Boss. In an incident borrowed from Henry Rider Haggard's *King Solomon's Mines* (1885), fortuitous knowledge that an eclipse of the sun is due to occur allows Sir Boss to escape death by proving he is a greater wizard than Merlin. Further humour comes from the Yankee's application of nineteenth-century technologies to defeat his enemies. These include gunpowder, pistols, electricity and bicycles. The most curious use of archaic weaponry comes when Sir Boss wins a tournament by lassoing his opponents.

Throughout the novel, Twain ridicules the contemporary obsession with medievalism. Sir Boss notes that many of the ladies and knights of King Arthur's court consistently use rude and indelicate language. This is no surprise to him, for having read early English novels like *Tom Jones* (Henry Fielding, 1749), he is familiar with how such lewd talk was common, even amongst the upper classes. He comments, however, on how this is not recognised in the supposedly historical *Ivanhoe* (Walter Scott, 1819):

> Suppose Sir Walter, instead of putting the conversations into the mouths of his characters, had allowed the characters to speak for themselves? We should have had talk from Rebecca and Ivanhoe and the soft Lady Rowena which would embarrass a tramp in our day.
>
> (Twain, 1889: 242)

A constant theme throughout the book is how life was tough and unfair in medieval times. The social order comes in for special ridicule and is portrayed as distasteful to any right-minded democratic American. Observing the fabled Knights of the Round Table, Sir Boss finds greed and violence rather than chivalry, recording that their conversation consists of:

> accounts of the adventures in which these prisoners were captured and their friends and backers killed and stripped of the steeds and armor ... these murderous adventures were not forays undertaken to avenge injuries, nor to settle old disputes or sudden fallings out; no, as a rule they were simply duels between strangers ... between whom existed no cause of offence whatever ... there did not seem to be brains in the entire nursery, so to speak, to bait a fishhook with.
>
> (Twain, 1889: 230)

Meeting a group of peasants, Sir Boss rails against the inequities of feudalism:

> The talk of these meek people had a strange enough sound to a formerly American ear. They were freemen, but they could not leave the estates of their lord or their bishop without his permission ... they could not sell a piece of their own property without paying him a percentage of the proceeds ... they had to harvest his grain for him gratis, and be ready to come in a moment's notice, leaving their own crop to destruction by the threatened storm ... there were taxes, and taxes, and taxes, and more taxes, and taxes again, and yet other taxes – upon this free and independent pauper, but none upon his lord the baron or the bishop.
>
> (Twain, 1889: 293)

Twain targets taxation without representation, an unelected and decadent elite, a single state-backed church, intemperance (the knights are prodigious drinkers), imprisonment without trial, capital punishment for theft and the lack of an education system as faults in this magical world. All of these elements of medieval society his Yankee hero finds appalling, and the intention is that his contemporary readers will also find these offensive to the values they hold dear. Wrapped in humour and buffoonery, Twain's message is that the imagined medieval world was a horror for most of its inhabitants.

The story concludes with Sir Boss engaging in a bloody battle. With Arthur killed by Mordred, the Yankee is declared an outlaw. Occupying a fortified hilltop, Sir Boss withstands massed charges of knights, who are slaughtered by the thousands by automatic weaponry. It is a very disturbing finale for what is often regarded as a lightweight, humorous tale. Twain's symbolism, however, is clear.

The final battle is very similar to Gettysburg, fought just a quarter of a century earlier. The massed knights charging up the hills towards murderous Yankee fire-power suggests Pickett's Charge. Once again, Twain highlights the Confederates' appropriation of medieval chivalry and argues that there is little place for such notions in a modern world.

The Vikings in America

Whilst southerners in North America sought to appropriate knighthood and chivalry, their counterparts in the north looked to the Vikings. In Europe, the growth of interest in the Norse was underpinned by scholars translating and interpreting a number of medieval texts, and some of these told of journeys to a fertile land to the far west that the Vikings called Vinland. If Vinland was the north-east coast of North America, then it gave Americans their very own medieval history. Newport, Rhode Island, became the centre of this cult, for it contained a ruined stone building called the Newport Tower. Though built in the seventeenth century as the base for a windmill, knowledge of its origins had been lost, and it looked like a castle.

It was the poet Henry Wadsworth Longfellow who popularised the idea that the Newport Tower was of Viking origin. His poem 'The Skeleton in Armour' (1841) married together the tower, Viking voyages to the west and the earlier find of a skeleton in Massachusetts, which appeared to have armour. The narrative was a romantic confection regarding a Viking warrior and a princess who elope. Blown off course by a storm, they land on Rhode Island, where he builds the tower and they live happily ever after. In 1882, the poem inspired heiress Catharine Lorillard Wolfe to build her mansion 'Vinland' at Newport. The interiors were designed by William Morris and Edward Burne-Jones – who she unsuccessfully tried to tempt to travel to the USA – and included stained-glass windows representing the Vikings sailing to America and the Norse gods of Odin, Thor and Frey (Morris, 1885; Sharpe and Kuchta, 2007; Wawn, 2000). In another manifestation of the cult of the Vikings, statues of Leif Erikson were erected at Boston (1885) and Milwaukee (1887), commemorating him as the discoverer of the Americas. Rather than imagining Erikson as a bearded warrior, these statues presented him as clean-shaven and in the style of a Greek hero from antiquity.

In 1892, Chicago hosted a World's Fair to commemorate the 400th anniversary of the arrival of Columbus, complete with replicas of his fleet sailing around Lake Michigan. The stage was set for the advocates of America's Viking history to undertake what today we would call ambush marketing. Norwegian newspaper owner Magnus Andersson commissioned a Viking longboat replica based on the archaeological find of a burial ship at Gokstad in Norway in 1880. This replica was then successfully sailed across the Atlantic Ocean to New York and then towed along the Erie Canal and into the Great Lakes. It was one of the star attractions of the World's Fair and was viewed by crowds in excess of 100,000 per day. Not everybody was happy with its intrusion, but it did provide an alternative version of American history (Andersson and Magelssen, 2017). It was not until 1960, however, that archaeological discoveries at L'Anse aux Meadows in Newfoundland confirmed that the Vikings reached the Americas 500 years before Columbus.

Into the twentieth century

The end of the nineteenth century and the Victorian era did not provide a sharp cut-off to the fascination with the medieval. Though new fashions and trends developed, interest with this period continued and formed a link with today's ongoing interest. A few examples illustrate how medievalisms continued to occur. The Woolworth Building (discussed earlier) was constructed between 1910 and 1913. Early in the twentieth century, Jeanne d'Arc became popular in the English-speaking world, albeit anglicised to Joan of Arc. Previously, she had not been viewed so favourably, with William Shakespeare characterising her as an evil witch. Accordingly, when in 1906 the National Gallery of Victoria in Melbourne purchased a large French statue of Joan, the local newspaper called it 'an act of almost inconceivable stupidity', which would 'make us a mock and laughing stock' (quoted in Hayes, 2016). World War I quickly changed these attitudes, for now the French were allies with the British and Joan was symbolic of French resistance to German invasion. On Bastille Day, 1917, local people 'organised a series of public events in solidarity with their French allies, centred on the Joan of Arc monument' (Hayes, 2016). Interestingly, the statue of Joan of Arc was situated to balance out a similarly sized one of St George and the Dragon, which had been purchased in 1889. In 1933, wealthy couple Virginia and Stephen Courtauld effected an extraordinary transformation to ruined Eltham Palace in suburban London, marrying the medieval and the new design trend of art deco (Figure 2.4). Whilst restoring the fifteenth-century medieval hall, they constructed modernistic living quarters. The sort of restoration that could not possibly be approved today, it is a powerfully effective juxtaposition.

The eve of World War II is perhaps an appropriate period to end this chapter. Three instances at this time demonstrate how the medieval period was continuing to be reimagined for modern tastes. The film *The Adventures of Robin Hood* (1938) was a huge success, presenting the medieval world in colour for the first time. Its retelling of the outlaw myth became widely seen as definitive and inspired a range of further medieval adventure films after the war. Another radical retelling of a medieval legend was *The Sword in the Stone* (White, 1938). This presented a completely new take on Arthur, focussing on his youth and incorporating magical realism, and inspiring future generations of writers including J.K. Rowling and Neil Gaiman. In 1939, one of the star attractions of the New York World's Fair was Lincoln Cathedral's copy of the Magna Carta. A number of copies had been made in the thirteenth century and distributed around England (see Chapter 7). Only four remained, and this was the first time any had left England. For the American audience, however, this was their national heritage rather than England's. The Magna Carta was widely viewed as one of the foundations of American democracy. Indeed, with the outbreak of the war, it was agreed that it needed to be kept safe by being retained in the USA, and it was stored in Fort Knox until 1947. Medievalism had not finished with the end of the Victorian age; it would continue to be a strong influence on contemporary society.

Figure 2.4 Medieval Hall in Eltham Palace.
Source: Jennifer Frost.

References

Alexander, M. (2007) *Medievalism: The Middle Ages in modern England*, New Haven, CT and London: Yale University Press.

Allen, D. (2012) 'England's 'Golden Age': imperial cricket and late Victorian society', *Sport in Society*, *15*(2), 209–226.

Andersson, A. and Magelssen, S. (2017) 'Performing a Viking history of America: The 1893 voyage and display of a Viking longship at the Columbus Quadricentennial', *Theatre Journal*, *69*(92), 175–195.

Anstruther, I. (1963) *The knight and the umbrella: An account of the Eglinton Tournament 1839*, London: Geoffrey Bles.

Bayless, M. (2012) 'Disney's castles and the work of the medieval in the Magic Kingdom', in T. Pugh and S. Aronstein (Eds.), *The Disney Middle Ages*, New York: Palgrave Macmillan, 39–56.

Byron, L. (1818) *Childe Harold's pilgrimage*, Project Gutenberg, https://www.gutenberg.org/files/5131/5131-h/5131-h.htm (accessed October 21, 2018).

Cosgrove, D. (1982) 'The myth and the stones of Venice: An historical geography of a symbolic landscape', *Journal of Historical Geography*, *8*(2), 145–169.

Fenske, G. (2008) *The Skyscraper and the city: The Woolworth Building and the making of modern New York*, Chicago and London: University of Chicago Press.

Finkel, R. (2010) '"Dancing around the ring of fire": Social capital, tourism resistance and gender dichotomies at up Helly Aa in Lerwick, Shetland', *Event Management*, *14*(4), 275–285.

Frost, M. (2014) *The lost companions and John Ruskin's Guild of St George: A revisionary history*, London: Anthem.

Frost, W. (2002) 'Heritage, nationalism, identity: The 1861–62 England cricket tour of Australia', *International Journal of the History of Sport*, *19*(4), 55–69.

Frost, W. and Laing, J. (2014) 'Fictional media and imagining escape to rural villages', *Tourism Geographies*, *16*(2), 207–220.

Graham, P.A. (1892) *The rural exodus: The problem of the village and the town*, London: Metheun.

Hayes, G. (2016) 'Melbourne's Joan of Arc', *State Library of Victoria – Our Stories*, https://blogs.slv.vic.gov.au/our-stories/joan-of-arc/ (accessed May 1, 2020).

Hill, R. (2007) *God's architect: Pugin and the building of romantic Britain*, London: Allen Lane.

Laing, J. and Frost, W. (2018) *Royal events: Rituals, innovations, meanings*, Abingdon and New York: Routledge.

Langford, N.P. (1905) *The discovery of Yellowstone Park: Journal of the Washburn Expedition to the Yellowstone and Firehole Rivers in the year 1870*, Lincoln, NE: University of Nebraska Press, 1972 reprint.

Longfellow, H.W. (1841) *The skeleton in armour*, Poetry Foundation, https://www.poetryfoundation.org/poems/44648/the-skeleton-in-armor (accessed March 9, 2020).

MacCarthy, F. (2015) *William Morris: A life for our time*, London: Faber & Faber.

Mackechnie, A. and Urban, F. (2015) 'Balmoral castle: National architecture in a European context', *Architectural History*, *58*, 159–196.

McGrory, D. and Gill, M. (2010) *The last judgement: The Coventry Doom Painting and Holy Trinity Church*, Coventry: Holy Trinity Church.

Morris, W. (1885) 'Letter to Catharine Lorillard Wolfe', 15 April, in N. Kelvin (Ed.), *The collected letters of William Morris: Volume II, 1885–1888*, Princeton, NJ: Princeton University Press, pp. 422–425.

Ortenberg, V. (2006) *In search of the Holy Grail: The quest for the Middle Ages*, London and New York: Hambledon Continuum.

Pionke, A. (2008) 'A ritual failure: The Eglinton Tournament, the Victorian medieval revival and Victorian ritual culture', in K. Fugelso and C. Robinson (Eds.), *Studies in Medievalism XVI* (pp. 25–45), Martlesham, UK: Boydell & Brewer.

Rider Haggard, H. (1885) *King Solomon's mines*, Oxford: Oxford University Press, 1991 reprint.

Rider Haggard, H. (1899) *A farmer's year: Being his commonplace book for 1898*, London: Cresset, 1987 reprint.

Rosenberg, J. D. (1987) 'Tennyson and the passing of Arthur,' *Victorian Poetry*, *25*(3–4), 141–150.

Sandbrook, D. (2016) *The great British dream factory: The strange history of our national imagination*, London: Penguin.

Scott, W. (1819) *Ivanhoe*, London: Dent, 1965 reprint.

Sharpe, A. and Kuchta. S. (2007) 'Rediscovering Vinland', *The Pre-Raphaelite Society Newsletter of the United States*, *17*, pp. 1–2.

Shirley, R. (2017) 'Festival landscapes: The contemporary practice of well-dressing in Tissington', *Landscape Research*, *42*(6), 650–662.

Stankiewicz, M.A. (1992) 'From the aesthetic movement to the arts and crafts movement', *Studies in Art Education*, *33*(3), 165–173.

Stiles, T. (2002) *Jesse James: Last rebel of the Civil War*, New York: Knopf.

Twain, M. (1889) *A Connecticut Yankee in King Arthur's court*, 1994 reprint in *Mark Twain Historical Romances* omnibus, New York: The Library of America.

Verne, J. (1864) *Journey to the centre of the Earth*, Ware, UK: Wordsworth, 1996 reprint.

Wawn, A. (2000) *The Vikings and the Victorians: Inventing the Old North in nineteenth-century Britain*, Cambridge: Brewer.

White, T.H. (1938) *The sword in the stone*, London: Harper Voyager, published in *The Once and Future King* omnibus 2015.

Williams, R. (1997) *The contentious crown: Public discussion of the British monarchy in the reign of Queen Victoria*, Aldershot, UK: Ashgate.

3 Medieval kingship
Hollow crown or tower of strength?

Introduction

The calibre of a king in medieval times carried great importance for the ongoing prosperity and security of their realm. Few who desired or attained kingship had the character or qualities needed to be a successful ruler, which are different to those that make a good warrior or knight. Thus, as Larrington (2016: 100) points out: 'Holding and ruling the kingdom justly is a very different matter from winning the throne through conquest … [and] medieval epics often contrast the strength of the hero with the wisdom of the king'. In the right hands, 'the king's name is a tower of strength' (Shakespeare, *Richard III*). The question of what makes a good king has been debated over centuries and is the centrepiece of much of the narratives throughout popular literature, film and television that we consider in this chapter.

Part of the fascination with kingship is the climb to power; the other part is the difficulty of holding on to the crown, with the potential for others to seek to seize it for themselves. As much as the throne is desired by many, it may also prove to be a poisoned chalice: 'for within the hollow crown / That rounds the mortal temples of a king / Keeps Death his court' (Shakespeare, *Richard II*). Some medieval kings suffered cruel or violent deaths, such as Edward II, who was rumoured to have been murdered through the incision of a red-hot-poker in his anus, and Richard II, who was said to have died of starvation in prison. Others died on the battlefield, such as Richard III at the Battle of Bosworth Field.

William Shakespeare, arguably the greatest dramatist in the English language, was repeatedly drawn towards writing about kings, both good and bad, imaginary and real; conveying their foibles, misdeeds and triumphs in prose that lives on centuries after his death. His portraits of some of these medieval kings have become the touchstone by which we think of these individuals (Norwich, 1999). The popular view of Richard III is of a man who is 'determined to prove a villain' (Shakespeare, *Richard III*) to gain power; which leads him inexorably towards evil actions such as murdering his two young nephews. By contrast, Henry V is linked in popular culture to his rallying cries to his troops at Agincourt, such as the famous St Crispin's Day speech – 'We few, we happy few, we band of brothers' – and the inspirational exhortations of, 'once more unto the breach, dear friends, once more' and 'God for Harry! England, and St George!' (Shakespeare,

Henry V). The film *Henry V* (1944), starring Laurence Olivier, was a tool of propaganda by the British government during World War II to boost patriotism and highlight English virtues of tenacity, courage and camaraderie against a common foe (Hilb, 2015). These soliloquies have entered the popular lexicon, with the television series *Band of Brothers* (2001), about soldiers in World War II, an example of the intertextuality that has resulted from their ubiquity.

Yet, Shakespeare was writing for his times, during the Tudor period, when it was politic for him to decry earlier monarchs as corrupt or inept, and our contemporary understanding of some of these kings is changing, due to new archaeological and historic evidence becoming available. He also focussed his plays around certain historical figures, but not others, so that we have plays about Henry V, King John and Richard III, but not Alfred the Great, Henry II or Richard the Lionheart. Interestingly, cinema and television have taken up this mantle in recent years. The role of Henry II in the murder of his archbishop Thomas Becket has been explored in a number of dramatic contexts, including plays and films. Most recently, it is Alfred who has received attention in the *Last Kingdom* book and television series. We consider in this chapter the way that the media has shaped our understanding of various medieval kings – focussing on Alfred the Great, Henry II and Richard III. In particular, we examine the contemporary shift in our thinking about Richard III, linked to the discovery of his remains and the rise of interest in King Alfred, and how this translates into tourism development at Leicester, York and Winchester.

The ideal of the medieval king is arguably King Arthur, and not just in current popular culture. He is viewed as noble, yet flawed; able to be duped, yet ultimately seeking the best in and for his people. We trace the origins of this mythic narrative and its metamorphosis in terms of how it is presented through modern media and explore the packaging of the Camelot myth for tourist consumption at Tintagel in Cornwall and Glastonbury. The relevance of the Arthur story for modern audiences is discussed, including recent attempts to pitch the story at youth. The chapter concludes by examining the continuing fascination with medieval kings, through the aegis of medieval-themed fantasy series such as *Lord of the Rings* and *Game of Thrones*.

The complex king – Alfred the Great

Alfred the Great's vision for one unified kingdom of England is a constant thread through Cornwell's *Last Kingdom* series, inspiring the name of the first book, which refers to Wessex as the final kingdom of the Saxons that has not fallen to the Danes. Alfred not only pushes back the tide but seeks to join the fallen kingdoms together to create 'Engalaland'. It is a monumental achievement for a man who was an unlikely king. King Alfred is described as having 'an undoubted authority in his eyes' (Cornwell, 2005: 9), although he is otherwise unprepossessing, being gaunt with illness and looking older than his years (Figure 3.1). Alfred has claimed the throne and usurped his nephew Aethelwold, after the death of the latter's father, Alfred's older brother Aethelred. This accession is done without bloodshed, but is pragmatic and accepted by the nobles, given the inept

Figure 3.1 Alfred the Great, ca. 1900–ca. 1950.

Identifier H27360. Source: State Library of Victoria.

Aethelwold's deficiencies. Alfred is portrayed as an intelligent, learned and devout man, who took part in pilgrimages to Rome, but is subject to a weakness for young women, which he constantly strives to overcome. He is therefore not perfect, but seeks to be good. This acknowledgement of his own imperfections gives him an insight into the motivations of others, and there is both flexibility and complexity in the way that he makes decisions that often confounds his enemies.

In *The Pale Horseman* (Cornwell, 2005), we see Alfred at his lowest ebb; hiding in the marshes from the Danes, ill with stomach complaints and fearful as to whether his son and heir Edward will survive. The apocryphal moment where Alfred burns the oatcakes is the result of his absorption in solving the problem of defeating the Danes and taking back Wessex. The story, while unlikely to be true, is an example of the common myth, 'where the unrecognised king goes among his people' (Horspool, 2006: 16). It also emphasises how Alfred is able to bring himself back from the jaws of defeat to an unlikely and important victory (Davis, 1971; Horspool, 2006). In this sense, it performs a similar function to the story of Robert the Bruce watching a spider's resilience in spinning a web, which inspired him to persevere and defeat the English at the Battle of Bannockburn in 1314.

Once Alfred decides to engage with the Danes at the Battle of Edington in 878, he must learn how to bring his people along with him, as 'the men liked what they heard, but the idea of England was in Alfred's head, not theirs. He had a dream of one country, but it was too big a dream for the army in the meadow' (Cornwell, 2005: 362). He has to promise that they will defeat their enemy without showing mercy and fight for their families rather than the abstract concept of 'all Saxons'. Alfred is shown to be willing to compromise his ideals to achieve a greater cause, and is thus a good strategic leader. He is also adept at self-promotion, or at least crafting the story that he wants to become the official narrative of his reign, through such tools as the manuscripts that form the *Anglo-Saxon Chronicle*, notably the *Winchester Chronicle*, and the *Vita Aelfredi regis Angul Saxonum* (Life of Alfred, king of the Anglo-Saxons), written by Bishop Asser in 893, who lived at Alfred's court under his patronage (Williams, 2017). In this respect, Alfred appears very modern – there are parallels in contemporary leaders harnessing the power of social media for PR purposes. Even his desire to encourage literacy amongst his populace can be attributed to his 'concern with shaping his own legacy', given, 'it was, after all, no good commissioning biographies and chronicles if nobody could read' (Williams, 2017: 135).

King Alfred was given the epithet of 'Great' during the sixteenth century, but it was during the Victorian era that he became 'England's darling' (Parker, 2017; Williams, 2017). This was partly attributable to the growing interest in the medieval period more generally (see Chapter 2) in the nineteenth century, but also coincided with the commemoration of 1,000 years since his death. The Alfred Millenary in 1901 led to a statue of Alfred being erected in Winchester and generated enthusiasm for a city museum to be built there two years later. The city's Mayor, Alfred Bowker, had argued for Winchester to be the site, as 'There lies the dust of the kings of his ancestors, and of the kings of his successors. Thirty five of his line made Winchester their capital' (quoted in Mead, 1902: 70). The unveiling ceremony was described by F. York Powell, Regius Professor in Modern History at Oxford University, who observed that it was important to finally acknowledge Alfred's achievements:

> Winchester is determined to do her best to honor him whom Gibbon was not afraid to style 'the greatest of English kings', one, too, especially associated with her own history. The callous and stupid neglect of the past is to be amply atoned for, and the generation that is of all since Alfred's most unlike his is prepared to do the highest honor to his name and fame.
>
> (York Powell, 1901: 519)

Despite this flourishing of attention on Alfred in the nineteenth century, popular culture in the twentieth century had largely overlooked the life of the king, other than the little-known film *Alfred the Great* (1969) starring David Hemmings in the title role and a young Michael York as the Dane Guthrum who is defeated by Alfred and later is converted to Christianity. It was neither a critical nor a box-office success. It was really Cornwell's *Last Kingdom* book and television series which has re-focussed attention on Alfred and his kingship. Along with Cornwell's success as an engaging writer of popular historical fiction, the television series has been acclaimed for its realistic locations and sets and strong cast. David

Dawson is a believable Alfred, portraying all the ambiguities and complexity of the character, and noting in an interview that his research led him to try to convey the idea to viewers that,

> far from being that typical warrior king, [Alfred] was this physically frail and yet fiercely intelligent diplomat … he could be the most dangerous man in a room because he was so fiercely intelligent and has an ability to manipulate people to get what he wants.
>
> (quoted in Friedlander, 2015)

Back in 2003, there were concerns raised when Winchester City Council removed Alfred from the official city tourism logo as part of a rebranding exercise. A representative of the Council stated, 'in changing the logo we are not dropping Alfred, but we want to show that there are other symbols, such as the Luminous Motion monument in the cathedral grounds' (Southern Daily Echo, 2003a). The counter-argument was articulated by a local bed-and-breakfast operator, who observed, 'the city's history is our greatest asset and if we don't stress the history we will lose out on people [tourists]' (Southern Daily Echo, 2003a). The *Southern Daily Echo* asked its readers, 'see today's Daily Echo to read some of the many letters we have received protesting about the proposed removal of King Alfred from the city's tourism logo. Do you back the campaign to Save King Alfred?' (Southern Daily Echo, 2003b). The result of the rebranding of Visit Winchester was a generically bland logo that did not reinforce the identity of some residents, who felt a strong connection to the king's role in their history.

Two decades later, Alfred-themed tourism is on the rise, with Winchester seemingly now keen to embrace the king's role in its history once more. The Visit Winchester website home page features a backdrop of the Alfred Statue, so prominent that it cannot be overlooked (Visit Winchester, 2021). It also promotes three separate self-guided walking tours, with the routes contained in a leaflet produced by Visit Winchester and available for downloading. The first, *Alfred's Final Journey*, follows the route that Alfred's remains took when they were moved from the New Minister to Hyde Abbey in 1110 (Visit Winchester, 2021). The second and third walks cover other medieval sites in Winchester such as Winchester Castle, the Cathedral, the High Street and the City Bridge (Visit Winchester, 2021).

Another interesting development taps into a thirst for knowledge about Alfred the Great, as inspired by Cornwell's stories. A company called The Cultural Experience planned to deliver a four-day tour called 'The Pale Horseman: The Wessex of Alfred the Great' in June 2021, led by historian Professor Ryan Lavelle, who was an historical adviser on the *Last Kingdom* series. Apart from Winchester, this tour would visit a number of places associated with Alfred, such as the sites of the Battles of Ashdown (871) and Ethandun (878) and the marshlands where Alfred hid from the Danes in exile. There is a strong educative purpose stated for the tour, which has its own recommended reading list of books about Alfred for participants. The tour website emphasises the importance of understanding the role of kingship during Alfred's reign:

we will try to understand how Anglo-Saxon kingship worked during this cru-
cial period in English history as the most famous son of Wessex, Alfred the
Great, fought for survival against his Viking enemies ... the tour allows us to
explore the reality behind Bernard Cornwell's popular novels.

(The Cultural Experience, 2021)

The flawed king – Henry II

Henry II, who was king from 1154 to 1189, will be forever associated with his
role in the assassination of his Archbishop of Canterbury, Thomas Becket.
Henry's irritation at Becket's assertion of the church's authority over the king led
him to allegedly say the fatal words, 'Who will rid me of this turbulent priest?',
although, 'no contemporary source quotes those words' (Weir, 1999: 192). Jones
(2013) argues that Henry's words were more opaque than the words popularly
attributed to him, 'What miserable drones and traitors have I nurtured and promoted in my household who let their lord be treated with such shameful contempt
by a low-born clerk!' (quoted in Jones, 2013: 78).

Nonetheless, the message behind Henry's angry outburst seems to have been
clearly received by his retinue. Four of Henry's knights slaughtered Thomas
within Canterbury Cathedral on 29 December 1170, an act which was met with
shock and revulsion across the land, and more broadly across Europe (Jones,
2013; Weir, 1999). Henry argued, rather unconvincingly, that he had not meant
his frustration with Becket to be construed as an order to kill the priest, but he
sought absolution from the Church for his sins. Nothing Henry subsequently did
as penance was able to remove the stain on his character, whereas Thomas, seen
as a martyr, was subsequently canonised in 1173, with the site of his death becoming a shrine for pilgrims (see Chapter 7).

It is unfortunate for Henry that this deed has outshone his achievements as a
ruler, as he united a kingdom that had been previously riven in two by the civil
war between King Stephen and Empress Matilda. This period has been labelled
the Anarchy (Jones, 2013; Matthew, 2002), or to quote the *Anglo-Saxon Chronicle*,
a time when, 'it was said openly that Christ was asleep, along with his saints'
(quoted in King, 1974: 180). The expression led to its use by Sharon Penman as
the title of her novel about the battle between these rival claimants – *When Christ
and His Saints Slept* (1994). Henry II was also known for 'his encouragement of
law, administration and learning on a scale that could not be imagined in the days
of his predecessor, King Stephen' (Vincent, 2007: 1).

Henry's fractured relationship with his Archbishop was dramatised in the film
Becket (1964). Both Peter O'Toole as Henry and Richard Burton as Becket were
nominated for an Academy Award for Best Actor; strangely, for overblown and
unconvincing performances. Part of the problem is the dialogue. Henry is constantly delivering weak witticisms and sniping at his wife and mother, and there
is no subtlety in the characterisation. The film does not seek to redeem Henry for
his actions against Becket, suggesting that Henry is a man who doesn't want to
grow up, with a quick temper and a dislike for being told the truth. He tells Becket
at one point, 'Why must you destroy all my illusions?' and is told in return,

Figure 3.2 Plaque Commemorating the Birthplace of St Thomas Becket in London.
Source: Jennifer Frost.

'Because you should have none, My Prince'. Henry seems unsuited to kingship, whereas Becket enjoys the power that accompanies his position of Archbishop and intends to use it to the full.

Canterbury Cathedral still attracts visitors wishing to see the spot where Thomas was killed, which is marked by a candle (see Chapter 7), and in London, a plaque commemorates his birthplace (Figure 3.2). The year 2020 marked the 850th anniversary of Thomas's death, although the coronavirus pandemic led to many of the commemorative events being cancelled or postponed. For example, the exhibition, *Thomas Becket: Murder and the Making of a Saint*, at the British Museum, was moved to 2021. In contrast, few tourism offerings focus on the life of Henry II outside his association with Thomas Becket. Henry's main residence was the Castle of Chinon in France, yet today, its association with women such as Marie d'Anjou and Joan of Arc is more prominent in the interpretation presented to visitors than the story of the men who lived within (see Chapters 4 and 6).

The rehabilitated king – Richard III

Wickham (2016) observes that English kings in the fourteenth century were generally either weak or 'inept' (p. 219) but makes an exception for Henry V and Edward IV, although noting that neither king lived a very long life. Edward IV might seem a curious choice as an effective king at first blush, given that his reign took place during the War of the Roses, in which the houses of York and Lancaster fought each other for power. Edward's ascension to the throne usurped the rights of the incumbent, Henry VI, and his son; and Edward also arguably had blood on his hands, with strong suspicions that he had Henry VI murdered in prison. He is acknowledged, however, as a supremely competent politician and soldier, with, 'an acute understanding of what lay at the heart of good kingship' (Jones, 2014: 285). He had a personality that enabled him to talk to anyone, from any social strata, and appeared to enjoy life to the full (Jones, 2014). This love of good living may have contributed to Edward's untimely death in 1483, leaving behind him a power vacuum, with his son and heir aged just 12 and another son, aged 9. Enter Edward's brother Richard of Gloucester; arguably, as Richard III, the most infamous king in British history. Until recently, the two kings – Edward and Richard – have been considered to be polar opposites.

Richard, protector of the young Edward V, seized the throne when the marriage between Edward IV and his queen Elizabeth Woodville was pronounced invalid and their children thereby illegitimate. Richard's two nephews were held in the Tower of London, until they suddenly disappeared, with no explanation (Jones, 2014). To this day, their bodies have not been found. A popular theory is that Richard ordered the boys to be killed; a narrative which suited the Tudors, who succeeded Richard after his death at the Battle of Bosworth Field, and which Shakespeare perpetuated with his portrait in *Richard III* of a man who is ruthless, scheming and hungry for power at any cost. The play also suggests that Richard poisoned his wife Queen Anne, after their only child and heir died, with the intention of marrying Elizabeth of York, his comely, younger and presumably fertile niece. Richard's cry on the battlefield – 'A horse, a horse, my kingdom for a horse!' – shows the desperation of a man who has lost everything in pursuit of his ambition. Elizabeth married Henry Tudor, thereby joining the House of York and the House of Lancaster to begin the Tudor dynasty.

References to Richard are made in the play using language such as 'poisonous bunch-backed toad' and 'bottled spider', which modern ears recoil from. Even Richard himself declares that he is 'not shaped for sportive tricks [nor] made to court an amorous looking glass' (Shakespeare, *Richard III*). While Williams (2009) argues that the play shows us that 'bodily difference may actually be enabling' and can be used by Richard 'to obscure his shrewd political maneuvers', an alternative view was advanced by some of Richard's supporters that his portrayal as a hunchback was inaccurate (Young and Light, 2018). In a twist on the story, archaeologists found that the skeleton of Richard III, discovered in 2012, displayed a distinct curvature of the spine, consistent with scoliosis (King *et al.*, 2014; Young and Light, 2018).

The alleged murder of the Princes in the Tower was probably the act that has most damned Richard in popular opinion, given the ages of the children and their vulnerability versus his position of trust as their guardian. In contrast, as Larrington notes, 'those who are charged with the killing of children in myth or folklore often baulk at the task' (2016: 226), aware of the particular heinousness of the crime. The prevailing view until recently was that 'the person who benefited most from [the boys'] disappearance was Richard III' (Jones, 2014: 301). He wanted to be king, and the two princes stood in his way. There is, however, an alternative argument that this version of the story does not make sense, and over time, Richard's evil reputation has been rehabilitated or at least cast into doubt through new evidence.

A number of literary works have tried to paint a more sympathetic picture of Richard. *The Sunne in Splendour* (Penman, 1982) traces the life of the man nicknamed Dickon by his family whose loyalty to his brother and king Edward is beyond doubt and who loved both his wife Anne and his niece Elizabeth of York; a love which is reciprocated in both cases. There is no suggestion made here that Richard killed either his wife or his nephews. The crime writer Josephine Tey utilises the convention of a detective solving a murder mystery to dissect the disappearance of the Princes in the Tower in her book *The Daughter of Time* (1951). Alan Grant, an inspector from Scotland Yard, spends his time while recuperating from a broken leg investigating the case, inspired by viewing a reproduction of a portrait of Richard III from the National Portrait Gallery. Grant feels that the portrait is not that of a killer without scruple or empathy, based on his experience of studying faces that he has used to solve crimes. He saw a man accustomed to suffering, conscientious and responsible, a worrier.

Inspector Grant decides to find out more about this man and discovers a number of things. First, the cover-up of the murders was not in Richard's interests, but it suited Henry Tudor, the next King of England. Henry had repealed the Act of Parliament that had declared the two princes illegitimate, in order to make his wife – the boys' sister Elizabeth – legitimate. This put Henry's claim to the throne at risk. Brent Carradine, an historical researcher, tells Grant:

> The *whole point* of Richard's killing the boys was to prevent any rising in their favour, and to get any benefit from the murder the fact of their deaths would *have* to be made public, and as soon as possible … But Henry … Henry's whole case depended on no one's knowing what exactly happened to the boys.
>
> (pp. 216–217, emphasis in original)

Second, contemporary evidence about Richard suggests he was devoted and loyal to his brother Edward. The act of killing Edward's sons appears out of character. Third, the damning accusations of Thomas More, often used as evidence of Richard's perfidy, were not contemporaneous with Richard's death. More was only eight years old when Richard III died and he therefore wrote a second-hand account of events – hearsay in legal parlance. Fourth, the Bill of Attainder brought against Richard after the Battle of Bosworth does not mention the murder of the princes amongst Richard's many crimes. Surely, this would have been front and centre if it were believed to be true?

The Richard III Society, founded in 1924, is an international organisation that has sought to clear Richard's name. It made the headlines in 2012 when the president of the Scottish Branch of the Richard III Society, Philippa Langley, precipitated the search for Richard's grave, which she believed was under a Leicester carpark, which had been built on the site of the old Greyfriars Church. Her years of painstaking research led her to raise money for the *Looking for Richard* project, with an archaeological dig conducted by academics from the University of Leicester, with the assistance of the local council (Langley and Jones, 2014). The local council also contributed to the cost of the excavations, with an eye to 'the potential of the discovery of Richard III to boost tourism in the city' (Young and Light, 2018: 99).

The dig was filmed for a documentary, *The King in the Car Park*, by Britain's Channel 4 (Day, 2013), and the cameras caught the moment when extraordinarily on the very first day, the skeleton of Richard III was uncovered and Langley called for Richard's royal standard to be draped on the box of remains that was dug up, as a mark of respect for the dead king. It was gripping and emotional television. Langley has now written a screenplay for a film on Richard III which she hopes will provide a more nuanced portrait, arguing,

> human beings are not 'saints' or 'sinners' but we each have qualities of both light and dark within us. This is ever our internal struggle and, for me as a screenwriter, makes our stories (our journeys) so interesting and profound.
>
> (quoted in Hughes, 2014)

Pictures of the discovery were everywhere, 'probably there are few skeletons or human remains which have received so much media coverage or which are so recognizable to the general public' (Young and Light, 2018: 94). Part of the fascination with the case involved the various tests that needed to be conducted to make sure that these were indeed the remains of Richard III. These included DNA testing on a descendent on Richard's maternal side. Scientists concluded 'that the evidence for the remains being those of Richard III is overwhelming' (King *et al.*, 2014: 1). Some of the research confirmed the historical hearsay, with scoliosis causing one shoulder to be raised higher than the other, and the injuries suffered by the individual were consistent with those that Richard was supposed to have sustained at the Battle of Bosworth Field (King *et al.*, 2014). Interestingly, we now have an idea of what Richard looked like, with a copy of his reconstructed face based on his skull now on display at the Richard III Visitor Centre in Leicester (Figure 3.3). It is, if anything, more appealing than the portrait that the fictional Inspector Grant looked at in *The Daughter of Time*, showing a man with a pleasant-looking face. Philippa Langley remarked on seeing his facial reconstruction, 'it doesn't look like the face of a tyrant. I'm sorry, but it doesn't' (BBC, 2013).

It was agreed that the remains of Richard III would be reinterred in Leicester Cathedral (see Figure 7.5 in Chapter 7), close to the site of the carpark where they were found. The then chair of the Richard III Society, Phil Stone, observed, 'I think for a medieval king reburied in the 21st Century, it's a fitting place' (BBC, 2015a). Actor Benedict Cumberbatch, who is related to Richard, read a poem during the interment service in 2015, attended by members of the royal family, and at night, 8,000 candles were lit and fireworks let off from the Cathedral's roof (BBC, 2015a). The tone of the service was one of conciliation. The Bishop of Leicester told the congregation,

> people have come in their thousands from around the world to this place of honour, not to judge or condemn but to stand humble and reverent … Today we come to give this King, and these mortal remains the dignity and honour denied to them in death.
>
> (BBC, 2015b)

Figure 3.3 Reconstructed Face of Richard III.
Source: Jennifer Frost.

The choice of Leicester for the grave was not universally popular, with some of Richard's descendants mounting a legal challenge to the decision, arguing that York Minster was a more fitting location for the king's remains, or even Westminster Abbey (BBC, 2015b; Young and Light, 2018). Richard grew up in Yorkshire and visited York on many occasions, as well as belonging to the House of York. The appeal failed, and Leicester also became the site of the new Richard III Visitor Centre, opened in 2014. The city had won the battle for the tourism that would flow from the discovery, given that, 'Richard III was now linked with Leicester in a way which no other place could replicate' (Young and Light, 2018: 100). York has attempted to link the city's history with Richard, with the Richard III Museum being rebranded as the Richard III Experience in 2014. It is difficult, however, to estimate how important this Richard III tourism is to York, given that the city traditionally enjoys high visitation rates due to other factors, such as its Viking heritage (see Chapter 9). In contrast, the benefits for Leicester appear clear, given the city was never a popular tourist destination in the past. Visitor numbers to the Visitor Centre in 2016 in Leicester were estimated at 70,000, with the director, Iain Gordon, stating, 'we have worked hard over the last four years to bring group travel business to the visitor centre and to Leicester' (quoted in Martin, 2018).

While the service of interment and the design of Richard's grave were generally seen as dignified and praiseworthy, the news that Leicester Cathedral planned to stage a production of Shakespeare's *Richard III* in 2017 was met with outrage. Philippa Langley felt that, while she had no problem with the play, 'to perform

[it] right beside this man's grave is quite frankly, a deliberate humiliation' (BBC, 2017). The Cathedral's website opined that 'cathedrals are principally places of Christian worship and witness but additionally they provide space for community events, exhibitions, concerts, dramas and debates. The sacred and the secular coexist as they have done since at least medieval times' (Leicester Cathedral, 2017). This argument for opening up cathedrals (see Chapter 7) misrepresents the core of what Langley was arguing – that it was the juxtaposition of the play with the grave that was distasteful to her, not the fact that it was being performed in a cathedral *per se*. The directors of the play, Ben Horslen and John Risebero, pursued a different line of reasoning, being keen to stress that this production could be viewed as a catalyst for prompting a broader discussion of Richard's character and actions:

> By bringing our production to Leicester Cathedral, the king's final resting place, we hope to entertain the audience with Shakespeare's version of his story, while encouraging them to look beyond it at the more nuanced assessment of Richard that is now emerging.
>
> (Leicester Cathedral, 2017)

Even before the Visitor Centre was completed, a temporary exhibition was housed in the Guildhall at Leicester for 16 months (Young and Light, 2018), which we visited during our early fieldwork in 2014. It was sparse in terms of what was presented, with the centrepiece being the reconstructed head of Richard III (see Figure 3.3), but it served its purpose in providing at least something to take advantage of the interest in Richard shown by visitors to the city. We then visited the Richard III Visitor Centre in 2017; three years after it was opened to the public. It is a state-of-the-art facility housed in a nineteenth-century Gothic Revival school building, partly built on the site of the Greyfriars church and incorporating the original site of Richard's grave, 'which has been transformed into a glass-floored contemplative space for visitors' (King Richard III Visitor Centre, 2021). It won the award for Best Museum at the UK Group Leisure and Travel Awards in 2018 (Martin, 2018), and it presents a skilful blend of historical artefacts and technology, to appeal to a diverse audience.

The story of how Richard's body was rediscovered is presented to visitors, alongside the different theories about Richard and contemporaneous events, including his involvement (or not) in the disappearance of the two princes from the Tower and their likely fate. The website exhorts the visitor to reach their own conclusion as to what really happened: 'Turn detective and travel back through time to uncover the plot lines, birth rights and family connections that combined to create an intricate story of medieval murder, mystery and mayhem' (King Richard III Visitor Centre, 2021). The interpretative material espouses various theories for visitors to mull over (Figure 3.4), following the favoured approach of modern museums of using multiple discourses or counter-narratives rather than one single narrative (Arnold-de-Simine, 2013; Cook, 2016; Laing and Frost, 2019a). The Centre also leverages off the modern interest in archaeology, with the website's reference to 'one of the greatest archaeological detective stories ever

Figure 3.4 Visitor Interpretation Providing Alternative Theories About the Disappearance of the Princes in the Tower at the Richard III Visitor Centre in Leicester.

Source: Jennifer Frost.

told' (King Richard III Visitor Centre, 2021). It shows how far archaeological research has come and how enduring the interest is in this medieval king.

The good king – King Arthur

The archetypal medieval king is surely King Arthur. His story is tragic – he is fated to be killed by his own son, his wife Guinevere is in love with his most trusted friend and knight, Sir Lancelot, and his kingdom and the Round Table have fallen. Arthur's doom is partly his fault, 'a king whose end is shown to derive directly from his sinful coupling with his half-sister Morgan' (Matthews and Matthews, 2008: 203) – and the fruit of that liaison – Mordred – will destroy the idyll that Arthur has built in Camelot. Despite that, Arthur's vision of a society that is just and pure is admirable, and the ideal of Camelot as a mythical Golden Age (Pugh and Weisl, 2012) has resonance even in a more cynical age. We know Arthur is flawed, yet that is part of his appeal. His indecision and misplaced faith in others make him human, but not a monster.

Jacqueline Kennedy used the Arthurian myth with reference to her late husband JFK's administration, telling *Life* magazine, 'there'll be great Presidents again … but there'll never be another Camelot again' (quoted in White, 1963). This was a deliberate attempt at a *political medievalism* (Pugh and Weisl, 2012), aligning President John (Jack) Kennedy with the flawed hero that was Arthur. Jackie explained to journalist Theodore White how Jack had loved the Knights of the Round Table as a child and, 'for Jack, history was full of heroes. And if it made him that way, if it made him see the heroes – maybe other little boys will see. Men are such a combination of good and bad' (quoted in White, 1963). She had an eye to Jack's legacy and wanted to stress that the President, while complex, had always striven to live up to 'Arthurian values' (Pugh and Weisl, 2012: 141).

Ironically, despite Jacqueline Kennedy's repeated references to history, we do not know if Arthur actually existed or where and how the Arthurian myth originated. There are theories that he was based on a Roman army officer stationed in Britain in the second century, while others place him in fifth- or sixth-century Britain (Higham, 2002; Matthews and Matthews, 2008). Several seminal texts helped the myth to spread, such as Geoffrey of Monmouth's *Historia Regum Britanniae* (History of the Kings of Britain) and Chrétien de Troyes's Arthurian romances in the twelfth century, which were probably inspired by the poems of travelling bards from Britain (Orange and Laviolette, 2010). The French romance tradition then led to the stories being taken all across Europe, including back to Britain (Wickham, 2016), in an early version of *intertextuality*, where references are made to previous versions while providing material for future versions, in an endless cycle of adaptation. The Arthur story has been retold again and again throughout the ages, in a fluid and dynamic process, particularly at a time when the printed book was not yet readily available. This fundamental 'instability' of the oral tradition was noted by the Swiss medievalist Paul Zumthor, who used the French term *mouvance*, defined as 'alive, "moving", unfixed' (cited in Driver, 2004: 20) to refer to this fluidity. Thomas Malory's *Le Morte d'Arthur* (the Death of Arthur), dating from the fifteenth century, is the version that we are most familiar with, containing much of the source material that we commonly associate with King Arthur, such as the sword drawn from the stone, and the Round Table (Matthews and Matthews, 2008).

The story is often updated to incorporate current issues or 'recast an older story in light of current tastes' (Driver, 2004: 20). A stronger backstory for the female characters such as Morgan and Guinevere is provided in *The Mists of Avalon* (1982) – see Chapter 4 – so that Arthur is not the focus of the tale and these women's traditional role as villainess or temptress is subverted (Pugh and Weisl, 2012). Another way of writing the tale to appeal to a younger audience is to have the characters as children or young adults. Both examples discussed here have a strong theme of *educating the king*. Arthur is a young boy in *The Sword in the Stone* (White, 1938). Known as Wart, a ward of Sir Ector, the young boy is provided with a series of lessons from his new tutor – Merlin. Wart is changed into various animals, birds and insects, which teaches him about the way that power should be exercised, the importance of camaraderie and to understand the nature of warfare. This education will help Arthur to become a king who tries to be fair and to stand up for the things he believes in. We only learn his real identity – King Arthur – in the last line of the book. In the television series *Merlin* (2008–2012), Prince Arthur (Bradley James) is good-looking, arrogant and impetuous, but underneath the bumptious exterior has a good heart. His two good friends – Merlin, his servant (Colin Morgan) and Gwen (Angel Coulby), the servant of his father's ward, Morgana (Katie McGrath) – teach him over time to be more humble and to develop his finer qualities, such as courage and tolerance. Merlin is the same age as Arthur, rather than an old man, which changes the dynamics of the narrative – Arthur is learning from his peers. He also does not realise until the final episode that Merlin is a wizard, which is a departure from the conventional story, but one which keeps the audience guessing as to when this reveal will occur (Sherman, 2015). It makes Arthur's story arc more interesting, in that his views on magic are his own, and not influenced by those of his friend. Arthur realises that he does not wish to be a king like his father Uther (Anthony Head), who has banished all magic from the kingdom of Camelot, and must stand up for the principles he believes in. Magic is used in *Merlin* as a metaphor for being different or espousing beliefs that are seen as subversive or dangerous. For Arthur, those who have the gift of magic should not be ostracised. This open-mindedness will ultimately lead to his doom; but the programme suggests that a good king should not fear opposition or difference of opinion.

The counterpoint to the success of *Merlin* is Guy Ritchie's *King Arthur: Legend of the Sword* – the film that Mumford (2017) described as an 'epic fail' both artistically and commercially. It tried to be relevant to modern audiences by making Arthur (Charlie Hunnam) a lout, hanging around with his gang of mates, who act more as hooligans than knights. The problem for many viewers was that 'the "blokes and banter" tone central to much of Ritchie's work takes precedence over the traditional romantic elements found in older interpretations of the legend' (Mumford, 2017), and the future king lacks any kind of redeeming feature that would gain the sympathy of the audience. The planned sequels were never made, and the lack of success of this proposed franchise suggests that reinvention of a popular myth can only go so far. When it undermines the qualities that have made the character of Arthur so beloved – his nobility – it appears that audiences will revolt. It can be contrasted with the most recent variant on the Arthur myth in *The Kid Who Would Be King* (2019). As with Wart in White's *The Sword in the Stone* (1938), young English schoolboy Alex (Louis Ashbourne Serkis) does not realise his destiny until he takes Excalibur out of the stone. He must destroy the evil Morgana, with the help of his band of young friends and former enemies, who must work together to save England from doom. It is a fun and fresh look at the story, an example of the medievalism of *national identities* (Eco, 1986), which could be viewed as a commentary on the failings of modern-day political leadership. While it didn't do exceptionally well at the box office, *The Kid Who Would Be King* received mostly positive reviews, perhaps because there was a moral to this story that appealed to people in an era of concerns over climate change and political change – that a strong community with a common cause will triumph.

In our research for this book, we visited Tintagel in Cornwall, which is often referred to as the birthplace of King Arthur (Laing and Frost, 2019b). Visiting its castle (Figure 3.5) requires a steep and somewhat treacherous climb, some of which is up stone steps cut into the rock, which tested both of us. We were surprised at the number and age of many of the visitors, who did not let the challenge of the activity stop them from visiting the castle. Unlike the Richard III Visitor Centre, mentioned earlier, the castle did not feature interpretation that incorporated 'competing theories of evidence' (Robb, 1998: 593). Instead, English

Figure 3.5 Ruins of Tintagel Castle, Cornwall.
Source: Jennifer Frost.

Heritage signage at Tintagel told us that 'it was probably the seasonal home of a regional king'. This sort of 'myth-busting' (Orange and Laviolette, 2010; Robb, 1998) disappoints visitors, particularly where they are not provided with an alternative theory as to its previous occupant (Laing and Frost, 2019b). What is undeniable is the magnificence of its location, perched high on cliffs over the sea and the romance evoked by its ruins. The ambience of Tintagel Castle still conjures up a mythical medieval past, despite English Heritage's attempts at creating a more prosaic narrative for visitors.

The town of Tintagel in 2017 did not appear to have changed substantially from the town that was examined in previous studies by Robb (1998) and Orange and Laviolette (2010). The street heading towards the castle was still lined with shops selling Camelot-themed souvenirs, including a bin of plastic 'Excalibur swords' priced at £1.99 each (Figure 12.4). We later found that similar swords with the same wording were featured in a photo contained in the article by Orange and Laviolette (2010), at a slightly cheaper price of £1.40. The Arthurian connection was emphasised by King Arthur's Café, a pub called King Arthur's Arms and its competitor, Ye Olde Malthouse Inn, complete with Guinevere's Restaurant. One of the more curious and long-lasting visitor attractions was King Arthur's Great Halls, complete with a round table and granite thrones, which has been open to tourists since 1933. The Halls were originally built for the Fellowship of the Knights of the Round Table of King Arthur, 'established in 1927 by Frederick Thomas Glassock, a custard millionaire' (Orange and Laviolette, 2010: 92). The attraction still features King Arthur's story narrated by actor Robert Powell; as documented by Robb (1998), which presumably hasn't been updated in the interim. Outside the Halls, there is a photo opportunity to pose with 'the sword in the stone' (Figure 3.6). Like Orange and Laviolette (2010), we also noted kitsch featuring magical characters such as mermaids, unicorns and fairies; crystals; Celtic jewellery; and a preponderance of *Lord of the Rings* souvenirs. The town would appear to be fossilised in time if it weren't for the presence of *Game of Thrones* official merchandise, including a replica dragon skull and mugs adorned with wolves. Our overall impression was that the town was tired and overcommercialised, although it could be argued that the latter is not a new phenomenon for Tintagel. The association with Camelot has been pushed to its limit since the nineteenth century. A faux castle hotel built for Victorian tourists, the King Arthur's Castle Hotel, is still operating but is now called the Camelot Castle Hotel. In that earlier era, a visitor 'descended from trains named Merlin, Lyonesse and Pendragon' (Orange and Laviolette, 2010: 90).

Two other places in England leverage tourism off the King Arthur story. The first is Winchester, which, apart from its links with King Alfred, discussed earlier, has a Great Hall in which hangs a Round Table (Figure 3.7). The table is thought to have been commissioned by Edward I, and 'its symbolic importance for his attempt to rule the whole of Britain and Scotland would not have been lost on his guests' (Matthews and Matthews, 2008: 222). The second destination is the town of Glastonbury in Somerset. Its association with Arthur has a long history. In 1191, the bones of Arthur and Guinevere were supposedly discovered at Glastonbury Abbey. According to a chronicler, Gerald of Wales, Henry II wanted to suppress

Figure 3.6 Retail Advertising in Tintagel Linked with Arthur.
Source: Jennifer Frost.

the Welsh myth that Arthur would return if needed and was keen to encourage excavation: 'The king had told the abbot on a number of occasions that he had learnt from the historical accounts of the Britons and from their bards that Arthur had been buried in the churchyard there' (quoted in Matthews and Matthews, 2008: 215). An alternative theory is that a monk was digging a grave and uncovered the coffin. Whatever the truth behind the discovery, it boosted pilgrimage and thus revenue to the site (Matthews and Matthews, 2008). The Abbey ruins can still be visited today (Figure 3.8) with signage referring to it as 'renowned as the legendary burial place of King Arthur and the earliest Christian foundation in Britain'.

As with Tintagel, souvenir shops in Glastonbury stock items with Celtic and magical associations, but with a pagan edge, linked with witchcraft, Gothic and even Viking sub-cultures. Signboards advertise the services of clairvoyants, mystics, healers, rune readers and shamans, and shops sport names such as 'Rainbows End Café', 'The Goddess and the Green Man', 'Cat and Cauldron' and 'Shield Maiden' (Figure 9.4). Marijuana is advertised overtly, such as the Bag End Grow Shop – named in homage to Bilbo's home in *Lord of the Rings* – which supplies

Figure 3.7 The Round Table in the Great Hall at Winchester.

Source: Jennifer Frost.

Figure 3.8 Glastonbury Abbey.
Source: Jennifer Frost.

bongs, pipes and seeds. This is a different medieval imagining, linked to the medievalism of *so-called tradition* (Eco, 1986) with its occult or hippy philosophies. It may also be encouraged as a result of the presence of the Glastonbury Festival, started in 1970 and mostly held annually, which brings in a wave of people in a liminal atmosphere of free expression and alternative sub-cultures.

The king is dead, long live the king

There is a direct line between the historical narratives and those kings portrayed in medieval fantasy fiction – notably Tolkien's *The Lord of the Rings* trilogy and Martin's *Game of Thrones* – but also with the Arthurian legends. In *The Lord of the Rings*, we have a wandering king-in-waiting (Aragorn) who is unsure about his readiness to rule, but who finally accepts his destiny to bring together the people of Middle-Earth, becoming the first High King of the Reunited Kingdom. In this way, there are parallels with Alfred the Great, in exile in the marshes. There are also strong similarities between the fictional Aragorn and the mythical Arthur:

> They are both raised in exile, unaware of their real identities. They are both the subject of prophecies that one day they will come to their true inheritance. They both state their claims to kingship by reclaiming their forefathers' swords … And both of them have their success, at least in part, to the tutelage of a wise old wizard.

> (Sandbrook, 2016: 196–197)

In *Game of Thrones*, we have King Robert Baratheon, who would have killed Lyanna Stark's baby Aegon, the son of the deposed heir to the Iron Throne, Rhaegar Targaryen, had the child not been smuggled away by Lyanna's brother Ned and brought up as his bastard son. The killing of innocent children who are threats to the succession of a usurper is reminiscent of the long-held belief that Richard III had killed his nephews to safeguard his claim to the throne of England. It is another example of *intertextuality*, with these stories resonating with fans because there is an authenticity that we recognise and respond to.

Even the recent reports of bad blood between Princes William and Harry have a Shakespearean quality to them – with echoes of the enmity between rival brothers and court intrigues. Without being conscious of it, the ideal of kingship and its extension into leadership in the modern era is deeply ingrained in us. Jacqueline Kennedy's reference to Camelot was indeed shrewd. Similarly, the places that we visit as tourists are consumed against this cultural backdrop, and thus cannot be understood without an appreciation of these deeper meanings for the visitor.

References

Arnold-de-Simine, S. (2013) *Mediating memory in the museum: Trauma, empathy, nostalgia*, Houndmills: Palgrave Macmillan.

BBC (2013) 'Richard III: Facial reconstruction show's king's features', *BBC*, 5 February, https://www.bbc.com/news/uk-england-leicestershire-21328380 (accessed January 12, 2020).

BBC (2015a) 'Richard III's tomb unveiled at Leicester Cathedral', *BBC*, 27 March, https://www.bbc.com/news/uk-england-leicestershire-32085532 (accessed January 5, 2021).

BBC (2015b) 'Richard III: Leicester Cathedral reburial service for king', *BBC*, 26 March, https://www.bbc.com/news/uk-england-leicestershire-32052800 (accessed January 5, 2021).

BBC (2017) 'Leicester Cathedral to stage "humiliating" Richard III play', *BBC*, 10 May, https://www.bbc.com/news/uk-england-leicestershire-39856414 (accessed January 5, 2021).

Cook, M. (2016) 'Counter-narratives of slavery in the Deep South: The politics of empathy along and beyond River Road', *Journal of Heritage Tourism*, *11*(3), 290–308.

Cornwell, B. (2005) *The pale horseman*, London: Harper Collins.

The Cultural Experience (2021) 'The pale horseman: The Wessex of Alfred the Great', *The Cultural Experience*, https://www.theculturalexperience.com/tours/the-pale-horseman-battlefield-tour/ (accessed January 5, 2021).

Davis, R. (1971) 'Alfred the Great: Propaganda and truth', *History*, *56*(187), 169–182.

Day, E. (2013) 'Philippa Langley: "I just felt I was walking on Richard III's grave. I can't explain it"', *The Guardian*, 8 December, https://www.theguardian.com/uk-news/2013/dec/08/philippa-langley-richard-third-car-park (accessed December 5, 2020).

Driver, M. (2004) 'What's accuracy got to do with It? Historicity and authenticity in medieval film', in M. Driver and S. Ray (Eds.), *The medieval hero on screen. Representations from Beowulf to Buffy* (pp. 19–37), Jefferson, NC: McFarland.

Eco, U. (1986) *Faith in fakes*, London: Seeker & Warburg.

Friedlander, W. (2015) 'The Last Kingdom's' David Dawson on learning his English history, *Variety*, 17 October, https://variety.com/2015/tv/news/last-kingdom-david-dawson-king-alfred-1201620614/ (accessed December 10, 2020).

Higham, N. (2002) *King Arthur: Myth-making and history*, London: Routledge.

Hilb, B. (2015) 'Contesting Olivier and JFK: The opposition to wartime propaganda in Orson Welles's *Chimes at Midnight*', *Interdisciplinary Literary Studies*, *17*(2), 164–188.

Horspool, D. (2006) *King Alfred: Burnt cakes and other legends*, Cambridge, MA: Harvard University Press.

Hughes, O. (2014) 'The search for the real Richard III: The king's grave with Philippa Langley', *Nerdalicious*, 2 June, https://nerdalicious.com.au/history/the-search-for-the-real-richard-iii-the-kings-grave-with-philippa-langley/ (accessed January 5, 2021).

Jones, D. (2013) *The Plantagenets: The kings who made England*, London: Harper Collins.

Jones, D. (2014) *The hollow crown: The Wars of the Roses and the rise of the Tudors*, London: Faber & Faber.

King, E. (1974) 'King Stephen and the Anglo-Norman aristocracy', *History*, *59*(196), 180–194.

King, T.E., Fortes, G., Balaresque, P., Thomas, M., Balding, D., Delser, P., ..., Schürer, K. (2014) 'Identification of the remains of King Richard III', *Nature Communications*, *5*(1), 1–8.

King Richard III Visitor Centre (2021) 'Discover an incredible story at the King Richard III Visitor Centre', *King Richard III Visitor Centre*, https://kriii.com/ (accessed January 3, 2021).

Laing, J. and Frost, W. (2019a) 'Presenting narratives of empathy through dark commemorative exhibitions during the centenary of World War One', *Tourism Management*, *74*, 190–199.

Laing, J. and Frost, W. (2019b) 'Imagining the medieval in the modern world: Film, fantasy and heritage', in C. Lundberg and V. Ziakas (Eds.), *The Routledge handbook of popular culture and tourism* (pp. 96–107), London: Routledge.

Langley, P. and Jones, M. (2014) *The king's grave: The search for Richard III*, London: St Martin's Press.

Larrington, C. (2016) *Winter is coming: The medieval world of Game of Thrones*, New York: IB Tauris.

Leicester Cathedral (2017) 'Antic disposition presents: Richard III', *Leicester Cathedral*, https://leicestercathedral.org/antic-disposition-presents-richard-iii/ (accessed January 6, 2020).

Martin, D. (2018) 'Richard III Visitor Centre in Leicester beats British Museum and Tate Britain to top tourism award', *The Leicester Mercury*, 15 October, https://www.leicestermercury.co.uk/news/leicester-news/richard-iii-visitor-centre-leicester-2103244 (accessed November 3, 2020).

Matthew, D. (2002) *King Stephen*, London and New York: Hambledon and London.

Matthews, J. and Matthews, C. (2008) *King Arthur: History and legend*, London: Folio Society.

Mead, E. D. (1902) 'The King Alfred Millennial', *Proceedings of the American Antiquarian Society*, *15*(April), 70–97.

Mumford, G. (2017) 'Epic fail: Why has King Arthur flopped so badly?' *The Guardian*, 17 May, https://www.theguardian.com/film/2017/may/16/epic-fail-why-has-king-arthur-flopped-so-badly (accessed December 5, 2020).

Norwich, J.J. (1999) *Shakespeare's kings: The great plays and the history of England in the Middle Ages: 1337–1485*, New York and London: Scribner.

Orange, H. and Laviolette, P. (2010) 'A disgruntled tourist in King Arthur's court: Archaeology and identity at Tintagel, Cornwall', *Public Archaeology*, *9*(2), 85–107.

Parker, J. (2017) *'England's darling': The Victorian cult of Alfred the Great*, Manchester: Manchester University Press.

Penman, S. (1982) *The sunne in splendour*, London: Penguin.

Penman, S. (1994) *When Christ and his saints slept*, London: Penguin.

Pugh. T. and Weisl, A. (2012) *Medievalisms: Making the past in the present*, London: Routledge.

Robb, J. (1998) 'Tourism and legends: Archaeology of heritage', *Annals of Tourism Research*, *25*(3), 579–596.

Sandbrook, D. (2016) *The great British dream factory: The strange history of our national imagination*, London: Penguin.

Sherman, J. (2015) 'Source, authority and audience in the BBC's *Merlin*', *Arthuriana*, *25*(1), 82–100.

Southern Daily Echo (2003a) 'Ditching our King Alfred will hit tourism', *Southern Daily Echo*, 17 June, https://www.dailyecho.co.uk/news/5591459.ditching-our-king-alfred-will-hit-tourism/ (accessed January 2, 2021).

Southern Daily Echo (2003b) 'Alfred is our hero', *Southern Daily Echo*, 13 June, https://www.dailyecho.co.uk/news/5591610.alfred-is-our-hero/ (accessed January 2, 2021).

Tey, J. (1951) *The daughter of time*, London: Arrow.

Vincent, N. (2007) 'Introduction: Henry II and the historians', in C. Harper-Bill and N. Vincent (Eds.), *Henry II: New interpretations* (pp. 1–23), Woodridge: Boydell.

Visit Winchester (2021) 'Follow in the footsteps of King Alfred', *Winchester City Council* https://www.visitwinchester.co.uk/listing/city-walk/ (accessed January 14, 2021).

Weir, A. (1999) *Eleanor of Aquitaine: By the wrath of God, Queen of England*, London: Pimlico.

White, T. (1938) *The sword in the stone*, London: Harper Voyager, published in *The Once and Future King* omnibus 2015.

White, T. (1963) 'For President Kennedy: An epilogue', *Life Magazine*, 6 December, https://www.jfklibrary.org/asset-viewer/archives/THWPP/059/THWPP-059-009#folder_info (accessed January 5, 2021).

Wickham, C. (2016) *Medieval Europe: From the breakup of the Western Roman Empire to the Reformation*, New Haven, CT: Yale University Press.

Williams, K. (2009) 'Enabling Richard: The rhetoric of disability in Richard III', *Disability Studies Quarterly*, *29*(4), https://dsq-sds.org/article/view/997/1181In (accessed January 14, 2021).

Williams, T. (2017) *Viking Britain: A history*, London: William Collins.

York Powell, F. (1901) 'The Alfred Millenary of 1901', *The North American Review*, *173*(539), 518–532.

Young, C. and Light, D. (2018) 'The corpse, heritage, and tourism: The multiple ontologies of the body of King Richard III of England', in M. Frihammer and H. Silverman (Eds.) *Heritage of death: Landscapes of emotion, memory and practice* (pp. 92–104), Abingdon: Routledge.

4 The princess in the tower?

Changing representations of
medieval women

Introduction: pretty in pink

Medieval castles are popular with tourists but must compete with other attractions and seek to engage a younger audience. We have noticed a trend to court young girls to visit castles, by linking them with the childhood appeal of fairy tales and princesses. Two examples stand out for us. The first is that while undertaking fieldwork at Warwick Castle in 2010 and 2011, we saw that its operators, Merlin Entertainments, had renamed the Watergate Tower as The Princess Tower, complete with a Barbie pink banner (Figure 4.1). There is a tongue-in-cheek sign (also in pink) as visitors approach that makes the target audience clear, 'Ye Boys, Dads, Grandads, Uncles, Nephews and Brothers. You may find the content of the Princess Tower offensive. You have been warned'.

The Princess Tower is promoted as the site of a love story between the legendary Guy of Warwick and his lady love:

> *Do you know someone who dreams of being a Princess? In our Princess Tower,*
> *wishes really can come true ... if only for a while.* Once upon a time the brave
> Guy of Warwick went on a fearful quest to win the hand of the beautiful Felice.
> After falling foul of an evil sorcerer, it is now up to Felice to break the curse to
> free her sweetheart. Join the princess to help to solve the riddle which will
> reunite Guy and Felice to live happily ever after.
>
> (Warwick Castle, 2020)

There may be a link here with Disney's *Tangled* (2010), a retelling of the Rapunzel fairy tale, where the princess is locked in a tower and uses her long hair like a rope to escape. Both the princess in *Tangled* and Merlin Entertainment's version of a princess are resourceful and resilient, rather than the passive 'damsel in distress', but still wear a medieval-style long gown and, in the Warwick version, a coronet. While visiting the Princess Tower, children can dress up like a medieval princess inside a human-sized replica of a 3D book cover, so that they can have a photo of themselves in their very own fairy tale. There is also a princess 'hall of fame', which includes Princess Isabella of Castille (1451–1504) alongside more recent examples of Princess Grace of Monaco and Princess Diana. The focus on the medieval female, while welcome in broadening the castle's appeal beyond a male-centric narrative, is based on fantasies connected to royalty, rather than

Figure 4.1 The Princess Tower, Warwick Castle.
Source: Jennifer Frost.

depicting the life of ordinary women of the time. This supports the observation by Dempsey *et al*. (2020: 365): 'Gendered interpretations of castles remain focused on the exceptional stories of named, elite women'.

Our second example is the Château de Chinon in the Loire Valley in France, which also uses motifs connected to the medieval princess that appear to be designed to appeal to young girls. Arguably its most famous association is with Joan of Arc. She met Charles VII at Chinon in 1429 and persuaded him of her avowed belief in the divine guidance she was given. He provided her with an army to fight and help conquer the English, who were laying siege to the town of Orléans, and the success of the strategy led to Charles being crowned King of France, with Joan at his side. Joan famously dressed as a soldier and became known as the Maid of Orléans for these exploits. Captured by the English, she was subsequently burnt at the stake in 1431 for various crimes, including witchcraft and dressing as a man. The King had failed to save her, perhaps because of her growing celebrity amongst the common people, but also due to fears that his reign would be tainted by association with a heretic.

While Chinon does present Joan's story in rooms inside the castle (Chapter 6), in the castle surrounds and occasionally inside, there is a greater focus on engaging young visitors through a less challenging story arc. The Chinon gardens are replete with Barbie pink signage and banners featuring pink crowns. They feature narratives such as 'When the Queen Goes Hunting' (Figure 4.2), which refers to the fifteenth-century Princess Madeleine, the daughter of Charles VII and Marie d'Anjou. Madeleine, 'recreates the afternoon's hunting outing with dolls gifted to her by her mother ... created in Paris, especially for the princess'. Other signs are headed '24 Hours in the Life of a Queen', 'At Marie's Table' and 'The Queen Is a Fashion Victim'. Again, the emphasis is on the high-born medieval lady or the princess. The life of King Charles's consort takes precedence over Joan of Arc.

In this chapter, we examine how medieval women are represented in the media and tourism and the evolving narrative about women's role in medieval society. We start with a discussion of the traditional emphasis in contemporary popular culture of narratives connected to high-born women of the medieval period and their connections with chivalry and courtly love. These real medieval women often have their fantasy equivalents, most notably in the book and television series *Game of Thrones*, which often depicts women who yearn after power, or who learn that they have to acquire it to survive in a man's world. Some of these are in the fairy-tale tradition of the wicked queen juxtaposed with the innocent princess who is the focus of jealousy by an older woman, as in *Snow White*. Others fit the trope of the high-born schemer. Campbell's (1949) *Hero's Journey* is a useful lens to understand these women, either as the heroine of their own narrative, or as an archetype of the goddess or the temptress. They can also be studied through the prism of medievalisms (Eco, 1986; Pugh and Weisl, 2012). Their stories may represent the romanticisation of the medieval world. In other cases, there is intertextuality in that their character acts as a vehicle for a commentary on contemporary issues such as feminine emancipation or disempowerment.

Figure 4.2 Princess-Themed Interpretation, Castle of Chinon, France.

Source: Jennifer Frost.

We will also explore the enduring interest in the medieval princess, which was originally framed by fairy tales. In the modern era, this can be understood through the construct of the *Disney Princess*; one of Disney's most popular and lucrative franchises. We consider the growth in the princess industry and its link with medievalisms, as well as the ways that tourism has appropriated or been built around this interest. This princess mythology – often linked to marriage and living 'happily ever after' – can be contrasted with the female warrior leader. These women embody a different narrative, where women decide their own paths and actively defend themselves and others or seek out what they want. It is a more nuanced story of women in the medieval period than previously seen, although generally still focussing on women of noble birth and influence.

The chapter concludes with a critique about the relative absence of low-born or peasant women in representations of the medieval period. The exceptions to this rule are often servants or companions to the aristocratic or high-born, and thus onlookers on a world of privilege. We examine the reasons why this might be the case and whether this has changed in recent times.

Beyond the damsel in distress

Ideals of chivalry were introduced by the Christian Church in their education of young men as a means of tempering or channelling violence and thuggish behaviour and encouraging protective instincts and a desire for justice and fairness (Wickham, 2016). Chivalry shaped a view of high-born medieval women as fragile creatures in need of protection in times of danger – the so-called 'damsel in distress'. In part, it reflects the archetype of the woman as a goddess (Campbell, 1949), in that she represents an object to guard or rescue through a quest. It is also an example of the medievalism of the Romantic Middle Ages (Eco, 1986), in that females of this era have often been idealised as virtuous and vulnerable.

The alternative to the romanticised medieval female is to paint her as a dangerous schemer – a dichotomy that Freud in the early twentieth century labelled the *Madonna/Whore Complex*, where women are either *Good* or *Bad* (Bareket *et al.*, 2018). This can also be seen in fairy tales, which Zipes (1988) argues has been exaggerated by Disney in *Snow White*, *Cinderella* and *Sleeping Beauty*, where, 'evil is always associated with female nature out of control – two witches and a bitchy stepmother with her nasty daughters' (p. 24). The archetype of the wicked queen in fairy tales does, however, have its roots in history. For a period in the ninth century, Anglo-Saxon wives of monarchs were not crowned as queens after the exploits of Queen Eadburh, wife of Beorhtric of Wessex, who accidentally poisoned her husband while trying to kill his favourite; just one of numerous 'troublesome and feisty medieval queens' (Larrington, 2016: 3). Some of these women are depicted as using their beauty and seductive qualities to influence their partners, often to the advantage of their own families. This reflects Campbell's (1949) archetype of the Temptress who tries to sway the hero from their course or path and must be resisted.

Both Elizabeth Woodville, who married Edward IV, and Anne Boleyn, who married Henry VIII, exemplified this archetype. Neither marriage was dynastically important, with each being a commoner who was selected as a consort because the king was attracted to them. This ability to bewitch a monarch was subsequently painted as a form of witchcraft. Richard, Duke of Gloucester, the future King Richard III, argued after Edward's death that Elizabeth's marriage was not legitimate, as Edward had been promised to another at the time. As a result, Elizabeth's sons were disinherited from the throne and subsequently disappeared from the Tower of London. Elizabeth retreated to Bermondsey Abbey – a convenient way for a medieval woman to save herself from trouble, but also a solution that ensured that she was both out of sight and out of mind. Elizabeth's eldest daughter, also called Elizabeth, was wed to Henry Tudor, later Henry VII, in a marriage that joined the Houses of York and Lancaster together and created the Tudor royal dynasty. In contrast to her mother, Elizabeth of York is generally viewed as a pawn whose marriage gave Henry's reign legitimacy (Jones, 2014; Seward, 1995), Elizabeth's daughter-in-law, Queen Anne Boleyn, had a more violent end, being beheaded in the Tower. Anne was accused of treason, but this was a convenient excuse for the king to rid himself of a wife who had only borne him a daughter – the future Elizabeth I – and no sons, and whose charms had now palled in comparison to the nubile Jane Seymour.

High-born women in the medieval period often presided over tournaments, where their favour was worn by combatants, but they did not generally take part in the jousting or a mêlée, nor were they commonly involved in warfare, in line with, 'the belief that fighting was men's business, in part because training for knighthood was so intensive that it had to start in childhood, which was never done for a girl' (Blythe, 2001: 245). They inspired rather than committed deeds of valour. Three exceptions are worth noting. The first was Joan of Arc, who commanded armies but is not believed to have engaged in combat. The second was Sichelgaita, wife of Robert Guiscard, the Norman Count of Apulia and Calabria. In 1081, the Normans invaded Byzantium, and Sichelgaita commanded the right flank. Under a savage assault from the Varangian Guard – the Byzantine emperor's bodyguard primarily composed of Anglo-Saxons who had fled England after the Norman Conquest – the Normans broke. Brandishing her spear, Sichelgaita rallied her troops and counter-attacked, winning the day (Norwich, 1995). The third was Eleanor of Aquitaine, who participated in the Second Crusade (1147–1149) and visited Antioch and Jerusalem (Weir, 1999).

Eleanor, then Queen of France, was keen to escape the ennui of court life, and her offer of her vassals to boost the numbers of crusaders made it difficult for her husband, King Louis VII of France, to refuse her request to join the campaign. Other women followed Eleanor's lead, but there is no evidence that any of them physically fought in any of the battles. There is a popular but now discredited tale that her and her ladies were, 'armed like Amazons and riding white horses' (Blythe, 2001: 247), wearing, 'white tunics emblazoned with red crosses, plumes, white buskins and cherry-red boots' (Weir, 1999: 51). This legend is, however, testimony to the fact that she was one of the most charismatic, highly educated and beautiful women of her time, and it was somewhat plausible that she would have attracted attention to herself in this manner.

Eleanor had a sophisticated and elegant upbringing as the heiress to the Duchy of Aquitaine. She was able to own and inherit property and enjoyed a greater social status and involvement in public life than was common for women at the time (Weir, 1999). It is not surprising that she found it difficult to conform to the role of a passive consort when she married and both of her marriages turned out to be disappointing. Her first husband, Louis, was overly pious and bored her. She is said to have developed strong feelings for her uncle Raymond while in Antioch, which drove a wedge between her and Louis, and the marriage was annulled in 1152. At the age of 30, which was unusually old for a bride of the times, she married King Henry, who was ten years her junior. This tempestuous union, which is said to have begun with passion on both sides, and which was certainly politically advantageous to both, ended in estrangement and became poisonous when Eleanor was accused of plotting against the king.

It is surprising that there have been few attempts to explore Eleanor's life in film or television. Those that do generally concentrate on the later years of her life when she was Queen of England, most notably *The Lion in Winter* (1968), with Katharine Hepburn as Eleanor. It was remade for television in 2003 with Glenn Close in the role. The plot focuses on Christmas 1183, when Eleanor, then aged 61, is temporarily let out of prison by her second husband, Henry II of England, and the couple argue over which of their sons should become Henry's heir apparent. The queen trades barbs with her husband and is presented as a political operator, enjoying the cut and thrust of court intrigue. In *Becket* (1964), Eleanor (Pamela Brown) and her mother-in-law Matilda (Martita Hunt), are critical of what the two women see as Henry's (Peter O'Toole) weakness with respect to his Archbishop Thomas Becket (Richard Burton). The two women snipe at Henry's lack of gumption as they sit over their embroidery hoops, like a medieval Greek chorus, adding to the rising tension he feels over the actions of 'this troublesome priest'. In *Robin Hood* (2010), Eleanor (Eileen Atkins) is in her mid-seventies, when her son John is crowned king and she tries, with limited success, to advise him.

In contrast, Eleanor's earlier life in France has largely been overlooked for its dramatic potential, particularly the cultural importance of her court at Poitiers and its encouragement of poets, musicians and writers. While ideas about *courtly love* spread throughout Europe, they are particularly identified with Eleanor's court. Rules of conduct were created which, 'deified women, according them superiority over men, and laid down codes of courtesy, chivalry and gentlemanly conduct' (Weir, 1999: 9), built around non-physical romantic relationships, where the normal power imbalance between men and women was reversed and women's desires held sway. This was in contrast to contemporaneous rules about marriage, where aristocratic women were often a pawn in arrangements that had dynastic or political implications. Eleanor's championing of the lot of women was therefore unusual, 'in a period when females were invariably relegated to a servile role' (Weir, 1999: 355).

Another French-born Queen of England with a colourful life was Isabella, wife of Edward II. She is depicted as an ingénue princess in *Braveheart* (1995), married to a weak heir to the throne who is more interested in his favourite, Piers Gaveston, than his wife. Isabella (Sophie Marceau) is sympathetic towards

William Wallace (Mel Gibson) and his cause and is carrying his child after their illicit affair. The liaison with Wallace is of course nonsense, as he died when she was just ten years old and she did not arrive in England for two more years. In *Knightfall* (2017–2019), a younger Isabella (Genevieve Gaunt) is shown as a jealous schemer, conspiring against her sister-in-law Margaret (Clementine Nicholson) to make it appear that she was engaged in adultery. Isabella is told by her father King Philip IV (Ed Stoppard), 'you must always be the wolf, never the sheep'; a portent of her future nickname of She-Wolf of France. After nearly 20 years of marriage, Isabella rebelled against her husband and raising an army with her lover Roger Mortimer forced Edward II to abdicate. He was replaced on the throne by his son King Edward III. Edward III later captured Mortimer and his mother at Nottingham Castle. Mortimer was executed for treason, including the murder of Edward II, who was reputedly assassinated on Mortimer's orders using a hot poker (Jones, 2013). Again, this is a story that is ripe for a film or television series, where Isabella is the protagonist and not simply a bit player in the drama.

From a tourism perspective, Isabella has been largely overlooked as a figure in Nottingham's history. As part of the Nottingham Underground Festival, a tour was conducted of Mortimer's Hole, the passageway under the castle through which Edward's soldiers are said to have secretly entered in order to arrest Roger Mortimer (Visit Nottinghamshire, 2020), while Isabella is mentioned in the city's Ghost Walks as haunting the Castle in sorrow over her lover's death. Nottingham Castle, which had provided a refuge for Mortimer and Isabella until their seizure by Edward III in 1330, was undergoing substantial redevelopments and revitalisation to make it a more engaging tourist attraction, including new galleries, a visitor centre and new visitor interpretation offering immersive digital experiences, and was scheduled to open in 2021 (Nottingham Castle Project, 2020). It will be interesting to see if Isabella's story features more prominently or in more depth as a part of the Castle's new visitor interpretation.

Some of the stories of real-life medieval women have become embroidered through the centuries, so that it is difficult to separate fact from fiction. One example is Lady Godiva, wife of Leofric, Earl of Mercia, in the eleventh century. In the famous legend, Godiva outwits her husband, after he imposed extortionate levels of taxation on the town of Coventry. When she asks Leofric to take pity on them, he laughingly replies that he will reduce the taxes if she rides naked through the streets. She then calls his bluff by agreeing to the ride and the citizens support her decision by agreeing not to look at her. Godiva's ride, with her nakedness covered only by her long hair, was supposedly witnessed by just one person – Peeping Tom – which is a monicker we use to this day. Like Robin Hood, she stands up for the common people, yet her story has rarely featured on screen, other than *Lady Godiva of Coventry* (1955), starring Maureen O'Hara. In the nineteenth century, the painters Edmund Blair Leighton (1892) and John Collier (1897) depicted Godiva through art as the quintessential Pre-Raphaelite beauty with tumbling hair down her body, although Leighton's Godiva was clothed, in a nod to Victorian morality. Her story remains inextricably linked with that of Coventry, and modern-day visitors can see a statue of Lady Godiva, which was unveiled in 1949 when the city was being rebuilt after its wartime bombing.

Fictional medieval women – a growing complexity

Fictional depictions of medieval women have tended to conform to the tropes or archetypes discussed earlier, particularly the wicked queen versus the fair maiden. We see this most obviously in fairy tales, with the queen in the fairy tale *Snow White* being jealous of her young stepdaughter, who the magic mirror tells her is, 'the fairest of them all' and seeking to have her killed with a poison apple. She is juxtaposed with the sweet innocence of Snow White; an example of the princess myth, discussed in the next sub-section. Here, we will examine other portrayals of medieval women in fiction, which is becoming less stereotypical and more nuanced in recent times.

Queen Guinevere

In the stories of King Arthur, Morgan le Fay/Morgana and Queen Guinevere are generally depicted using the archetype of the temptress. In the case of Morgana, she gives birth to Mordred, the child of her stepbrother Arthur, who later defeats his father in battle. Guinevere commits adultery, generally with Lancelot but with Mordred in Geoffrey of Monmouth's *History of the Kings of Britain* (1136), and in doing so, betrays her husband King Arthur (Samples, 1989). Guinevere in Malory's *Le Morte d'Arthur* (1469–1470) is to be killed for her crime until she is rescued by Lancelot. In 1536, Guinevere's story was seen as a precedent for the execution of Queen Anne Boleyn, meaning that, 'the conceptual groundwork for killing a queen through an accusation of treasonous adultery lay not in legal or historical precedent, but in habits of reading inculcated by late medieval and early modern romance' (Lexton, 2015: 223). Guinevere's character is unsettling in that she challenges societal norms by pursuing an adulterous love and makes Arthur a cuckold, thereby emasculating the king in the eyes of his subjects (Barczewski, 2001).

Other than her role as one of the catalysts for Arthur's downfall, Guinevere is typically not given a large part to play in the story, including most cinematic and television versions of the Camelot legend. This reflects that 'female characters [in general] are often relegated to the margins in medieval film' (Driver and Ray, 2004: 8). In *Excalibur* (1981) and *First Knight* (1995), Guinevere is young and decorative – a worthy consort for Arthur because of her beauty and the alliance she brings with her marriage, but destined to bring him unhappiness. In this way, she resembles the goddess who is generally a source of support to the hero during a time of trial, although she might also tempt him in some instances (Campbell, 1949). The 35-year age gap between the actors playing Guinevere (Julia Ormond) and Arthur (Sean Connery) in *First Knight* also bodes trouble for the match, with Arthur looking more like her grandfather than her husband. In *King Arthur* (2004), Guinevere (Keira Knightley) is a Celt who joins Arthur and Lancelot in battle scantily clad in a plaited leather cropped top and blue war paint, which is a far cry from the ethereal way that Guinevere is usually depicted, whether on screen or in the Pre-Raphaelite paintings of the nineteenth century. Knightley, like Ormond's Guinevere, is also much younger than the actor who plays Arthur (Clive Owen), although the difference here is less (21 years). The photographs for the film's posters were controversially digitally enhanced to make Knightley's breasts appear larger (Noah, 2012), which added to the perception that the role lacked depth and was gratuitously sexualised.

There have been attempts to give the role of Guinevere more gravitas, such as in *Merlin* (2008–2012). Guinevere (Angel Coulby) is a servant known as Gwen, dressed in simple and modest garb, who marries Arthur because he values her courage, resourcefulness and wisdom; not because it is politically expedient to do so. This is an unusual portrayal as Guinevere rises in rank through marriage from being a maid to Morgana, ward of the King, to being Arthur's Queen. This seems a nod to the Cinderella rags-to-riches myth, and in fact many fictional stories about medieval women are built intentionally around this story, such as *Ever After* (1998) with Drew Barrymore and *Ella Enchanted* (2004) with Anne Hathaway. Where a low-born male becomes the hero, such as William Thatcher (Heath Ledger) in *A Knight's Tale* (2001) and the blacksmith Balian (Orlando Bloom) in *Kingdom of Heaven* (2005), they do not rely on marriage to complete their journey to good fortune.

The mini-series *The Mists of Avalon* (2001) is based on a book of the same name by Marion Zimmer Bradley (1983), and focuses on the women of Camelot – Morgaine (Juliana Margulies), Morgause (Joan Allen), Igraine (Caroline Goodall), Viviane, the Lady of the Lake (Anjelica Huston) and Gwenhwyfar (Samantha Mathis). There is a strong focus here on women taking part in rituals such as Beltane and acting as priestesses to the Mother Goddess; although when we first meet Gwenhwyfar, she is a nun, setting up a clash between the old pagan ways and the introduction of Christianity. Morgaine, in this retelling of the story, makes love with a young man during the May Day festivities or Beltane. Neither is aware of the other's identity until afterwards, as Morgaine has not been brought up with Arthur, even though they share the same mother. This makes the character of Morgaine (Morgan le Fay) more sympathetic than is normally the case – she eventually gives birth to Arthur's child, but not due to any premeditation or intention to bring down Arthur.

The emphasis on spells, prophecies and magic in the story draws upon the medievalism of *so-called tradition* (Eco, 1986), with a number of female characters possessing the powers of enchantment and sorcery. While the depiction of women as witches is often to vilify them, in *The Mists of Avalon*, these women are strong, independent and empowered by their gifts, which allow them to control the destiny of others, particularly men. For this reason, the book is often referred to as a feminist text, even though Zimmer Bradley did not describe herself in these terms (Paxson, 1999). Allegations of sexual abuse made against her by her children have besmirched her reputation since her death and led some to argue that this background must affect how we read the book and some of its passages (Rosenberg, 2014).

Maid Marian

Like Guinevere, the character of Maid Marian in *Robin Hood* is usually underwritten in screen and television adaptations of the legend, although she is treated more sympathetically, possibly because she does not break sexual rules so blatantly. As Barczewski notes, even in nineteenth-century depictions, she is emancipated by current standards, such as 'she lives as an equal companion of the Merry Men and takes an active part in their activities, including hunting and other traditionally masculine pursuits' (2001: 9). In *The Sword in the Stone*, she is described as 'an accomplished soldier', able to 'move on all fours or even wriggle like a snake' (White, 1938: 114); the kind of girl who Wart (the future King Arthur) ironically muses that he would like to marry one day. Marian is a good sport, while seemingly remaining chaste from Robin's attentions. Interestingly, this representation of Marian is in contrast with her origin in popular carnivalesque stories of the bawdy wench accompanied by the fool (Cohoon, 2007), although consistent with the view that Marian is a secularised version of the Virgin Mary or Queen of the May (Clouet, 2001–2002; Tracy, 2012). In the twentieth century, she has remained virtuous, even being shown as an ageing nun (Audrey Hepburn) in *Robin and Marian* (1976), although her portrayal has veered from the restrained high-born elegance of Olivia de Havilland in *The Adventures of Robin Hood* (1938) to the tomboy played by Mary Elizabeth Mastrantonio, who wields a sword in *Robin Hood: Prince of Thieves* (1991), and the widow rather than an ingénue, played by Cate Blanchett in *Robin Hood* (2010). Possibly the most surprising characterisation of Marian is in the television series of *Robin Hood* (2006–2009). Marian (Lucy Griffiths) is a feisty and intelligent woman, whose desire to help Robin leads her to play with the affections of Guy of Gisbourne (Richard Armitage), at a terrible cost. Marian has promised to marry Gisbourne, who is jealous and suspicious of her feelings for Robin, but she keeps putting off the day, using her proximity to Gisbourne to gather intelligence for Robin. This cat-and-mouse game ends with her murder at Gisbourne's hands in a shock ending to the second series. This Marian is both clever and an innocent; not realising the full extent of the danger that Gisbourne represents if he is thwarted.

Game of Thrones

The dichotomy of Madonna/whore or goddess/temptress is gradually being tempered by a more nuanced depiction of medieval womanhood, and a backstory is often provided for these fictional women, which provides a rationale for at least some of their behaviour. This is exemplified by the female characters in *Game of Thrones*, who are central to much of the action and have a complexity to them that makes their stories far more interesting and relevant to modern audiences than was previously the case. Queen Cersei (Lena Headey) is jealous of her son Joffery's bride-to-be Sansa (Sophie Turner) and later her son Tommen's bride Margaery (Natalie Dormer), but this is partly due to Cersei's fear of the prophesy given to her by the witch Maggy – 'You will be queen, for a time … until there comes another, younger and more beautiful, to cast you down and take all that you hold dear'. Her father Tywin (Charles Dance) marginalises her and sees her essentially as a consort for men who can bestow or entrench power for the Lannister family. Cersei has conducted an incestuous liaison with her twin brother Jaime (Nikolaj Coster-Waldau) through most of her adult life, and other than her children, he appears to be the only person she truly loves. She is complicit in the death of her husband King Robert (Mark Addy) by instructing the king's squire to make sure he drinks too much wine during a hunt, resulting in a boar killing the king. The death of her children Joffrey (Jack Gleeson) and Myrcella (Aimee Richardson) starts to unhinge her mind. After her infamous walk of shame through the streets of King's Landing (based on an historical incident; see Chapter 7), she exacts revenge by having the Great Sept of Baelor and all those in it killed by exploding wildfire, including her daughter-in-law Margaery. Margaery's distraught husband Tommen, who was saved from this fate, jumps to his death when he realises that his wife has been killed, as his mother watches him.

While she is cruel, ruthless and increasingly unpredictable in her actions, there are redeeming features in Cersei that save her from being a pantomime villainess. Her fierce love for her children is one of them; a second is her indomitable will, which leads her to take charge of her own narrative, even if it is often twisted or misguided. Even the beleaguered Sansa, after observing that the queen will never stop trying to bring down her enemies, comments, 'I learned a great deal from her'. When Cersei dies with her brother and lover Jaime by her side amidst the rubble of the destruction of King's Landing, there is pathos in her demise. It is a curiously passive way for such a proud and decisive character to die. While we initially baulked at the notion that her brother has returned to be with her in her final hours, this also suggests that there is more to Cersei than just being an evil queen. She inspires love – and loyalty – from her twin, who will not let her die alone.

Sansa arguably has the biggest story arc of any woman in *Game of Thrones*. She begins as a romantic young girl who dreams of being a future queen, but reality intrudes in the form of the nightmare that is Prince Joffrey and the death of her father Ned Stark (Sean Bean) at the hands of the Lannisters. She is a pawn in the hands of others for much of the series, 'the beleaguered fairy-tale princess, imprisoned in the tower, praying for rescue by – whom?' (Larrington, 2016: 4). The Machiavellian court advisor Littlefinger (Aidan Gillen) helps her escape King's Landing in the confusion of Joffrey's assassination, only to give her as a bride to the deranged Ramsay Bolton (Iwan Rheon), who rapes her on her wedding night. Again, a man helps her to escape – this time, Theon Greyjoy (Alfie Allen), who is atoning for his betrayal of the Stark family, as well as running from his own hell at Ramsay's hands. Fleeing from Ramsay's men, Sansa is then saved by the female warrior Brienne (Gwendoline Christie), another strong female character. She ends up back where she started – Winterfell – which suggests Campbell's (1949) hero's journey, where Sansa has experienced separation from home, initiation through confronting an antagonist and the return. This is a common pattern for some fairy tales (Swann Jones, 1995) but less likely to be used in a story arc for women than for men in fantasy narratives.

Through the course of her suffering, Sansa is transformed from the 'little bird' or 'little dove' who is vulnerable in the eyes of her enemies, to a woman who makes her own decisions and seeks retribution for past wrongs, orchestrating the deaths of both Ramsay and Littlefinger. Sansa is not the 'good princess' but nor is she the evil queen. She is, correctly as it turns out, cautious about the intentions of others, notably Daenerys (Emilia Clarke), who she suspects will stop at nothing to claim the Iron Throne. As we see Sansa evolve, she becomes a far more interesting character, but we are never sure what her next move will be. As her second husband Tyrion Lannister (Peter Dinklage) remarks, 'Many underestimated you. Most of them are dead now'. Sansa becomes the Lady of Winterfell and requests that the North remain independent from the Seven Kingdoms, ultimately leading to her becoming Queen of the North. While it could be argued that Sansa had earned the right to rule Westeros, it was in some way fitting that she would choose loyalty to the people she grew up with and freedom to forge her own path.

While Larrington (2016) argues that, 'neither Theon/Reek nor Brienne and Pod are exactly the stuff of a maiden's – or a knowing no-longer maiden's – dreams' (p. 4), Brienne is the closest approximation to a knight in shining armour in *Game of Thrones* and is knighted by Ser Jaime on the eve of battle. Brienne is everything that most high-born men in Westeros are not – scrupulously fair and honest, just, considerate and trustworthy. She has sworn an oath to Sansa's mother Catelyn (Michelle Fairley) to look after her daughters and we are never in doubt that she will honour that promise. Brienne leads men into battle, before being appointed as Commander of the Kingsguard, and is thus an example of the female warrior who has come to the fore in medieval-themed narratives, discussed in greater detail at the end of this chapter. The interesting aspect of Brienne is that she combines brains with brawn, but more than that, she has integrity and good sense. We are left with the sense that the city's protection is in good hands.

Brienne can be contrasted with another warrior woman in Daenerys, who takes revenge on King's Landing by burning it to the ground with her dragons, in an act of genocide. This side of her is not unexpected, as Daenerys has demonstrated a number of times that she is capable of malice against those who cross her. She burnt a number of victims who would not 'bend the knee', and treated enemies as cruelly as they did to others, which makes her morally questionable. Her destruction of King's Landing, however, suggests that she no longer recognises right from wrong and has even descended into madness, reminiscent of her father's rule as King of Westeros. Daenerys is the least appealing female character in *Game of Thrones*, in that her lust for power is not tempered by any great love or loyalty towards others, and she appears to be set on an inexorable course of self-destruction. Like Marian in *Robin Hood* (2006–2009), she is killed at her lover's hands; yet apart from her remaining dragon, few mourn her death. Instead, there is relief at being spared yet another tyrant as a ruler.

The Letter for the King

During the Covid-19 pandemic, one of the most-watched series on Netflix was *The Letter for the King* (2020), based on the 1962 book by the Dutch children's author Tonke Dragt. There were a number of changes, particularly with regards to the character of Lavinia (Ruby Ashbourne Serkis). In the book, Lavinia is introduced to the hero Tiuri (Amir Wilson) when he stays at her father's castle en route to delivering a letter that will warn the King about his son's treason. She tries to help Tiuri escape from the Grey Knights who believe that the boy has killed one of their brethren, the Knight with the White Shield. Lavinia later tells Tiuri, 'Father says I'm too curious and that I talk too much. But I also know when to be silent. Secrets are safe with me' (Dragt, 1962: 159). This is a stereotypical 1960s portrait of a young girl who outwardly likes to gossip and chatter, although she will keep Tiuri's presence at the castle a secret. At the end of the book, Piak – Tiuri's companion – asks, 'you know, I think she likes you … Do you like her too?' (p. 507), to which Tiuri agrees. We are left with the suggestion that the pair may marry one day.

The television series turns this storyline on its head. Lavinia accompanies Tiuri on his quest, while the fictional Piak is given a far lesser role as the brother of one of Tiuri's fellow knights-in-training. It appears that Tiuri has magical powers and Lavinia encourages him to learn how to harness and exercise them, which he initially finds frightening (there is no magic in the book). The twist comes when we realise that it is Lavinia who wields these powers – she has conjured up a windstorm to escape their enemies and prevented Tiuri from being burnt in the flames by the Red Riders. Lavinia is therefore the key to the pair being able to successfully deliver their letter and prevent the kingdom from falling to dark forces. She uses her magic to repel Prince Viridian (Gijs Blom) in the final episode. The importance of magic to the plot again suggests the medievalism of '*so-called tradition*' (Eco, 1986), and once again, it is a woman who is instrumental in using magical forces. Additional female characters created for the series include knight-to-be Iona (Thaddea Graham) and Queen Alianor (Emilie Cocquerel), who shows that not all rulers need be men.

Changing the plot to give women greater prominence made sense against a backdrop of the #MeToo movement and female empowerment, and it also met with the approval of the (female) author. Her concerns with the proposed adaptation lay in other directions (Collin, 2020):

> I immediately said no to a couple of [changes Netflix had planned]. No torture! They wanted to remove shield-bearer Piak from the story but I said: Piak stays. And they wanted to make Tiuri's background more interesting, but I was against that—he is a regular boy. Children must be able to think: that could happen to me. Will I keep the promise [to deliver the letter]?

These examples of fictional women suggest that female characters, rather than remaining on the periphery, are increasingly taking centre stage in medieval-themed narratives. They are often shown wielding swords and fighting battles, and they shape their own destiny as much as the men do. Where does this leave the fairy story of the princess who lived happily ever after? As we consider in the next section, even the Disney princess is evolving in the face of modern mores that expect her to do more than sleep on a pea or marry a handsome prince.

The Disney princess

It is difficult to examine the princess myth in the contemporary era without reference to Disney's role in sustaining it. The official Disney Princess franchise covers 12 characters (Table 4.1) and was created in 2000 to bring all the different female leads in Walt Disney films together under one promotional umbrella. Each princess has her own coloured frock and distinct look. It is therefore a branding exercise, which achieved great success by tapping into the fantasy of being a princess. Disney executive Andy Mooney had noticed that little girls attending the Disney on Ice shows were dressing up like princesses in their own creations, and he saw a niche in the market for 'princess' merchandise (Smale, 2018;

Table 4.1 The Official Disney Princess Franchise

Character	Disney Animated Film	Original Inspiration
Snow White	*Snow White and the Seven Dwarfs* (1937)	*Schneewittchen* or *Snow White* from *Grimms' Fairy Tales* (1812).
Cinderella	*Cinderella* (1950)	There are many versions of this tale, but most would acknowledge the influence of *Cendrillon ou la petite pantoufle de verre* (1697) by Charles Perrault, translated as *Cinderella or the Little Glass Slipper*. The Italians also have a version called *Cenerentola* (1634).
Aurora	*Sleeping Beauty* (1959)	*Perceforest* in the fourteenth century, which was then published by Giambattista Basile in the *Pentamerone*, his collection of fairy tales, in the seventeenth century. Variants were also incorporated into fairy-tale collections published by Perrault (*La Belle au Bois Dormant* or *The Sleeping Beauty in the Woods)* and the Brothers Grimm (1812) (*Dornröschen* or *Little Briar Rose*).
Ariel	*The Little Mermaid* (1989)	*The Little Mermaid* (1837) by Hans Christian Anderson
Belle	*Beauty and the Beast* (1991)	*La Belle et la Bête (Beauty and the Beast)* (1740) *by* Gabrielle-Suzanne Barbot de Villeneuve Beauty.
Jasmine	*Aladdin* (1992)	*One Thousand and One Nights* or *The Arabian Nights* (traditional Arabic).
Pocahontas	*Pocahontas* (1995)	Historical. Pocahontas was a Native American woman who assisted the Jamestown settlers in the seventeenth century.
Mulan	*Mulan* (1998)	Chinese folklore – *The Ballad of Mulan* (fourth to sixth centuries)
Tiana	*The Princess and the Frog* (2009)	*Der Froschkönig* or *The Frog Prince* by the Brothers Grimm (1812), adapted for the more recent book *The Frog Princess* (2002) by E. D. Baker.
Rapunzel	*Tangled* (2010)	*Rapunzel* (1812) by the Brothers Grimm. This tale can be traced back to Basile's *Petrosinella* (1634) and even further to the eleventh-century Persian tale of *Zāl and Rudabeh*.
Merida	*Brave* (2012)	Original screenplay.
Moana	*Moana* (2016)	Original screenplay.

Whelan, 2014). Sales of the Disney Princess range hit US$3.4 billion in 2006, spanning everything from costumes and dolls to play castles, video games and bedroom décor (Bayless, 2012). The range inspired other popular children's brands to follow suit, such as Mattel's Barbie doll, which saw her regularly clad in 'silver spangles and tiaras' (Orr, 2009: 13).

Disney has its 'elitist critics' who fear its 'power to charm, to cast a spell, to make us unreflective and accepting' (Rollin, 1987: 90). For example, Zipes refers to *Cinderella* as a film that, 'reeks of sexism, sentimentality and sterility' (1979: 115). Yet, the popularity of the brand and its characters is undeniable. Similarly, while children enjoy dressing up as fairy-tale characters, research suggests that they can generally distinguish reality from fantasy, which includes Disney's portrayal of gender roles (Pugh, 2012). It is their parents who must often 'adopt critical blinders when enjoying the corporation's entertainment' (Pugh, 2012: 3), even where they have fond memories of watching the films as children (Pagès, 2017).

At Disney's theme parks, girls are encouraged to dress up like their favourite fairy-tale character, with Princess Parties that allow them to 'step into a quasi-medieval past' (Pugh, 2012: 5). Disney's Bibbidi Bobbidi Boutique takes this a step further for youngsters aged between 3 and 12 years, offering a one-stop shop for those who want to look like their favourite princess or knight (Bayless, 2012). This includes hairstyles, makeup, shoes, jewellery and costumes, with children primped and pampered in front of mirrors, until they emerge ready to be photographed (Figure 4.3). Bayless argues that this is the child's equivalent of a bride's preparations, in that a 'wedding is the ultimate bibbidi-bobbidi-boo of the adult woman' (2012: 52). The ultimate princess bride was Princess Diana, whose lavish wedding to Prince Charles at St Paul's Cathedral in 1981 was watched by millions of viewers worldwide (Otnes and Pleck, 2003), with the bride wearing a full-skirted gown and a diamond tiara to hold her veil.

The Disney dress-up concept has now been extended to 'Character Couture' makeovers for adults at the Disney theme parks, although they must bring in their own outfit, 'inspired by their favourite characters' (Romano, 2018), rather than purchasing an official outfit. This is to prevent adults masquerading as or being confused with official Disney employees. *The Big Bang Theory* (2007–2019) satirises this rule, when three female characters, aged in their twenties, visit Disneyland. Bernadette (Melissa Rauch) decides, 'I'm gonna make a beeline for the place that gives you a princess makeover' and after telling the other two to, 'pick your princess', she claims the right to be Cinderella. The others are forced to choose a different princess look, much to their chagrin. For two of the women, their princess attire is sexually arousing for their nerdy boyfriends, who can't believe what they are seeing. The third woman, Amy (Mayim Bialik), dressed as Snow White, lies on the couch and tries in vain to get a kiss from her partner Sheldon (Jim Parsons) to make her 'wake up'. Interestingly, a Cinderella-themed wedding 'is the most requested type of "fantasy wedding" at Walt Disney World' (Otnes and Pleck, 2003: 53).

All the Disney Princesses are the main or title character of their own films and all but two of the characters are born royal or marry into royalty. The exceptions are Mulan, the young female Chinese warrior, and Pocahontas, the daughter of a

Figure 4.3 Dressing Up as a Princess at Walt Disney World.
Source: Jennifer Frost.

Native American chief. While Pocahontas might arguably be considered to be American 'royalty', the extension of the franchise to a non-princess provides as broad an audience as possible for the princess fantasy and thus makes economic sense, as well as encapsulating the idea that, 'girlhood and princesshood [are] tightly intertwined' (Whelan, 2014: 174). This also represents an attempt to create a more ethnically, racially and socially diverse pantheon of princesses, alongside the African American restaurateur Tiana in *The Princess and the Frog* (2009), set in New Orleans, and the title role in *Moana* (2016), who is the daughter of a Polynesian chief (Craven, 2012). These animated films are progressively being remade by Disney as live action versions, starring well-known female actors such as Angelina Jolie as the evil queen from *Snow White* in *Maleficent* (2014), and Emma Watson as Belle in *Beauty and the Beast* (2017). This presumably brings another audience for these popular stories. Our focus in this chapter, however, is on the animated canon, which is the most beloved and well-known.

The origin of most of these films is not medieval, nor are they necessarily set in that historical era. For example, the costumes worn by the characters are also a pastiche of different eras – with the princesses often wearing crinoline-style dresses that more properly date to the nineteenth century than medieval times (Sturtevant, 2012). *Sleeping Beauty* was 'the most consciously modeled on medieval art and design' (Bradford, 2012: 176), with the film's designer, Eyvind Earle, describing one of his key inspirations as the Duc de Berry's *Très Riches Heures* or *Book of Hours* in the fifteenth century (Coyne Kelly, 2012; Sturtevant, 2012). This is an illuminated manuscript of exquisite delicacy, which contains prayers to be said at different times of the day. Even the famous Sleeping Beauty Castle, now enshrined as the Castle at Disneyland, resembles those depicted in its calendar – the Château de Saumur and the Louvre in Paris (Coyne Kelly, 2012). The film places the action within a precise medieval time period as the prince comments, 'now, father, you're living in the past. This is the fourteenth century'. Despite this attempt to establish its medieval *bona fides*, the fairy-tale elements are stronger.

Many of these films employ a common 'framing narrative' (Sturtevant, 2012: 89) in their title scenes. *Snow White* begins with a book reminiscent of a medieval illuminated manuscript complete with Old English lettering, with the pages flipped over as if by magic and the words 'Once upon a time'. *Sleeping Beauty* displays an illuminated book containing the words 'In a far away land long ago', to the strains of a song that is set to the waltz from *The Sleeping Beauty* ballet by Tchaikovsky, which was also based on Perrault's fairy tale (Coyne Kelly, 2012); an example of the circle of culture (see Chapter 1). Both books in these title scenes feature castles prominently in their illustrations, which links with the castle spire that forms an integral part of the iconic Walt Disney logo (Mitchell-Smith, 2012; Sturtevant, 2012). We are drawn into a fantasy of the medieval world as we imagine it in storybooks (Coyne Kelly, 2012). For Walt Disney, a love of fairy tales represented, 'nostalgia for the vanished past' (Schickel, 1971: 175).

The ultimate expression of a Disney 'pseudomedieval' world is its film *Enchanted* (2007), which 'refuses any historical anchor' (Sachiko Cecire, 2012: 244). This has also been labelled *neomedievalism*, where a fantasy medieval world has been created, complete with anachronisms and a pastiche of old and new, in a postmodern approach to portraying the medieval (Robinson and Clements, 2009). This is often playfully done with a knowing wink at the audience and references to popular culture. For example, *Ella Enchanted* (2004), set in a medieval-style village, contains a parody of the modern shopping mall or galleria experience, with hand-operated escalators and shop names that spoof their real-life equivalents; while in *Shrek* (2001), Princess Fiona (Cameron Diaz) utilises modern martial arts moves. Even the director of *Enchanted* was unclear how many times he paid homage to a Disney film across the course of the movie. Counting these references (and feeling smug about it) forms part of the fun of watching these films (Sachiko Cecire, 2012).

The characterisation of the princesses themselves is important in understanding the appeal of these films. As Fjellman observes, 'The problem with lead [Disney] characters such as Cinderella, Snow White ... is to make them interesting ... Disney's sweet heroines and heroes ... come to life most successfully not in animation but as embodied as live actors at the theme parks' (1992: 263). Many of these early screen princesses are dull, and criticised like many Disney creations for their 'sexless sexiness' (Schickel, 1971: 233). Perhaps that is the point. The Disney Princess may represent safety for young children, particularly girls, and is therefore comforting, in that they seem to remain innocently happy, regardless of the often-threatening adult situations they are faced with, and achieve a happy ending to their story, in that good always triumphs over evil.

Disney announced that *Tangled* (2010) was its last fairy-tale film, 'for the fore-seeable future', although the genre could be revived, according to Pixar Animation Studios chief Ed Catmull, if, 'someone has a fresh take on it' (Chmielewski and Eller, 2010). It did not take them long however to find a new fairy-tale story to turn into a film, and it became a global phenomenon. *Frozen* (2013) and its sequel *Frozen II* (2019) were inspired by Hans Christian Anderson's *The Snow Queen* (1844) and feature two new princesses – sisters Elsa (Idina Menzel) and Anna (Kristen Bell) – who surprisingly were not included in the official canon of Disney princesshood. It has been surmised that the films became so popular that it was feared that these characters would overshadow the other princesses if they were included in the same franchise. The sisters are, like Rapunzel in *Tangled*, feisty and independent. *Frozen* has become famous for the power ballad 'Let It Go', which won the Oscar for Best Original Song in 2014, in which Elsa sings of her decision not to continue to hold back on using her magic powers, which can turn things into ice and snow. She decides to leave her kingdom to protect her people, rather than continue to suppress who she really is. The song at one level is a celebration of emancipation, with the songwriters Kristen Anderson-Lopez and Robert Lopez creating it as a response to 'the pressure to be perfect' (Shapiro, 2019). More broadly, it has also been embraced as an 'anthem of acceptance … [for people] on the margins, all identifying with the tale of a queen in hiding, who learns to shed her shame and accepts the things that make her different' (Shapiro, 2019). These are princesses for a new generation of girls who look for sassiness and courage in their screen heroines.

The female warrior

This chapter began with a vignette about Chinon Castle's connection with Joan of Arc, where Joan's history has become secondary to the princess myth. This is not surprising, given the ubiquity of the princess myth, linked to romantic notions of the medieval world as a time of chivalry and courtly love. This has meant that the female warrior has been largely downplayed in medievalisms that celebrate the bravery and physical prowess of the male knight, even though, 'women engaged in, or financially supported, major political and religious battles throughout the Middle Ages, shaping the course of history' (Driver, 2004: 91). Joan's life is an exception, in that it has been filmed on a number of occasions, although the focus is more on her piety and less on the revolutionary nature of her ideas, which, 'proposed nothing less than a radically new political settlement in which military power served the needs of the state … rather than the interests of those wielding it' (Benson, 2004: 230).

Another female warrior in a medieval fantasy is Eowyn (Miranda Otto) in *The Lord of the Rings* film trilogy (2001–2003). Eowyn is a shield-maiden, who tells Aragorn (Viggo Mortensen), after he compliments her 'skill with the blade', that, 'the women of this country learned long ago, those without swords can still die upon them. I fear neither death nor pain'. She defeats the Witch King, who repeats the prophecy to her that no man can kill him, taking off her helmet and declaring, 'I am no man'. Eowyn can be contrasted with Arwen (Liv Tyler), the Elven princess who is a more traditional medieval heroine. While Sir Peter Jackson flirted with the idea of making Arwen a warrior, like Eowyn, he left her role much as it was originally written by Tolkien, although giving her some additional scenes such as when she rides Frodo (Elijah Wood) to safety and escapes the Ringwraiths, and having the shards of Narsil, 'the blade that was broken', reforged as a sword and given to Aragorn so that he can fulfil his destiny as King of Gondor. Her form of courage is to refuse to sail to the West and to 'choose a mortal life' with the man she loves.

The reference to shield maidens in *The Lord of the Rings* is potentially based on historical fact. Jesch (1991) notes that there are examples of Viking women buried with weapons, although there is conjecture that axes, for example, could be simply examples of practical tools used around the house, while weapons might have a symbolic function, rather than suggesting that they were used by women for fighting purposes. Yet in 2017, a Viking skeleton that had been found in Sweden in the nineteenth century and presumed to be a man, due to the weapons with which it was found, was subjected to DNA testing and found to be a woman (Hedenstierna-Jonson *et al.*, 2017). There are also references to female warriors in *History of the Danes* (c 1200) by Saxo Grammaticus, who 'dressed themselves to look like men and spent almost every minute cultivating soldiers' skills' (quoted in Jesch, 1991: 176).

Saxo mentions the likes of Lathgertha, the former wife of Regner Lothbrog, who gives him military aid when he needs it. This narrative is dramatised in *Vikings* (2013–2021), where Lagertha (Katheryn Winnick) often fights in battle alongside other female characters such as Torvi (Georgia Hirst) and Gunnhild (Ragga Ragnars) and is as fierce and brave as her male compatriots. Lagertha is cast aside by her husband for another woman because she cannot bear him any more sons, but becomes Queen of Kattegat through her own ingenuity. Long and Williams refer to her as an 'anti-hero', because they argue that she 'is morally questionable, creates conflicted feelings regarding her (often violent) actions, and behaves with ruthlessness, intelligence, and ambition' (2020: 140). Yet we see her conflicted by some of the things she has done to gain power (Long and Williams, 2020). The character of Lagertha is therefore representative of a changing depiction of women in medieval society as complex rather than one-dimensional. The actress Katheryn Winnick is proud of changing popular perceptions of Viking women, noting:

> I was told this is a male-dominated network and the male demographic is stronger than female. This is a show about Vikings and you are just the wife. I remember thinking that was not the way I was going to play it.
>
> (quoted in Bentley, 2015)

The creator of *The Vikings*, Michael Hirst, has also been vocal about the importance of the series focussing on women's involvement in Viking conquest and settlement, as part of a broader understanding of this age (Frankel, 2019).

The growing emphasis on the female warrior has given female characters a more active and central involvement in medieval-themed narratives. *The Last*

Figure 4.4 The Béguinage at Ghent.
Source: Warwick Frost.

Kingdom (2015 onwards) includes female characters such as Brida (Emily Cox), a Saxon girl who is brought up by the Danes and becomes one of their leaders in battle, and Hild (Eva Birthistle), who is introduced as a nun who is raped by the Vikings and later fights against them as a warrior. Aethelflaed (Millie Brady), Lady of Mercia and daughter of Alfred the Great, is another strong female in the cast, who is shown fighting in battles, although this level of involvement in warfare is open to conjecture. We do know that she became the sole ruler of Mercia after the death of her husband Aethelred around 911 and that military campaigns were carried out in her name which led to the conquest of Danish strongholds (Wickham, 2016). In *The Last Kingdom*, Aethelflaed is depicted as clever and strategic, having received special tutelage from her father in statecraft, who sees her marriage as playing a key role in Wessex and Mercia joining forces against the Viking threat and ultimately achieving his dream of a united England. Aethelflaed tells the Mercian nobles that she will remain celibate as their ruler, which will prevent an outsider from marrying her and taking over power in Mercia by default. This decision will also allow her to control her own destiny, and it exemplifies her skill at diplomacy and political intrigue. Aethelflaed is increasingly recognised as an important figure in British history, akin to the contemporary rise of interest in Alfred (see Chapter 3).

Where are the real women?

As pointed out earlier, real women from medieval times are absent from our screens, and this is not just the case for royalty like Eleanor of Aquitaine or Queen Isabella of England. Lives of everyday medieval women are rarely dramatised, perhaps because their lives would be too prosaic or spartan for modern tastes, given that 'the world of medieval movies is deeply dyed in the colors of romance and folktale' (Woods, 2004: 43). Even with regard to the social strata below monarchy, little has been shown of a medieval woman's lot, despite the existence of well-documented source material on which to base it. For example, there is currently no screen dramatisation of *The Book of Margery Kempe* (c 1438). Written by a Christian mystic, it is a rare example of a female autobiography in the Middle Ages, and possibly the first autobiography written in English (Beckwith, 1996). Much of her life was uncommon for a woman in her times, such as her pilgrimages and travel without her husband and her 'highly personal style of ecstatic Christianity' (Wickham, 2016: 188). We see little on screen about female nuns, despite the ubiquity of their male equivalents in such dramatisations as *Cadfael* (1994–1998), the story of a medieval brother who solves mysteries, based on the books by Ellis Peters; or *The Name of the Rose* (1986), the film based on Eco's 1980 novel. Notable exceptions are the nun Hild in the *Last Kingdom* series and the nuns, particularly Sister Caris, in Ken Follett's *World Without End* (2007), who both featured in the screen versions of these books. Another overlooked example of medieval women involves the *béguines*, groups of lay religious women who lived communally in order to dedicate themselves to God. The Flemish béguinages are now designated as World Heritage areas (Figure 4.4), yet we do not see the lives of their occupants reflected in our medieval screen narratives. The Paston Letters (1422–1509), a collection of correspondence between Margaret Paston, a Norfolk gentlewoman, and her family, also seem to be begging for dramatisation, given that they cover some of the most colourful periods of British history such as the War of the Roses and show how women coped at home when men went off to battle, defending and maintaining their homes and livelihoods (Driver, 2004).

We get glimpses of the importance of women to the economic and social prosperity of the Viking world in the novel *The Last Kingdom* (Cornwell, 2004), although this point has not been translated to the television series. Women, at a very practical level, had the responsibility of spinning and weaving the thread for the sails of boats, which allowed the Vikings to conquer and settle new territories, 'and so the women worked every hour the gods sent' (p. 46). We also see their role in defending their territory or conquest over the new, in more recent shows like *The Vikings*, mentioned earlier.

The new princess

Disney's announcement that in 2010 that they would stop creating new films within their Princess franchise did not prevent them from creating *Frozen* just three years later. While Sachiko Cecire (2012: 257) observes that 'this seems to herald the end of Disney's iconic Princess culture', the success of *Frozen* suggests that the princess myth is not dead – just reinvented for a new audience. As discussed in this chapter, the twenty-first-century princess is more likely to be a warrior woman, or at least shown as possessing courage, guile and resourcefulness in the face of danger, rather than being a lovely but passive prize for which the hero must risk all. There is a greater complexity in the way that she is portrayed, as exemplified by many of the women in *Game of Thrones*, such that she is generally not wholly good nor wholly bad, possessing flaws as well as virtues.

The ongoing interest in princesses arguably manifested itself in the intense adoration of Diana, Princess of Wales, which made her one of the most famous women in the world before her untimely death in 1997 (Laing and Frost, 2018). Even today, stories about the lives – and fashion – of her daughters-in-law Kate, Duchess of Cambridge, and Meghan, Duchess of Sussex, are ubiquitous in the media, with the women often depicted in terms of archetypes from fairy tales – Kate the 'good' princess for choosing duty, and Meghan the 'bad' fairy who ran away from her royal responsibilities and is jealous of her sister-in-law. There is thus a disconnection between the way that real royalty is portrayed in the media and the latitude given to their fictional counterparts. It is difficult to say that we have moved on as a society in our representations of women, when these one-dimensional tropes continue to be employed.

While women are becoming more prominent in our understanding of the medieval period, there are opportunities to foreground their stories more strongly. Given the wealth of historical material that is available that shows a number of women who led action-packed lives, or suggests the indispensable role played by ordinary women in medieval society, it is puzzling that it is only recently that their voice has been heard. Rather than an endless series of films about Robin Hood or King Arthur, there is scope to move the focus onto their women (Maid Marian or Queen Guinevere), or indeed, interesting real-life medieval women such as Eleanor of Aquitaine or Margery Kempe. Similarly, the tourism industry, in capitalising on the appeal of the medieval period for visitors, could devote more resources and attention to showcasing medieval women, in all guises and walks of life (Dempsey *et al.*, 2020). As our archaeologists learn more about the history of these times, it is hoped that this leads to a concomitant increase in stories that place real women at the centre rather than on the periphery of events.

References

Barczewski, S. (2001) *Myth and national identity in nineteenth-century Britain: The legends of King Arthur and Robin Hood*, Oxford: Oxford University Press.

Bareket, O., Kahalon, R., Shnabel, N., and Glick, P. (2018) 'The Madonna-whore dichotomy: Men who perceive women's nurturance and sexuality as mutually exclusive endorse patriarchy and show lower relationship satisfaction', *Sex Roles*, 79(9–10), 519–532.

Bayless, M. (2012) 'Disney's castles and the work of the medieval in the magic kingdom', in T. Pugh and S. Aronstein (Eds.), *The Disney Middle Ages* (pp. 39–56), New York: Palgrave Macmillan.

Beckwith, S. (1996) 'A very material mysticism: The medieval mysticism of Margery Kempe', in J. Chance (Ed.), *Gender and text in the Later Middle Ages* (pp. 195–215), Eugene, OR: Wipf and Stock.

Benson, E. (2004) 'Oh, what a lovely war! Joan of Arc on screen', in M. Driver and S. Ray (Eds.), *The medieval hero on screen: Representations from Beowulf to Buffy* (pp. 217–236), Jefferson, NC and London: McFarland.

Bentley, R. (2015) 'Lagertha a trail blazer', *The West Australian*, 18 March, https://thewest.com.au/entertainment/tv/lagertha-a-trailblazer-ng-ya-387362 (accessed January 3, 2020).

Blythe, J. (2001) 'Women in the military: Scholastic arguments and medieval images of female warriors', *History of Political Thought*, *22*(2), 242–269.

Bradford, C. (2012) '"Where happily ever after happens every day": The medievalisms of Disney's princesses', in T. Pugh and S. Aronstein (Eds.), *The Disney Middle Ages* (pp. 171–188), New York: Palgrave Macmillan.

Campbell, J. (1949) *The hero with a thousand faces*, London: Fontana, 1993 reprint.

Chmielewski, D. and Eller, C. (2010) 'Disney animation is closing the book on fairy tales', *Los Angeles Times*, November 21, https://www.latimes.com/archives/la-xpm-2010-nov-21-la-et-1121-tangled-20101121-story.html (accessed November 5, 2020).

Clouet, R. (2001–2002) 'The Robin Hood legend and its cultural adaptation for the film industry: Comparing literary sources with filmic representations', *Journal of English Studies*, *3*, 37–46.

Cohoon, L. (2007) 'Transgressive transformations: Representations of Maid Marian in Robin Hood retellings', *The Lion and the Unicorn*, *31*(3), 209–231.

Collin, B. (2020) '*The Letter for the King* gets the Netflix treatment', *24 Oranges*, 29 February, http://www.24oranges.nl/2020/02/29/the-letter-for-the-king-gets-the-netflix-treatment/ (accessed January 5, 2020).

Cornwell, B. (2004) *The last kingdom*, London: HarperCollins.

Coyne Kelly, K. (2012) 'Disney's medievalized ecologies in *Snow White and the Seven Dwarfs* and *Sleeping Beauty*', in T. Pugh and S. Aronstein (Eds.), *The Disney Middle Ages* (pp. 189–207), New York: Palgrave Macmillan.

Craven, A. (2012) 'Esmeralda of Notre-Dame: The Gypsy in medieval view from Hugo to Disney', in T. Pugh and S. Aronstein (Eds.), *The Disney Middle Ages* (pp. 225–242), New York: Palgrave Macmillan.

Dempsey, K., Gilchrist, R., Ashbee, J., Sagrott, S. and Stones, S. (2020) 'Beyond the martial façade: Gender, heritage and medieval castles', *International Journal of Heritage Studies*, *26*(4), 352–369.

Dragt, T. (1962) *The letter for the king*, London: Pushkin, 2020 reprint.

Driver, M. (2004) 'Iron maidens: Medieval female heroes on film', in M. Driver and S. Ray (Eds.), *The medieval hero on screen: Representations from Beowulf to Buffy* (pp. 91–93), Jefferson, NC and London: McFarland.

Driver, M. and Ray, S. (2004) 'Preface: Hollywood knights', in M. Driver and S. Ray (Eds.), *The medieval hero on screen: Representations from Beowulf to Buffy* (pp. 5–18), Jefferson, NC and London: McFarland.

Eco, U. (1986) *Faith in fakes*, London: Seeker & Warburg.

Fjellman, S. (1992) *Vinyl leaves: Walt Disney World and America*, Boulder, CO: Westview.

Frankel, S. (2019) '"The gods will always smile on the brave women" Exploring the heroines of History Channel's *Vikings*', in V. Frankel (Ed.), *Fourth wave feminism in science fiction and fantasy: Volume 2. Essays on television representations, 2013–2019* (pp. 62–74), Jefferson, NC: McFarland.

Hedenstierna-Jonson, C., Kjellström, A., Zachrisson, T., Krzewińska, M., Sobrado, V., Price, N., ..., Storå, J. (2017) 'A female Viking warrior confirmed by genomics', *American Journal of Physical Anthropology*, *164*(4), 853–860.

Jesch, J. (1991) *Women in the Viking age*, Woodbridge, UK and Rochester, NY: Boydell.

Jones, D. (2013) *The Plantagenets: The kings who made England*, London: William Collins.

Jones, D. (2014) *The Hollow Crown: War of the Roses and the rise of the Tudors*, London: Faber & Faber.

Laing, J. and Frost, W. (2018) *Royal events: Rituals, innovations, meanings*, London: Routledge.

Larrington, C. (2016) *Winter is coming: The medieval world of Game of Thrones*, New York: IB Tauris.

Lexton, R. (2015) 'Reading the adulterous/treasonous queen in early modern England: Malory's Guinevere and Anne Boleyn', *Exemplaria*, *27*(3), 222–241.

Long, A. and Williams, S. (2020) 'Rogue bodies: Disabled antiheroes and the pop-culture saga in Vikings', *The Journal of Popular Culture*, *53*(1), 129–147.

Mitchell-Smith, I. (2012) 'The United Princesses of America: Ethnic diversity and cultural purity in Disney's medieval past', in T. Pugh and S. Aronstein (Eds.), *The Disney middle ages* (pp. 209–224), New York: Palgrave Macmillan.

Noah, S. (2012) 'Keira Knightley's anger at airbrushed picture', *The Independent*, 13 November, https://www.independent.co.uk/arts-entertainment/films/news/keira-knightley-s-anger-airbrushed-picture-8312991.html (accessed January 5, 2020).

Norwich, J. (1995) *Byzantium: The decline and fall*, London: Viking.

Nottingham Castle Project (2020) *Nottingham Castle Project*, https://www.nottingham-castle.org.uk/ (accessed November 5, 2020).

Orr, L. (2009) '"Difference that is actually sameness mass-reproduced": Barbie joins the princess convergence', *Jeunesse: Young People, Texts, Cultures*, *1*(1), 9–30.

Otnes, C. and Pleck, E. (2003) *Cinderella dreams: The allure of the lavish wedding*, Berkeley: University of California Press.

Pagès, M. (2017) 'You can't do this to Disney! Popular medievalisms in the classroom', in G. Ashton (Ed.), *Medieval afterlives in contemporary culture* (pp. 58–66), London: Bloomsbury.

Paxson, D. (1999) 'Marion Zimmer Bradley and *The Mists of Avalon*', *Arthuriana*, 110–126.

Pugh, T. (2012) 'Introduction: Disney's retroprogressive medievalisms: Where yesterday is tomorrow today', in T. Pugh and S. Aronstein (Eds.), *The Disney middle ages: A fairy tale and fantasy past* (pp. 1–18), New York: Palgrave Macmillan.

Pugh, T. and Weisl, A. (2012) *Medievalisms: Making the past in the present*, London: Routledge.

Robinson, C. and Clements, P. (2009) 'Living with neomedievalisms', in K. Fugelso (Ed.), *Defining medievalism(s) II* (pp. 55–75), Cambridge: Brewer.

Rollin, L. (1987) 'Fear of faerie: Disney and the elitist critics', *Children's Literature Association Quarterly*, *12*(2), 90–93.

Romano (2018) 'You no longer have to be a kid to get a princess makeover at Disney world', *Travel & Leisure*, 20 July, https://www.businessinsider.com/adults-can-now-get-a-princess-makeover-at-disney-world-2018-7?r=AU&IR=T#:~:text=Salons%20 at%20Walt%20Disney%20World,around%20the%20parks%20in%20costume (accessed December 5, 2020).

Rosenberg, A. (2014) 'Re-reading feminist author Marion Zimmer Bradley in the wake of sexual assault allegations', *The Washington Post*, 28 June, https://www.washingtonpost. com/news/act-four/wp/2014/06/27/re-reading-feminist-author-marion-zimmer-bradley-in-the-wake-of-sexual-assault-allegations/ (accessed January 2, 2020).

Sachiko Cecire, M. (2012) 'Reality remixed: Neomedieval princess culture in Disney's *Enchanted*', in T. Pugh and S. Aronstein (Eds.), *The Disney middle ages* (pp. 243–259), New York: Palgrave Macmillan.

Samples, S. (1989) 'Guinevere: A re-appraisal', *Arthurian Interpretations*, 106–118.

Schickel, R. (1971) *The Disney version: The life, times, art and commerce of Walt Disney*, New York: Simon & Schuster.

Seward, D. (1995) *The Wars of the Roses: Through the lives of five men and women of the fifteenth century*, London: Penguin.

Shapiro, J. (2019) 'For many with disabilities, 'Let It Go' is an anthem of acceptance', *NPR*, 22 January, https://www.npr.org/2019/01/22/686690655/frozen-let-it-go-disabilities-american-anthem (accessed October 5, 2020).

Smale, W. (2018) 'How one man's eureka moment earns Disney $3bn a year', *BBC News*, 24 December, https://www.bbc.com/news/business-46546014 (accessed November 4, 2019).

Sturtevant, P. (2012) '"You don't learn it deliberately, but you just know it from what you've seen": British understandings of the medieval past gleaned from Disney's fairy tales', in T. Pugh and S. Aronstein (Eds.), *The Disney Middle Ages: A fairy-tale and fantasy past* (pp. 77–96), New York: Palgrave Macmillan.

Swann Jones, S. (1995) *The fairytale: The magic mirror of imagination*, New York: Twayne.

Tracy, L. (2012) '"For Our dere Ladyes sake": Bringing the outlaw in from the forest – Robin Hood, Marian, and normative national identity', *Explorations in Renaissance Culture*, 38(1–2), 35–65.

Visit Nottinghamshire (2020) *Mortimer's Hole cave tour with a touch of history at Cave City 2019: Nottingham Underground Festival*, https://www.visit-nottinghamshire.co.uk/whats-on/mortimers-hole-cave-tour-with-a-touch-of-history-at-cave-city-2019-nottingham-underground-festival-p739001 (accessed November 10, 2020).

Warwick Castle (2020) *What is the Princess Tower?* https://support.warwick-castle.com/hc/en-us/articles/360002073351-What-is-The-Princess-Tower- (accessed August 13, 2020).

Weir, A. (1999) *Eleanor of Aquitaine: By the wrath of God, Queen of England*, London: Pimlico.

Whelan, B. (2014) 'Power to the princess: Disney and the creation of the twentieth-century princess narrative', in A. Howe and W. Yarbrough (Eds.), *Kidding around: The child in film and media* (pp. 167–192), New York and London: Bloomsbury.

White, T.H. (1938) *The sword in the stone*, London: Harper Voyager, published in *The Once and Future King* omnibus 2015.

Wickham, C. (2016) *Medieval Europe*, New Haven CT: Yale University Press.

Woods, W. (2004) 'Authenticating realism in medieval film', in M. Driver and S. Ray (Eds.), *The medieval hero on screen: Representations from Beowulf to Buffy* (pp. 38–51), Jefferson, NC and London: McFarland.

Zimmer Bradley, M. (1983) *The mists of Avalon*, New York: Ballantine Books.

Zipes, J. (1979) *Breaking the magic spell: Radical theories of folk and fairy tales*, London: Heinemann.

Zipes, J. (1988) *The Brothers Grimm: From enchanted forests to the modern world*, New York: Routledge.

5   Medieval knights and chivalry

Introduction: *A Knight's Tale* (2001)

Ulrich von Liechtenstein (Heath Ledger) is the classical heroic knight. He is handsome, dashing, fearless and loyal. In best fairy-tale fashion, he wins the heart of Lady Jocelyn (Shannyn Sussamen), earns the respect of the Black Prince (James Purefoy) and defeats a villainous rival in Count Adhemar (Rufus Sewell). Being a post-modern take on the classic medieval story, it contains some interesting tweaks and anachronisms that either enchant or infuriate audiences depending on one's point of view. Most prominent is the use of modern music, included to provide a sense of excitement and engagement for modern audiences. This includes Queen's "We Will Rock You" in the opening tournament scene and David Bowie's "Golden Years" as the soundtrack for a medieval ball. A completely fictional tale, it includes some real people in von Liechtenstein (who was a thirteenth-century knight and poet), the Black Prince (Edward of Woodstock, son of Edward III) and Geoffrey Chaucer (Paul Bettany) slumming it as a herald due to gambling losses. Finally, it is a medieval caper film. Von Liechtenstein is not a knight. He is actually just a servant called William Thatcher. When his master dies, he pretends to be a knight simply to earn the money to return home. Once successful, the pretence is kept up, particularly with the help of the charismatic Chaucer creating an imagined noble pedigree (Haydock, 2002; Jewers, 2004).

Such ambivalence about medieval knights is not uncommon in films. How to present knighthood raises critical issues for film-makers. Is their nobility paramount? Can an ordinary person become a knight? How important is chivalry? While *A Knight's Tale* grapples with all these questions, they have also been in the subject matter for other films. For example, commoner Alan Ladd pretended to be a knight in *The Black Knight* (1954), and even in the recent *The Kid Who Would Be King* (2019), ordinary teenagers unexpectedly find that they have the qualities to be knights. In *The Letter for the King* (1962), squire Tiuri (Ami Wilson) gives up his chance to be a knight in order to fulfil a vow he has made to the dying Black Knight. In doing so, he demonstrates that he is a true knight, showing he has courage, persistence and loyalty to a worthy cause. One of his fellow novices, Iona (Thaddea Graham) is a skilful and brave warrior in battle, but she betrays Tiuri and becomes an outlaw. She has failed the test. Another knight-in-training is Arman (Islam Bouakkaz), a bully who eventually finds the strength to stand up to his corrupt father. His transformation as a character means that he is eventually worthy of standing beside Tiuri as a candidate for knighthood. There is a moral dimension to being a knight that runs strongly through these narratives, which is part of the mythology of knighthood.

The evolution of knighthood

While the media and tourism attractions tend to present knights in a quite unified way, the historical reality was that this was a complex and highly dynamic institution. From an English perspective, knighthood was virtually unknown before the Norman Conquest. In Europe, a knight was originally a mounted warrior, in Germanic languages known as a 'knecht' (meaning vassal) and in French as a 'chevalier' (horseman). For most of the early medieval period, armies were mainly composed of infantry, and while those of higher rank might have ridden to the battlefield, they fought on foot. From around the eighth century onwards, some Frankish warriors began to fight on horseback, taking advantage of the introduction of the stirrup from central Asia, which allowed them greater balance and the ability to use a lance whilst mounted. This creation of mounted cavalry gave great military advantages, though it was expensive; requiring horses, specialised equipment and extensive training. The inability of monarchs to effectively maintain central control in the face of external and internal threats led to the devolution of power to a variety of regional lords, thereby creating demand for the services of knights in these multiple small armies and castle garrisons. Those warriors that made the transition to becoming mounted knights quickly became aware of their elite status and began to claim special honours, privileges and rituals, constructing a hegemonic ideal of themselves as part of an exclusive and noble brotherhood of arms (Collins, 2013; Saul, 2011; Wickham, 2017).

In the twelfth through the fourteenth centuries, knighthood became increasingly expensive and bound up within newly invented traditions. Armour became heavier. Training and practice consumed much of their time, so that most knights were professional soldiers attached to the retinues of kings and nobles. In the twelfth century, the first tournaments began as a method of improving training and testing military prowess. Notions of chivalry and courtly love flowed down from their masters, and knights were keen to gain status by appropriating these ideals for themselves.

The age of chivalry

As knights developed as a military elite, the concept of chivalry took hold across medieval Europe. In essence, chivalry was a shared ideal that knights should be more than just warriors, but also should exhibit courage and honour and have a responsibility to protect the weak. In part, the concept of chivalry was developed to rein in the more destructive urges of the warrior caste and direct it towards ensuring social stability and order. It was also, as Saul describes it, 'an aristocratic value system' (2011: 4), to which knights willingly subscribed in order to claim a higher status in society. Rather than being mere military vassals or soldiers-for-hire, knights looked to the nobility and constructed an identity that was similar. Crudely put, chivalry allowed for social climbing through adopting the ideals and outward markers of the upper orders in a highly class-bound society. Accordingly, chivalry evolved so it:

> Embraced both ideology and social practice. Among the qualities central to it were loyalty, generosity, dedication, courage and courtesy, qualities which were esteemed by the military class and which contemporaries believed the ideal knight should possess.
>
> (Saul, 2011: 3)

From the twelfth century onwards, institutions and practices developed to reinforce chivalry and the privileged place of knights in the social order. The first was that tournaments shifted from being merely military practice to an elaborate set of rituals and displays. The second was that being recognised as a knight developed as a process culminating in being 'dubbed' a knight by the king or appropriate lord. Over time, this became an elaborate ceremony emphasising the worthiness of the candidate and involving ritualised bathing, a special costume, a parade and feasting. This was often a major court event, as in the Feast of Swans in 1306, where Edward I dubbed 267 knights at Westminster Abbey. The third was the invention of heraldry, in which noble and knightly provenance was recorded by a set of officials and then signified through the display of a coat of arms on banners and shields. This allowed a knight's credentials to be displayed and acknowledged.

Chivalry was celebrated through medieval poetry and literature, which had a major trope of knights engaging in brave deeds and the quest for honour. Examples include de Troye's *Lancelot, ou Le Chevalier à la Charrette* (Lancelot – the Knight of the Cart) in the twelfth century, *Sir Gawain and the Green Knight* in the fourteenth century and Malory's *Le Morte d'Arthur* in the fifteenth century. At court, chivalry was often played out through interaction with noble women. A knight at a tournament, for example, might compete wearing a lady's token, signifying that he was her champion. Prizes at tournaments included keeping these tokens and in some cases even being rewarded with a kiss. All of this was meant to be platonic – part of 'courtly love' – though it sometimes went further (Saul, 2011).

While chivalry developed as a means to allow knights to move upwards through the social order, it also affected the higher classes. Kings, in particular, came to be expected to have the knightly qualities of courage, honour, justice and compassion (Asbridge, 2014; Lewis, 2013) In England, monarchs such as Richard I, Edward I and Edward III consciously appropriated knightly values and incorporated them into their own regal identities. Conversely, some kings were seen as failing to live up to some ideals (for example, John), or even rejecting them (Richard II). The blurred concept of the 'good' and 'bad' King is discussed in Chapter 3.

Chivalry was essentially a fantasy, even in the medieval period. Romantic tales of chivalrous heroes living lives of honour and sacrifice and protecting the weak were highly popular. Kings, nobles and knights readily subscribed to these shared notions of how they should behave, but this did not mean they actually always followed these principles. The result was paradoxical:

> The ideal was a vision of order maintained by the warrior class and formulated in the image of the Round Table ... King Arthur's knights adventured for the right against dragons, enchanters and wicked men, establishing order in a wild world. So their living counterparts were supposed, in theory, to serve as defenders of the Faith, upholders of justice, champions of the oppressed. In practice, they were themselves the oppressors, and by the 14th century the violence and lawlessness of men of the sword had become a major agency of disorder.
>
> (Tuchman, 1978: xxi)

Even the supposedly chivalrous kings – such as Richard the Lionheart, Edward I and Edward III – were all capable of cruelty and savagery. Richard, for example, ordered the massacre of 3,000 unarmed prisoners after the capture of Acre during the crusades (Miller, 2005). Knights might follow the conventions of chivalry at courts and tournaments, but on military campaigns, such ideas were quickly jettisoned.

The chivalric cycle in cinema of the 1950s

Whereas the nineteenth-century media valorised chivalry, in the early twentieth century it was somewhat out of fashion. Up to 1950, chivalry was satirised and lampooned in film versions of Mark Twain's *A Connecticut Yankee in King Arthur's Court* (novel 1889, filmed in 1921, 1931 and 1948) and treated seriously only in Robin Hood films, Robin being a knight who becomes an outlaw to protect the weak (Richards, 2008). However, all this changed between 1952 and 1955, when Hollywood made a series of films about medieval knights and chivalry. These were successful at the box office as they presented a romanticised fantasy of knighthood and chivalry at a time when American society was under strain. In part, this emphasis on chivalry, values and honour was an antidote to growing concerns about juvenile delinquency and declining morals in the prosperous post-war economic boom. Equally, these films drew on Cold War tensions, with common plots of 'the overthrow of legitimately constituted and genuinely popular authority by subversive cabals in the higher echelons of society' (Richards, 2008: 170). In the face of such dangers, these films featured a 'White Knight', returning home to defeat the enemy within, restore order and protect the weak. Such elements could also be seen in other genres of cinema, such as Westerns like *Shane* (1953) (Frost and Laing, 2015).

Whilst the chivalric cycle celebrated the heroic knight, the films also constructed an evil 'Black Knight' as the counterpart. The Black Knight was the villain par excellence. Not only were they opposed to the good hero, but their character and behaviour were also the opposite. Accordingly, whereas the chivalrous knight was brave and honest, the black knight was cowardly and treacherous. The hero valued honour, the villain sought money or power. The hero was in love, the black knight was lecherous or frustrated. Finally, whereas the hero was transparent and honourable, the black knight was cunningly adept at disguise and trickery, often pretending to be worthy and chivalrous whilst secretly plotting away.

Ivanhoe (1952)

Based on the Sir Walter Scott novel (1819), this film begins with Sir Wilfred of Ivanhoe returning home after the Crusades to find England in chaos. As played by American actor Robert Taylor, Ivanhoe is brave, handsome, well-mannered and gracious – attributes that the conservative Taylor valued and saw himself as representing in his films (Tranberg, 2011). The trusted friend of King Richard, Ivanhoe is equally at home with the serf Wamba. Without thinking, he rushes in to save Isaac from robbers. That Isaac is Jewish means nothing to Ivanhoe, and Isaac exclaims that it is the first time ever that he has shaken hands with a Gentile. When his friends are captured, Ivanhoe offers himself as a hostage in their place. When Rebecca (Elizabeth Taylor), the daughter of Isaac, is accused of witchcraft, Ivanhoe volunteers to fight as her champion. Everything Ivanhoe does is brave, noble and selfless.

Working against Ivanhoe are Prince John (Guy Rofe) and his henchmen Sir Brian De Bois-Guilbert (George Sanders) and Sir Hugh De Bracy (Robert Douglas). There is nothing chivalrous about Prince John. Sedentary, conniving and cruel, Rofe provides the most evil Prince John in cinema. The two knights talk of chivalry and bravery, but are driven by baser desires. Sir Hugh reveals that he wants to force the imprisoned Saxon princess Rowena (Joan Fontaine) to marry him, telling her, 'I have a taste for beauty and a love of money and you have both'. Sir Brian accepts Ivanhoe's surrender, but then casts him into a dungeon and refuses to release the other prisoners as agreed. He simply cannot believe that Ivanhoe is so gullible as to accept his word of honour. Brian's weakness is that he is besotted by Rebecca. When she calls him a, 'false coward, who believes in nothing, least of all your vow of chivalry', he replies that, 'on the contrary my vows of chivalry bid me slay the infidel [that is, her], but my heart is stronger than my sword'. Rejected by Rebecca, he fights as Prince John's champion in a trial by combat, knowing that if he defeats Ivanhoe, she will be executed. Nonetheless, just before the combat begins, he offers to forfeit and leave England as a 'degraded knight' if she will marry him. Mortally wounded, Sir Brian shows remorse and is happy that Rebecca will not die. Nollen argues that Sanders's portrayal of Brian exhibited, 'much more depth than Scott's literary version', for he created an aristocratic, 'villain capable of hatred and evil, yet he also possesses qualities of chivalry, grace and occasional gentleness' (1999: 128–129). It was also a courageous portrayal of a man overcoming his anti-Semitic prejudices at a time when the world was still reeling from the Holocaust during World War II.

The first of the cycle, the Cold War aspect, is not really present in *Ivanhoe*. Instead, it is an adaptation of Scott's post-Napoleonic War novel to the Second World War. Prince John suggests Hitler. Sir Hugh reinforces this in telling Rowena that he is part of a 'New Order'. Ivanhoe leads a group of allies in opposition. Anti-Semitism must be defeated to win the war and Robin Hood and his Saxons are the resistance. However, as the cycle developed, these elements would change to point towards future rather than past conflicts.

Prince Valiant (1954)

Hiding in exile, King Aguar of Scandia sends his son Valiant to the court of his friend King Arthur. As a prince, Valiant hopes to be made a Knight of the Round Table, but Arthur quickly explains to him how chivalry and knighthood works:

> It is clear you have little knowledge of what knighthood means. In how many tournaments have you fought? What deeds have you done? Have you killed any enemies of our realm? Knighthood cannot be had for the asking. It is not enough to be high-born ... I will give you whatever lies within my power. But knighthood must be won. If that is where your aim lies, you must start by becoming a squire.

As played by Robert Wagner, Valiant is clean-cut, wholesome and honest. With beautiful manners – he always calls his elders 'sir' – he epitomises an idea of what American youth should be like in the 1950s. He is appointed as squire to the legendary warrior Sir Gawain (Sterling Hayden), and a strong bond develops between the two. Indeed, so loyal is Valiant, that when it becomes apparent that both of them are in love with Princess Aleta (Janet Leigh), he steps aside for the older man.

Juxtaposed with the chivalrous Sir Gawain is the villainous Sir Brack (James Mason). While pretending to be a loyal Knight of the Round Table, Sir Brack is secretly the disguised Black Knight plotting with Vikings to launch an invasion and seize power. He has, however, two key weaknesses that ultimately lead to his downfall. The first is that he lusts after Aleta and this distracts him from his mission and leads to his second mistake. He has an *Austin Powers*–Doctor Evil moment after capturing Valiant. At this stage, Valiant only knows him as the Black Knight, but Brack lifts his visor to reveal his identity and gloatingly tells his romantic rival all his evil plans. Not surprisingly, Valiant escapes and is later able to unmask the traitor. Having achieved all that Arthur had earlier set out to him, Valiant is knighted.

In *Prince Valiant*, there is no ambiguity between the hero and the villain – Valiant is the antithesis of the Black Knight in every way and appears to possess no weaknesses or character flaws. This polarisation between good and bad characters starts to change with films like *The Black Knight* (1954) released in the same year.

King Richard and the Crusaders (1954)

Based on the Walter Scott novel *The Talisman* (1825), the story is set in 1191 during the Third Crusade. The crusaders should be united but have broken up into factions. Conrad of Montferrat (Michael Pate) engineers an assassination attempt, in which Richard the Lionheart (George Sanders) is wounded by a poisoned arrow. Sir Kenneth (Laurence Harvey) warns King Richard that there are plots against his life, but Richard refuses to believe that any of the Christian knights would put their personal interests before their sacred duty. Though the traitors try to silence the honest and virtuous Sir Kenneth, in the end he succeeds in convincing King Richard of the enemies within. Like *Prince Valiant*, the hero is tested, but not because he is tempted to go to the dark side. Instead, he must stay true to his ideals as a knight in the face of pressure and ridicule.

The Black Knight (1954)

John (Alan Ladd) is a commoner, who, disguised as the Black Knight, undertakes heroic deeds. In essence, this idea comes from the novel *Zorro* and has become particularly popular in comics. Examples include *The Black Knight* (created by Stan Lee in 1955 after this movie was made) and *The Dark Knight*, a retelling of the Batman story. In the case of this film, the Black Knight foils a plot to overthrow King Arthur. As with a number of the chivalric cycle films, this involves an outwardly loyal King Mark of Cornwall (Patrick Troughton) secretly plotting with foreign powers to stage a surprise invasion. There is an interesting inversion in this story in that the Black Knight is an outlaw who is actually good, a tradition continued in the various media versions of Batman and Zorro.

The film is strongly tainted with the McCarthyism of the era. John is recruited to become a sort of undercover agent by Sir Ontzlake (André Morell), who explains that, 'there is treason all about us and it must be stamped out before all of us – you, I and King Arthur himself – are overwhelmed'. Only by going outside the law can the country be preserved from the conspiracies of ruthless foreign powers. While Aberth argues that this is a poor production, he nominates it as 'perhaps the most politically driven film ever set in the Middle Ages' (2003: 13).

The Court Jester (1955)

Though not included in Richards's (2008) cycle of chivalry, *The Court Jester* is worthy of consideration for its representation of knighthood, court rituals, tournaments and chivalry. A spoof of the characteristics and conventions of Hollywood medieval films, it was made to cash in on the popularity of the 1950s chivalric cycle (Koenig, 2012). It starts with the revelation that King Roderick (Cecil Kellaway) has usurped the throne, massacring all the royal family. The exception is a baby, who the new king is determined to murder. Despite such horrific crimes, a sort of collective amnesia surrounds the court, with most of the knights and nobility quite happy with the new regime. The only resistance comes from a band of forest outlaws. Their leader is the Robin Hood-like Black Fox (Edward Ashley, an Australian who reputedly got the part because he was vaguely like Errol Flynn).

Hubert (Danny Kaye) is a former carnival performer who has joined the outlaws. Useless as a fighter, his job is to care for the royal infant. His commander is Captain Jean (Glynis Johns), who has been raised to fight like a man. When the opportunity arises, Hubert and Jean infiltrate Roderick's castle, with Hubert impersonating the new court jester Giacomo. Complicating matters, it turns out that the jester is meant to be an assassin, hired by the villainous Sir Ravenshurst (Basil Rathbone). As the action progresses, Hubert is revealed as 'a shifting, liminal figure whose ambiguous identity generates considerable narrative anxiety' (Bayless, 2009: 185). Hubert takes on a range of persona, from cowardly fool to skilful actor and even – under the magic of a sorceress – daring swordsman. The concept of a man taking on multiple roles and personalities was common in Danny Kaye's film performances – including *Wonder Man* (1945), *The Secret Life of Walter Mitty* (1947), *On the Riviera* (1951) and *Knock on Wood* (1954) – as it allowed free reign for his range of manic characters and improvisational style.

As court jesters were allowed to be, Hubert is the only one at court who may speak bluntly to the king and tell the truth. Such a role, however, comes with dangers as there is always the possibility that the jester may go too far. Adding to the sense of unease, the real Giacomo (John Carradine) is a foreigner played by an actor with a strong American accent, an assassin posing as an entertainer and his name – pronounced 'Jackamo' – is suggestive of the violent fourteenth-century peasant uprising of the Jacquerie. As he enters more deeply into the deception, Hubert is 'challenged to repudiate his unmanly, ambiguous and ultimately queer ways and prove he is a hero, a role coterminous with [1950s] masculinity' (Bayless, 2009: 185). Similarly, Jean is transformed from a trouser-wearing warrior to a feminine role acceptable to 1950s audiences. With Roderick defeated, the film concludes with Hubert and Jean as the surrogate parents of the royal infant, in a world that has returned to an American vision of domestic normalcy.

Hubert's transformation comes through the process of knighthood. Roderick and Ravenshurst suspect that Hubert is the Black Fox and scheme to have their erstwhile ally Sir Griswold (Robert Middleton) kill him in mortal combat at the tournament. Under the laws of chivalry, however, Griswold can only fight another knight. Ravenshurst proposes as a solution that Hubert be quickly knighted so that he can be challenged by Griswold. This leads to the two great set pieces of the film. First, the solemn medieval rituals of knightly training and investiture are reduced to a farce as the protesting Hubert is whisked through them at break-neck speed. Second, the tournament is disrupted by Hubert and Griswold's efforts to remember that they must avoid a 'poisoned pellet in the vessel with the pestle', or possibly the, 'flagon with the dragon', whereas the, 'chalice with the palace has the brew that is true'. It is after these hijinks that Hubert is transformed into the White Knight of 1950s cinema. Miraculously, he unhorses Griswold. Sparing his defeated foe, Hubert demonstrates chivalry. Griswold recognises that he has misjudged Hubert and sees him as a truly worthy knight, pledging him his loyalty.

Hubert then defeats Ravenshurst in a swordfight. Watching Danny Kaye prevail over Basil Rathbone stretches all credulity. However, Rathbone was now well into his sixties and struggled to keep up with an athletic Kaye who was 20 years younger, necessitating some shots to be filmed with an unconvincing stand-in (Koenig, 2012). When Griswold returns, he repays Hubert's chivalry by listening to his story, and it is when Griswold accepts that the infant is the true king that the rebellion is successful. In all of this, once Hubert is ritually anointed as a knight, he actually behaves and prevails as a heroic knight, completing his transformation. Unfortunately, the film-makers did not have a happy ending. The film went massively over budget and it was a major financial failure. It was only after it was released to television to recoup some of the losses that *The Court Jester* became such a popular comedy (Koenig, 2012).

Changing representations of knights and chivalry in cinema

The chivalric cycle of the 1950s burnt out quickly. Cardboard representations of good and evil quickly lost their appeal. Audiences demanded something more complex than what was being increasingly dismissed as juvenile fare, and increasing competition from television pushed film-makers to explore deeper and darker issues than could be presented on the small screen. A trend for more psychological explorations of heroism was apparent in many genres, including medieval-themed films.

The Seventh Seal (1957)

This Swedish production was especially popular amongst more intellectual audiences in the USA, serving as a marker of sophisticated cinematic tastes (Peary, 1983). Director Ingmar Bergman was inspired by medieval church paintings that he had seen in his youth. Particularly influential was one at Täby on the outskirts of Stockholm. By Albertus Pictor, it depicted a knight playing chess with Death (Aberth, 2003; Peary, 1983). In the film, knight Antonius Block (Max Von Sydow) has just returned from ten years on the crusades, when he is confronted by Death (Bengt Ekerot). Antonius challenges Death to a game of chess. He knows he probably cannot win, but it gives him a few more days of life. As Death notes, Antonius now has a short reprieve; what can he do with it? Can he achieve 'one meaningful deed'? The knight is war-weary and spends the interludes between playing chess trying to better understand the nature of existence. He journeys through a bright and sunny landscape, which contrasts with the collapse of society as the Black Death takes hold. Indeed, it is quite possible that Antonius is spreading the plague to the communities he visits. He is increasingly frustrated by his inability to find answers, but eventually takes the opportunity to distract Death, allowing his companions Mia (Bibi Andersson) and Jof (Nils Poppe) to escape.

Antonius is nothing like the other 1950s representations of chivalrous knights. He does not engage in any battles. He considers freeing a woman who is to be burnt as a witch, but changes his mind when he realises that she is mad. His existential crisis cripples him, so that his only positive act is the clumsy upsetting of the chessboard which allows Mia and Jof to sneak away while Death is smirking at what he sees as a pathetic effort to keep the game going. Nor is this film neatly plotted or clear in its symbolism and message. As Peary noted:

> It was a revelation to see a picture that required the audience to search for the director's meaning, just as the Knight searches for the meaning of life, in Bergman's vivid imagery and intriguing symbols, as well as his dialogue and events. And it was compelling that we didn't fully grasp Bergman's meaning at the film's conclusion or even after several viewings.
>
> (1983: 140)

As with the films of the chivalric cycle, this medieval tale is a means of reflecting on modern concerns. The knight 'embodies a mid-twentieth century angst' and had been deeply affected by years of war (Aberth, 2003: 217). Interestingly, Ingmar Bergman made these connections very clear in the program notes he wrote for test audiences, explaining how:

> In my film the crusader returns from the Crusades as the soldier returns from the war today. In the Middle Ages, men lived in terror of the plague. Today they live in terror of the atomic bomb.
>
> (quoted in Aberth, 2003: 227)

The War Lord (1965)

In the eleventh century, the Duke of Flanders appoints Sir Chrysagon (Charlton Heston) as feudal lord of a small coastal village. Chrysagon is annoyed that his reward for 20 years of loyal military service is so paltry. He is attracted to a young peasant girl, Bronwyn (Rosemary Forsyth). When he finds out that she is to be married, he invokes his feudal right of 'first night' or 'Droit du Signeur', through which the lord was allowed to have sex with a bride. A similar plot device is contained in *Braveheart* (1995) and is a catalyst for the Scots to rebel against the English. Whether such a practice ever existed is contested by historians and it may have been a form of revenue raising to accept payment for its waiving. In this case, it is not enough. Sir Chrysagon wants to keep Bronwyn, and this flouting of custom leads the peasants to revolt and besiege the keep.

Charlton Heston was attracted to the film because, 'it was a *small story* ... there were no teeming thousands of extras sacking cities, no kings or dukes ... only a penniless, landless knight ... with twenty men-at-arms ... [and] a sodden village of some sixty souls' (Heston, 1995: 311). The film received an award from the American Historical Association for its historical accuracy. Aberth described it as 'one of the best depictions of the complex culture of feudalism and manorialism on film', emphasising that while the knight has lordly privileges, he also has 'the surly manner of a lord who knows he has obligations' that he finds tiresome and beneath him (Aberth, 2003: 300). The knight was the type of character that Heston specialised in, a brave and highly trained warrior who is flawed, disaffected and even vulnerable (Frost and Laing, 2015). In his auto-biography, Heston reflected that he made this film in between *Major Dundee* (1965) and *Khartoum* (1966) and that there was a 'growing gallery of dark, driven men that seemed increasingly to define the fictional characters I played' (Heston, 1995: 334).

The modern cinematic imagery of knighthood

Recent cinema and television representations of knighthood draw on the multiple images of past productions. Some knights may be shown as brave and chivalrous, though this is often in comedies, such as Sir Godefroy (Jean Reno) in *Les Visiteurs* (1993). Or it may be that the brave knight is not really a knight, but a commoner engaging in a subterfuge. These are variations on the Hero's Journey (Campbell, 1949), in which circumstance catapults the reluctant hero into a mission or quest. Examples include William Thatcher in *A Knight's Tale* (2001) and common sol-dier Robin Longstride (Russell Crowe) pretending to be Sir Robin of Locksley in *Robin Hood* (2010). In both these instances, the pretence is adopted to allow the heroes to return home from abroad, but they quickly find themselves trapped within their disguise. Furthermore, as there must be a villain to oppose the hero, variations of the Black Knight still abound, just as cunning, duplicitous and vicious as their predecessors in the 1950s. Examples of these include Count Adhemar in *A Knight's Tale* and Sir Godfrey (Mark Strong) in 2010's *Robin Hood*. The ambivalent manner in which knighthood is presented in modern pro-ductions is well illustrated in the various knights portrayed in the successful tele-vision series *Game of Thrones*.

Game of Thrones (2011–2019)

This fantasy television series takes place in the kingdom of Westeros, where a number of noble houses battle for the throne. This is essentially the medieval world of Western Europe, for there are armoured knights (albeit with the title Ser), castles, troubadours and tournaments (Frost and Laing, 2016). Within the intrigues and changing allegiances, knights are but pawns in the game. None are simply brave and chivalrous; rather, they are complex and morally ambiguous. A common narrative for these characters is redemption, often through undertaking a quest. Three knightly characters are worth considering.

Ser Jaime Lannister (Nikolaj Coster-Waldau) is the head of the King's Guard and regarded as one of the greatest warriors in the kingdom. Initially cruel and merciless, he cheerfully pushes the young Brandon Stark out of a castle window, to try to avoid the boy telling others of his guilty secret – his incestuous love for his sister Cersei. Jaime's nickname of Kingslayer comes from him killing the former King Aerys just as rebels were flooding into the capital of King's Landing. Accordingly, he is shunned and disliked by other knights for such blatant treach-ery. However, as the series unfolds Ser Jaime is brought low. He is captured in battle, has his sword hand lopped off and has to journey through a war-torn land-scape to return to safety (a classic *katabasis* or mythological descent into hell).

Here we start to see the softer side of his nature, which emerges through suffering but also by the vulnerability of no longer being surrounded by his powerful family. It is gradually revealed that he was effectively a hostage at court and that he killed Aerys when he realised that the king planned to unleash wildfire on King's Landing, incinerating not only the rebels, but most of the population. His haughty demeanour is a front, and he is saddened that he is seen by his peers as a traitor rather than one who defended the common people.

Ser Jaime's companion on his nightmarish journey is Lady Brienne of Tarth (Gwendoline Christie). Brienne longs to be a knight. Often dismissed as being merely a woman, her height and strength allow her to defeat most opponents (Christie is 1.91 metres in height) and she is the epitome of the chivalrous knight, with a strong moral code. She accepts the task of escorting the captive Jaime to King's Landing, so that he can be exchanged for the Stark daughters. Initially, she is scornful of the Kingslayer, but on the road comes to understand and admire him. In the final series, the two acknowledge their feelings for each other and there is a suggestion that Jaime will find redemption with a 'good woman'. He even knights her, thus fulfilling her lifelong wish. In the end, Jaime does not feel he is worthy of her love. He has been responsible for too much evil and cannot be washed clean, even by the pure heart of Brienne. He returns to his sister when King's Landing is being besieged, so that she will not be alone, and dies by her side. In the end, Jaime redeems himself by this knightly act.

Ser Jorah Mormont (Iain Glen) is a noted warrior, who once bested Ser Jaime in a tournament; he flees into exile after being condemned to death for slavery. He joins the service of Princess Daenerys Targaryen (Emilia Clarke), the pretender for the throne of Westeros, becoming her most trusted general and advisor. Ser Jorah, however, is a spy and is supplying information about Daenerys's progress to King Robert in the hope of receiving a royal pardon. When he sends a message that Daenerys is pregnant, assassins are despatched to kill her. Jorah foils the attempt. Now in love with the princess, he decides to stop spying on her. Nonetheless, eventually the story of his deceit is revealed and the devastated knight is banished again. He is infected by the greyscale disease, a metaphor for the despair he feels at failing to live up to a knight's code of honour. Jorah is cured by the actions of Samwell Tarly, who like Lady Brienne is one of the few truly honourable characters. Both Jorah and Jaime find their road back to knighthood through meeting someone they can have faith in, in front of whom they have reached their lowest ebb. Redemption comes for Jorah when he is forgiven by Daenerys and he dies bravely defending her from the White Walkers at the Battle of Winterfell. The paradox for the television viewers is that the woman he gave his life for ultimately proves not to be worthy of his sacrifice. She is subsequently responsible for a massacre of the innocent inhabitants of King's Landing and revealed as mad like her father Aerys (see Chapter 4). His bravery at Winterfell has tragic consequences for Westeros.

These three knights in *Game of Thrones* were very popular with fans. This was because they were complex characters rather than cardboard heroic stereotypes. They each came with a backstory that was revealed only piecemeal and often surprised viewers. Their storylines changed, with issues of failure and redemption defining and redefining their characters. Whilst they were pawns in the 'game of thrones' – often manipulated and lacking control – they generally tried to do what they thought was best by their own personal values. They were constructed as knights for the early twenty-first century, their nobility tinged with darkness and tragedy. In many ways they were akin to the superheroes of the Marvel Universe, that great cinema franchise of the modern era. In addition, they also tapped into the narrative of the dutiful soldier being sacrificed by uncaring politicians, a staple of the film noir of the 1940s and 1950s that has re-emerged in popular culture this century.

Knights as warriors

The primary function of knights was as mounted warriors who served as the decisive shock troops in battle. Charging en masse, they could smash through the ranks of foot soldiers, turning military order and discipline to chaos. As Morillo argues, 'against a solid infantry formation, a cavalry charge was a psychological weapon', which, 'had to depend on frightening at least some of the foot-soldiers into breaking ranks or fleeing' (1994: 156). If the enemy broke, the highly mobile knights caused havoc amongst soldiers retreating in disorder. Up until the eleventh century, the infantry shield-wall had been the most effective battle tactic, but mounted knights made this tactic an anachronism. Eventually, new tactics would be developed to defeat charging knights (as discussed later in this chapter), but for at least 200 years they remained supreme on medieval battlefields, and it was this deadly effectiveness that was the source of their elite status.

Medieval battles on screen

Visual media representations of such mounted charges have tended to be limited, mainly because their re-creation is expensive. The introduction of CGI (computer-generated imagery) technology has lifted some of these restrictions, allowing thousands of warriors to be seen on screen without the cost of actors or the dangers of simulating warfare, though virtual battles can still tend towards being clunky. Perhaps the best modern portrayals have been the charge of the Rohan in *The Lord of the Rings: The Return of the King* (2003) and the Battle of the Bastards in *Game of Thrones* (season 6, episode 9, 2016). The latter is reputed to have been the most expensive ever single episode of a television series.

However, while *Game of Thrones* has provided some extraordinarily powerful and effective battle scenes, it has also gained notoriety for one of the worse seen on screen. This was the much-awaited Battle of Winterfell in its final season (2019). On a pay-for-view streaming service, the picture quality of the night-time battle was extremely poor. While the battle, 'was just as dramatic and horrifying as we'd been warned it would be', Coy (2019) complained, 'the only trouble was most of us could not tell what was going on' and, 'the extreme darkness … sparked a tidal wave of viewer complaints'. Watching it, we found it incomprehensible, with large sections in the pitch-dark with little dialogue and no sense of what was happening to our favourite characters. Going online, we found instructions that the episode could be better watched by turning the brightness of the television up to its maximum level. This was much better and revealed a well-crafted and engaging episode.

Faced with a public relations disaster, the show's maker came out with some curious explanations. Cinematographer Fabian Wagner argued that the fault was with the streaming services and the quality of television sets that viewers were watching on. This was a somewhat surprising claim given that the series was specifically made for pay-TV streaming. It did beg the question of when the 22 producers of *Game of Thrones* realised that this episode was unwatchable on the normal televisions that their pay-TV customers were using. Wagner went further, explaining that it was, 'intended for the lengthy battle scenes to appear claustrophobic and disorientating to make them realistic' (Coy, 2019). Such a view highlights a long-standing debate as to how warfare should be portrayed on screen and to what extent realism should be sacrificed to narrative (or vice versa).

Faced with the logistical and financial difficulties of filming large-scale battle scenes, it is more common in cinema and television to focus instead on the conflict between two protagonists within a battle. Historically, once a charge had been undertaken, fighting tended to break up into individual pairings. Such man-on-man combat provided opportunities for knights to gain status in defeating a renowned foe. In terms of media representations, the battle between two knights offers dramatic potential in two ways. The first is that the conflict is represented in a personal way to which the audience can better relate. A compelling example of this is the battle scene in *Henry V* (1989), which was staged with the focus on approximately a dozen key actors. Director and star Kenneth Branagh made the film for a fraction of the cost of most Hollywood films of this genre, yet the result of this parsimony was to heighten the audience's engagement with what is happening and to allow a dramatically visceral picture of warfare in all its horror. Second, there is the opportunity for a final resolution between hero and villain. To increase the dramatic tension, the two protagonists must be closely matched. This is well illustrated with the swordfight which is the finale of *The Adventures of Robin Hood* (1938). As the Saxons attack the Normans in Nottingham Castle, an intensely personal duel takes place between Robin Hood/Sir Robin of Locksley (Errol Flynn) and Sir Guy of Gisbourne (Basil Rathbone). Arguably, this is the greatest cinematic swordfight, although others may argue for that between Westley (Cary Elwes) and Inigo Montoya (Mandy Patinkin) in *The Princess Bride* (1987). Certainly *The Princess Bride* swordfight is a delight, but its protagonists are not bitter enemies, and it accordingly lacks the underlying hatred that provides the dramatic tension for the Robin Hood classic.

In some cases, single combat clashes were watched by opposing armies. These typically occurred before a battle, when knights sought to enhance their reputation by challenging individual opponents. An extraordinary example of this occurred at Bannockburn (1314). As King Robert the Bruce of Scotland was deploying his forces, Sir Henry de Bohun rode out and challenged him to single combat. Probably Sir Henry intended only to show off through the public taunting and shaming of the Scottish king. However, the king accepted his challenge, possibly because the king recognised Henry's coat of arms and sought revenge for his

English estates having been confiscated and given to the de Bohuns. With the assembled armies watching on, the two warriors clashed, and King Robert killed Sir Henry with a single blow. Judged by modern standards, such an occurrence seems highly foolhardy, an 'excess of chivalry', but was consistent with the medieval notions of knightly behaviour (Laing and Frost, 2018: 64).

The media has tended to ignore such duels before battles, possibly because they stretch the credibility of the audience (would a leader foolishly risk all in a single combat?) Where fights between two knights have been represented on screen or in literature has been in the case of trial by combat. Adding to the dramatic tension is that the hero is often opposed by a champion warrior who is expected to win; a David-and-Goliath struggle. Two examples are worth considering.

Ivanhoe (1952)

Rebecca (Elizabeth Taylor) is accused of witchcraft, and Ivanhoe (Robert Taylor) steps forward as her champion. Prince John maliciously nominates Sir Brian (George Sanders) as his champion. The underlying tensions are that Sir Brian hates Ivanhoe and loves Rebecca, forcing him to face a terrible choice. If he kills Ivanhoe, she will be burnt at the stake. She can only be saved if he loses. The combat is on horseback, and for much of the battle Brian appears to be winning. In the end, Ivanhoe prevails and Rebecca is saved. The ending is not clear-cut, leaving open the possibility that Brian deliberately loses (Nollen, 1999).

Game of Thrones (George Martin, 1996)

Tyrion Lannister is falsely accused of attempting to kill Bran Stark. There are howls of laughter when he asks for trial by combat, due to his size, for he is a dwarf and is likely to be pitted against a man twice his size. Watching this unfold, Bran's mother Catelyn is uneasy, for she fears a vendetta against other members of her family and she is not even certain that Tyrion is guilty. Her uneasiness grows when Tyrion nominates a mercenary soldier Bronn as his champion. Ser Vardis, his impressive opponent, is 'encased in heavy plate armor over mail ... [with a visor] with a narrow slit for vision'. In contrast, 'Bronn was so lightly armored he looked almost naked beside the knight' (Martin, 1996: 422). Yet, Catelyn notes that Bronn is taller, with longer reach and 15 years younger. The combat takes place in a ceremonial courtyard, with an uneven slope and obstacles such as statues. The light-footed Bronn takes advantage of this terrain, moving constantly backwards. Whilst most of the crowd shout, 'Stand and fight, coward', Catelyn realises that Bronn's tactics are superior, 'he wants to make Ser Vardis chase him. The weight of armor and shield will tire even the strongest man' (Martin, 1996: 424). Using a statue as a shield, Bronn starts to inflict wounds on Ser Vardis. Weakened by the loss of blood, the knight makes a sudden charge, but Bronn tips the statue on to him. The onlookers are staggered that a knight could be defeated in this unchivalrous way, but Tyrion has earnt his freedom.

Practicing warrior-craft: tournaments

A major part of the mounted knights' military advantage was that they engaged in many years of training in developing their skills with horses and weaponry. In this sense they were professionals. In contrast, their infantry opponents – particularly between the eleventh and thirteenth centuries – were less experienced in drilling and working in unison (Morillo, 1994). To hone their martial skills, prospective knights served for years as squires and engaged in competitive practice. At first this was informal and local, but as knights became an increasingly important weapon, there was an impetus to engage in centralised competitions and mock battles. From the twelfth century onwards, tournaments began to be staged. These allowed the knights to come together to perfect their techniques, gain repute, engage in exclusive and high-status rituals and enjoy the camaraderie of an elite class. For some, the round of tournaments provided economic opportunities (through claiming the horses and armour of defeated foes) and the means to gain a strong reputation (Saul, 2011). The case of Sir William Marshal is a good example of this. As a younger son of a lord, he had no access to land. Initially a member of a knightly retinue, he faced dim prospects when he fell out of favour with his lord. Turning to tournaments, he gradually built up his expertise and eventually became known as one of the greatest knights in Europe. He then joined the tournament retinue of Prince Henry – the son of Henry II – and forged a position of comrade in arms and advisor. In time, he was made an earl and rose to become regent for the young Henry III (Asbridge, 2014).

Tournaments combined a number of competitions. The chief ones were the *melee* and the *joust*. The melee was a mock battle which tended to be a free-for-all. The term comes from the French 'mesler', meaning to mix or mingle. Sometimes the contestants formed teams, whereas at other times there was little order or formality; the various knights battled away until only a single victor was left (Figure 5.1). Generally, the knights paired off, though in some cases two or three knights would combine to take on a particularly strong contender. The joust involved two knights charging at each other on horseback. With their lances blunted with tips, the aim was to unhorse one's opponent. Again the term 'joust' came to English from French, being an adaptation of 'joster', meaning to meet or approach. Jousting was a highly specialised sport, testing horsemanship and balance rather than just strength and fury. It became an extremely popular spectator event, which could be staged in a field close to viewing tents and pavilions and involve chivalric relations with ladies of the court. Jousting was also extremely dangerous, with many deaths recorded.

As knighthood and chivalry developed over time, the uses and meanings of tournaments changed. In England, the first tournaments tended to be unruly and disorganised, so that they were even banned for most of the twelfth century. They were reintroduced by Edward I in 1267. He was involved in expansionary military campaigns and needed to recruit more knights. His grandson Edward III followed suit, emphasising tournaments as key activities of his court and linking them to chivalric rituals and symbols. He was obsessed with promoting King

Figure 5.1 Modern Re-enactment of a Melee, Battle, England.
Source: Warwick Frost.

Arthur, and in a 1334 tournament he appeared costumed as Sir Lionel, one of the Knights of the Round Table. Like a number of medieval kings, Edward III enthusiastically took part in tournaments on equal footing with his knights, believing that the ideal ruler combined warrior skills, chivalry and masculinity. His successor was Richard II, who had other ideas. He believed that the king should be seen to be well above his subjects and accordingly did not take part in tournaments but rather presided over them as a regal spectator. Richard II's views on kingship and tournaments were not popular, and he was overthrown by the more martial Henry Bolingbroke (Laing and Frost, 2018; Lewis, 2013; Saul, 2011).

In the modern world, competitive tournaments have become popular amongst medieval re-enactors and audiences. For participants, re-enacting is a form of *serious leisure*, in which they gain satisfaction and status through their skill, costuming and adopted identity (Emery, 2017). We viewed such tournaments at Battle in 2011. Organised by English Heritage, these competitions comprised the morning's program, with the afternoon given over to a re-enactment of the Battle of Hastings (Frost and Laing, 2013).

Cinematic representation of tournaments has tended to focus on jousting. A melee is described in detail in *Ivanhoe* by Sir Walter Scott (1819), but this was not included in the 1952 Hollywood version. The likely reason that jousting is usually depicted in films is that it offers an attractive combination of spectacle and dramatic tension between two combatants. One is the heroic knight, often hampered by injury or outnumbered. The other is his nemesis, usually aristocratic, but so desperate to win that they will engage in cheating.

These tropes are well illustrated in two cinematic examples. In *Ivanhoe* (1952), King Richard is imprisoned in Austria. His friend Sir Ivanhoe (Robert Taylor) is charged with raising the ransom. Ivanhoe reasons that he can publicise his cause by participating in the grand tournament at Ashby. Four Norman knights have won through to the final round when Ivanhoe appears. Asked to challenge one, he audaciously challenges all four. The crowd is enraptured by the Saxon champion's spirit and this will help him in raising the ransom. Ivanhoe defeats the first three knights, but is unhorsed by the last. This is his enemy Sir Brian, against whom he will clash with later in the film. In *A Knight's Tale* (2001), the final championship in London sees William facing Count Adhemar. The count cheats by using a specially sharpened lance, which injures William severely. Rather than withdraw, William insists on having his lance strapped to his arm. In the best tradition of medieval romances, he wins against the odds.

The military decline of knights

Paradoxically, just as knighthood reached its peak, the military advantage of heavily armoured warriors began to decline. Even though the evolution of thicker and stronger armour continued to give knights an advantage, infantry also evolved rapidly and were eventually able to defeat mounted knights even in open fields. The changes that swung the advantage to infantry were organisational rather than technological. Indeed, victorious infantry in battles in the late Middle Ages were essentially using the same weaponry as soldiers a thousand years before. What changed was that they became more professional, better drilled and able to effectively use new offensive and defensive skills. On the continent, the first successes came with the Swiss Pikemen, highly valued, skilled mercenaries whose defensively arrayed pikes could stop charging knights. The English first experienced such tactics in Scotland, where they were defeated by William Wallace at Falkirk (1294) and Robert the Bruce at Loudoun Hill (1307) and Bannockburn (1314). The Scots used a 'schiltron' to great effect, essentially a circular shield wall or phalanx with massed pikes. Importantly, the Scottish infantry maintained its disciplined formation against the overconfident English knights. Under Edward III, these lessons were adapted for use in the Hundred Years War with France, with the English putting greater emphasis on professional troops of archers and armoured infantry. These were decisive factors in victories against larger French armies at Crécy (1346), Poitiers (1356) and Agincourt (1415). Such battles demonstrated that disciplined foot soldiers could defeat armoured knights (Jones, 2013; Morillo, 1994).

These changes in the medieval balance of power are picked up in media representations. The Scottish defeat of the English knights at Loudoun Hill was impressively staged for *The Outlaw King* (2018). In the novel *Timeline*, Marek watches a group of fourteenth-century English archers practising. He notes that they practice every day and can fire 20 arrows a minute. He comments to his companion:

'noble knights have been the determining factor in warfare, until now. Now it's over'. He pointed to the archers in the field. 'Those men are commoners. They win by coordination and discipline. There's no personal valour. They're paid a wage: they do a job. But they're the future of warfare – paid, disciplined, faceless troops. The knights are finished'.

(Crichton, 1999: 238)

Bosworth Field (1485) was the last major battle of the medieval period in England. In the death of Richard III, we may possibly see the final rites of medieval knights and chivalry. Details of the battle are scanty, but the critical moment came when Richard led a small contingent of his household troops in a charge against his opponent Henry Tudor. At this stage, Richard outnumbered Henry and was doing well; so why would he engage in such an all-or-nothing attack? One possibility was that he was disconcerted by the decision of Lord Stanley to not engage his troops to support him. Fearing treason, Richard wanted to settle the battle quickly (Seward, 1995). Such an explanation paints Richard as a rational and calculating general.

An alternative theory is that Richard was influenced by notions of chivalry (as outlined in the archaeological documentary series *Time Team* in 2011). Seeing Henry exposed, he opted for a heroic charge and man-to-man combat. Victory in this manner would cement his reputation as a courageous knight. Unfortunately, his charge took him into swampy ground where mounted knights were ineffective. Now, Richard was vulnerable. Stanley changed sides, attacking Richard, who was killed. Richard's rashness – or desire to craft a reputation as a chivalrous knight – led to this being the only instance since 1066 in which an English king died in battle.

References

Aberth, J. (2003) *A Knight at the movies: Medieval history on film*, London and New York: Routledge.

Asbridge, T. (2014) *The greatest knight: The remarkable life of William Marshal, the power behind five English thrones*, New York: Harper Collins.

Bayless, M. (2009) 'Danny Kaye and the "fairy tale" of queerness in *The Court Jester*', in K. Kelly and T. Pugh (Eds.), *Queer movie medievalisms* (pp. 185–199), Farnham and Burlington, VT: Ashgate.

Campbell, J. (1949) *The hero with a thousand faces*, London: Fontana, 1993 reprint.

Collins, P. (2013) *The birth of the West: Rome, Germany, France, and the creation of Europe in the tenth century*, New York: Public Affairs.

Coy, B. (2019) 'GoT cinematographer hits back at complaints episode was 'too dark', *News.com.au*, 1 May 2019, https://www.news.com.au/entertainment/tv/game-of-thrones/got-cinematographer-hits-back-at-complaints-episode-was-too-dark/news-story/874566ea2aef97fe087de6e67467f9d5 (accessed May 2, 2019).

Crichton, M. (1999) *Timeline*, London: Century.

Emery, E. (2017) 'Medieval Times: Tournaments and jousting in twenty-first-century North America', in G. Ashton (Ed.), *Medieval afterlives in contemporary culture*, (ebook, no page numbers), London: Bloomsbury.

Frost, W. and Laing, J. (2013) *Commemorative events: Identity, memory, conflict*, London and New York: Routledge.

Frost, W. and Laing, J. (2015) *Imagining the American West through films and tourism*, London and New York: Routledge.

Frost, W. and Laing, J. (2016) 'Travel and transformation in the fantasy genre: *The Hobbit, A Game of Thrones* and *Doctor Who*', in P. Long and N. Morpeth (Eds.), *Tourism and the creative industries: Theories, policies and practices* (pp. 164–176), London: Routledge.

Haydock, N. (2002) 'Arthurian melodrama, Chaucerian spectacle, and the waywardness of cinema pastiche in *First Knight* and *A Knight's Tale*', in T. Shippey and M. Arnold (Eds.), *Film and fiction: Reviewing the Middle Ages* (pp. 5–38), Cambridge: D.S. Brewer.

Heston, C. (1995) *In the arena*, London: HarperCollins.

Jewers, C. (2004) 'Hard day's knights: *First Knight, A Knight's Tale* and *Black Knight*', in M. Driver and S. Ray (Eds.), *The medieval hero on screen: representations from Beowulf to Buffy* (pp. 192–210), Jefferson, NC: McFarland.

Jones, D. (2013) *The Plantagenets: The kings who made England*, London: William Collins.

Koenig, D. (2012) *Danny Kaye: King of jesters*, Irvine CA: Bonaventure.

Laing, J. and Frost, W. (2018) *Royal events: Rituals, innovations, meanings*. Abingdon and New York: Routledge.

Lewis, K. (2013) *Kingship and masculinity in late medieval England*, London and New York: Routledge.

Martin, G.R.R. (1996) *A game of thrones*, London: Harper Voyager, 2011 reprint.

Miller, D. (2005) *Richard the Lionheart: The mighty crusader*. London: Phoenix.

Morillo, S. (1994) *Warfare under the Anglo-Norman kings 1066–1135*, Woodbridge, UK: Boydell.

Nollen, S. (1999) *Robin Hood: A cinematic history of the English outlaw and his Scottish counterparts*, Jefferson, NC and London: McFarland.

Peary, D. (1983) *Cult movies 2*, New York: Delta.

Richards, J. (2008) 'Robin Hood, King Arthur and Cold War chivalry', in H. Phillips (Ed.), *Bandit territories: British outlaws and their traditions* (pp. 167–195), Cardiff: University of Wales Press.

Saul, N. (2011) *For honour and fame: Chivalry in England, 1066–1500*, London: The Bodley Head.

Scott, W. (1819) *Ivanhoe*, London: Dent, 1965 reprint.

Seward, D. (1995) *The Wars of the Roses: Through the lives of five men and women of the fifteenth century*, London: Penguin.

Tranberg, C. (2011) *Robert Taylor: A biography*, Albany, GA: Bear Manor Media.

Tuchman, B. (1978) *A distant mirror: The calamitous 14th century*, London: Papermac, 1992 reprint.

Wickham, C. (2017) *Medieval Europe: From the breakup of the Western Roman Empire to the Reformation*, New Haven, CT and London: Yale University Press.

6 Medieval castles and walled cities

Introduction

The silent film *Robin Hood* (1922) created the archetype of the cinematic castle. An intensely personal project for its star Douglas Fairbanks, it was a huge success, 'creating an early prototype of the movie "blockbuster"' (Vance and Maietta, 2008: 125). Fresh from hits with *The Mark of Zorro* (1920) and *The Three Musketeers* (1921), Fairbanks was keen to make another historical swashbuckler. The initial idea was for a film version of Sir Walter Scott's novel *Ivanhoe*, but this led to an alternative suggestion of Robin Hood. The two ideas were analysed by the New York marketing department of United Artists, who decided that Robin Hood was likely to be the more commercially viable option (Vance and Maietta, 2008).

Fairbanks wanted the movie to be a great spectacle, authorising large sets and a huge budget for the day. This included a 90-foot-high Nottingham Castle set, built at the Pickford-Fairbanks Studio in Hollywood. At the time, this was the largest set ever built by a studio. When Fairbanks first saw it, he panicked and threatened to abandon the film, objecting that, 'I can't compete with that ... I can't work in a great vast thing like that'. However, when director Allan Dwan demonstrated a stunt in which he slid down a giant 40-foot curtain to escape Norman guards, Fairbanks changed his mind, realising that the massive set would assist and even enhance his acrobatic style (Vance and Maietta, 2008: 134).

Visually, *Robin Hood* set the scene for how medieval castles would be represented in the media. They are physically dominating structures, immense and daunting, dark and brooding. Often they embody danger for the hero, as in *Robin Hood*. They can be the seat of power of the villain, a base for an oppressive military force, the potential trap for the hero or a place of captivity. Despite the darkness of Nottingham Castle, ultimately it is the venue for the happy ending, where the wicked are vanquished, Robin and Marian are reunited, and King Richard has returned to restore order. A similar narrative occurs with princesses undergoing a romance or transformation within the precincts of the castle. There is often a fairy tale element to most media representations of castles, with the castle as a zone for epic struggles and transformation. This romantic media imaginary spills over into tourism. Whilst sites of historical importance, castles are often packaged up for tourists in terms of these media representations. Enchantment and romance are just as equally in evidence as tales of kings and knights. For heritage managers, this sometimes leads to issues as they try to balance the historical and the media narratives in satisfying the expectations of visitors.

The historical development of castles

In antiquity, cities and towns were often protected by walls, and these continued to be maintained and even extended in times of peace. Armies often made temporary use of stockades, but these were not intended to be permanent. It was not until about the tenth century that kings, lords and knights began to build castles. Initially, most castles were developed as defensive strongholds, primarily earthworks with timber walls and just a central stone keep. Over time, these were strengthened and extended, heading towards our modern conception of a castle. In simple terms, the common features of most castles were a moat and stone outer wall and an inner bastion ('keep' or 'donjon') placed atop a raised mound or 'motte'.

In England, castles were introduced from Europe by the Normans in the eleventh century. They engaged in major programs of castle-building as they extended their power and sought to subjugate the local Saxon populations, the most famous of their constructions from this period being the Tower of London, which was intended to dominate this key city and port (Pounds, 1990). In later centuries, further programs of castle-building were implemented to control border zones in Scotland, Wales and Ireland. At their peak in the twelfth century, there were approximately 1,200 castles in England. This growth was primarily due to the insecurity arising from the civil war between King Stephen and Empress Matilda, which encouraged lords and knights to construct strongpoints that they could retreat to and defy their enemies (Saul, 2011).

Castles were intended to both physically and symbolically dominate a region, serving as an administrative and military base. Towns and markets developed around these castles, taking advantage of the protection they offered. Castles varied in scale from small frontier outposts to elaborate and palatial conurbations. For example, the thirteenth-century castle of the French Coucy family had five towers, and its donjon at 180 feet high was the tallest in Europe. Its building took only seven years – at a time when nearby cathedrals took 50 to 150 years to complete. An estimated 800 stonemasons and another 800 craftsman were employed for its construction. One particularly striking innovation in its design was the inclusion of individual rooms for the high-born, for previously all occupants had shared the lord's great hall (Tuchman, 1978).

Militarily, castles were used either as defensive strongholds or as bases for raids upon enemies. Castle Coucy, for example, was designed to withstand major sieges with its massive stone walls ranging from 18 to 30 feet thick. It could hold an army of up to 1,500 men-at-arms, and its permanent garrison of 500 included 50 knights (Tuchman, 1978). Effectively constructed and garrisoned castles and walled towns were usually able to see off most attackers. Armoured knights – deadly on the open battlefield – were of little value against such defensive structures. Attacking forces consisted of foot soldiers with scaling ladders, and their casualties were high if the defenders were well organised. Long sieges tended to be rare, as the attacking armies were exposed and quickly ran through their supplies. There was also a real possibility of being caught between the defenders and a relieving force. The Battle of Lincoln in 1217, which decided who would succeed King John, was a telling example of this. The army of barons supporting the French claimant were attacking the castle when they were surprised by a relieving force under William Marshal. They emerged from a gate in the city walls that was thought to be blocked up and were upon the besiegers before they fully realised what was happening (Asbridge, 2014).

Apart from direct assaults, a range of other options existed to attack the occupants of a castle. These included digging underneath walls so that they would collapse, giving bribes to defenders to surrender and even engaging in ruses to trick one's way in. Military leaders used castles defensively to control areas and delay their opponents, so that campaigns were often attritional. Richard I, for example, took part in many sieges but fought only one full-scale battle in his whole military career. Running counter to this, however, was the desire for many knights to win glory and honour through battles in the open with massed charges. This latter strategy could often led to disaster, as in the defeat of seemingly superior forces at Bannockburn, Crécy, Poitiers and Bosworth Field (Asbridge, 2014; Saul, 2011).

Castles, however, were more than military encampments. Recent historical research has tended to concentrate more on their other functions:

> While popular perceptions of medieval castles are often dominated by their presumed military significance and role in contemporary warfare, the defining feature of the medieval castle was, rather, that it served a number of diverse needs. All castles were built, at least to some degree, to serve as high-status private residences and estate centres as well as military strongpoints … As evocative symbols of lordship, they represented a powerful ideological force, and their construction must have re-shaped the landscape in the minds of contemporaries. Perhaps of even greater significance was the influence that the owners of castles exerted over territories under their jurisdiction. A castle did not exist or function in isolation to its surroundings. Most lay at the hub of a wider network of estates rendering services and rents that sustained the seigneurial centre.
>
> (Creighton, 2002: 1)

The multifunctionality of castles may be seen in the various sites chosen for their construction. Despite popular imaginaries, desolate crags and clifftops were not common options, for while they might make the castle impregnable, they created major difficulties with access and supply. Instead, the tendency was often to site castles in reasonable defensive positions close to areas that were desired to be controlled. Accordingly, they were often near fertile lands, prosperous settlements, trade routes (such as old Roman roads) and strategic river crossings. In England, the Normans sometimes built their castles on previously occupied Saxon sites as a way of claiming legitimacy (Creighton, 2002). Walled towns sheltered a range of activities, sometimes leading to tensions between competing interests. Merchants and artisans, for example, benefitted from protection but sometimes found that the emphasis on defence restricted their options for economic development. During the Hundred Years War, there were even complaints that improving defences made towns more strategically important and increased the likelihood of their being attacked (Reyerson, 2000).

Some medieval castles were built or rebuilt in order to express status. For example, in 1227, Tintagel was purchased by Richard, the Earl of Cornwall and brother of King Henry III, who proceeded to build a castle. The site was heavily associated with Arthurian legends (see Chapter 3), and 'this acquisition effectively allowed the Earl to appropriate and exploit Tintagel's famed past through the physical act of castle-building, despite the site's absolute lack of military and other strategic significance' (Creighton, 2002: 71–72).

As with knights, there was a tendency in the late medieval period towards elaborate and ornate displays as castles became more symbolic and less practical. Developments in weapon technology – particularly gunpowder and cannons – made castles obsolete from a military standpoint, though they continued as markers of power and status. There were even instances of what we might term *fantasy castles*, built with deliberate anachronistic references. At Bodiam and Kenilworth in England, the castles were situated amongst lakes and waterways in a purely aesthetic rather than defensive placement. Furthermore, intentionally narrow windows and walkways made defence impractical (Creighton, 2002; Saul, 2011). The castle at Cooling was situated close to the River Thames in order to be seen and admired. This so compromised any defensive capabilities that it was notably besieged and captured in a single day in 1554 (Saul, 2011). There was also a growth of what have been termed combination palace/castles such as Alnwick, Kenilworth and Warwick (Pounds, 1990).

Media representations of castles

In the media, castles are often used as markers of the medieval, signifying to readers and audiences that this is the distinct historical time period the story is set in. Having established that this is a medieval space, other elements and characters – including knights – are introduced and fill the landscape. Such is the strength of castles as a signifier of the medieval, that there is an expectation that they will figure prominently and be a key part of the story. This leads to castles functioning as a background setting in which plot developments occur. Within the walls of the castles, there is pomp and ceremony, feasting, courtiers and nobles plotting, knights jousting and swaggering and lovers having clandestine meetings. Outside, armies assemble or conspirators plot to gain entry.

The expense of recreating castles has tended to restrict how they are used in cinema. The construction of the Nottingham Castle set for *Robin Hood* (1922) added enormously to that film's budget, and later film-makers were often wary of such risk-taking. Instead, a range of strategies were utilised with varying degrees of success. Most common was the skilful use of painted backdrops. For *Ivanhoe* (1952), an elaborate castle set was constructed at the MGM British Studios at Borehamwood. The cost of this was then spread by using it again the next year for Camelot in *Knights of the Round Table* (1953). Another option was that second units could cheaply film exteriors on location at castles in England, and this could then be blended with interiors filmed on soundstages. In more recent years, there has been a tendency towards the use of castles in Europe, particularly France, Hungary and the Czech Republic. This is part of the trend towards *runaway productions*, where films are set in one place, but the filming takes place in countries with cheaper costs or tax incentives (Frost, 2009). For example, the television series *Merlin* (2008–2013) used the Chateau de Pierrefonds (100 kilometres north of Paris) for Camelot.

In cinema, castles offer spectacle. The cost of constructing an elaborate castle set or shooting on location forces film-makers to utilise the dramatic possibilities. Attacks on castles stand out as an action highlight in cinema, often the most spectacular – and expensive – of scenes. Examples of this include the Saxon attack on the Norman castle in *Ivanhoe* (1952) and the Viking assaults in *Prince Valiant* (1954) and *The Vikings* (1958). In all three films, the attack is divided into two parts. The first is the main battle, with action-packed set pieces utilising a large number of actors. The second is a more intimate sub-story, in which during the attack, the chivalrous hero infiltrates the castle to free the captive heroine. The resulting fall of the castles in these three films is transformative. The hero survives a test and is shown to be worthy and heroic. The villain is defeated, and his castle and his cause are overthrown.

The action of a lone hero or a small group bravely infiltrating the castle is a common plot device. Secret doorways and passages abound. In part, this represents the hubris of the defenders, usually led by an aristocratic villain who is so overconfident in the strength of their impregnable castle that they are blind to potential weaknesses. In *The Adventures of Robin Hood* (1938), King Richard and Robin Hood's men gain access to Nottingham Castle disguised as hooded monks. The same ruse is used in *The Court Jester* (1956). In *Prince Valiant* (1954), the eponymous hero escapes from his cell within the castle and lowers the drawbridge to allow his men in. In *Game of Thrones* (2011–2019), there are two instances in which supposedly impregnable fortresses fall after a small group of attackers enter through the sewers. In *Knightfall* (2017–2019), the Knights Templar are able to return to their captured castle and retrieve their lost treasure through a secret passage. In the novel *Timeline*, Lord Oliver is urged to retreat to the castle of La Roque, which is strong enough to withstand a siege by his enemy Arnaut. Lord Oliver, however, is worried that there is a secret passage, which Arnaut will use. He explains why the castle was built with a secret passage:

> La Roque has a weakness. There is a passage I cannot find … [Bishop] Laon was architect at La Roque … That old bishop was crafty, and whenever he was called upon to give assistance rebuilding a town, or a castle, or a church, he left behind some secret known only to him. Every castle had an unknown passage, or an unknown weakness, which Laon could sell to an attacker, if need arose. Old Laon had a sharp eye for the interest of Mother Church – and a much sharper eye for himself.
>
> (Crichton, 1999: 258)

Occasionally, fictional media might feature in detail the multiple roles and characteristics of castles. This is particularly the case in novels, which have the space for such expositions. Such an approach is quite different to that of just presenting the castle as a setting for action. An example of this more complex representation occurs in the novel *The Pillars of the Earth*.

The Pillars of the Earth (Ken Follett, 1989)

In the twelfth century, Tom the stone-mason is seeking work. He journeys to the castle of Earl Bartholomew. At first he is told by the steward that there is no work, so he tries a desperate gambit, telling the steward in a voice loud enough that the lord can hear that, 'I just hope you're not expecting to do battle soon'. As it happens, that is a possibility, so the lord – 'irritated but attentive' – asks him to elaborate. The mason explains:

> Your defences are in bad repair … The mortar in the gatehouse walls has come away in places. This leaves an opening for a crowbar. An enemy could easily pry out a stone or two; and once there's a hole it's easy to pull the wall down … also, all your battlements are damaged. They're level in places. This leaves your archers and knights unprotected … The keep has an undercroft with a wooden door. If I was attacking the keep I'd go through the door and start a fire in the stores.
>
> (Follett, 1989: 201)

As the earl is involved in a plot to overthrow the king, being told of these weaknesses is daunting. He hires Tom to make the repairs. One of Tom's companions is the teenage Jack, who has never seen a castle. He has only heard about them as romantic places in poems. Now, he finds that:

> The real thing was amazing: it was so big, with so many buildings and such a host of people, all of them so *busy* – shoeing horses, drawing water, feeding chickens, baking bread, and carrying things, always carrying things, straw for the floors, wood for the fires, sacks of flour, bales of cloth, swords and saddles and suits of mail. Tom told him that the moat and the wall were not natural parts of the landscape, but had actually been dug and built by dozens of men all working together. Jack did not disbelieve Tom, but he found it impossible to imagine how it had been done.
>
> (Follett, 1989: 203–204)

While the castle is presented as a place of habitation and work, it eventually returns to the more conventional role of a place of action and betrayal. The castle is infiltrated by William of Hamleigh, who hopes to take over the earldom. Opening the drawbridge, his men flood in and capture the castle. Ironically, the castle has not fallen because its defences were too poor to withstand a siege – as Tom had indicated – but rather due to overconfidence and carelessness amongst its defenders. With Earl Bartholomew now a prisoner, there is no work for Tom, and he must move on.

Castle tourism

Castles function as central markers for tourism. Many are large, professionally operated tourist attractions with tours and activation programs. We consider three examples of such heritage tourism operations – Warwick, Alnwick and Chinon Castles – examining how they are marketed, the tourism experiences offered and their interconnections between media and heritage. The three castles chosen here are all high-status examples. They were constructed as palace/castle combinations to be used by royalty or great lords. Through the accidents of history they have survived virtually intact into the modern era (in contrast, the grand Castle Coucy referred to earlier was destroyed in World War I).

Warwick Castle

Warwick Castle began to draw tourists in the eighteenth century. Sir Walter Scott visited in 1828 and declared it 'the most noble site in England' (quoted in Westwood, 1989: 235). The advent of a rail connection made it even more popular, and it is notable that in Mark Twain's *A Connecticut Yankee in King Arthur's Court* (1889), the story starts with the author undertaking a guided tour of Warwick Castle. By the late 1960s, it was one of the most visited castle attractions in Britain with 150,000–200,000 visitors a year. In 1978, its annual visitation exceeded 500,000, but financial difficulties saw the Earl of Warwick sell it to Madame Tussauds. This led to greater capital investment, financing much-needed repairs, developing new attractions and seeing a fivefold increase in marketing expenditure between 1979 and 1985 (Westwood, 1989). One particularly noteworthy campaign from this period advertised Warwick Castle as 'Britain's Greatest Medieval Experience', with the provocative byline of '*NOT* SHOWING AT YOUR LOCAL CINEMA' (Ortenberg, 2006: Plate 6). In 2007, Madame Tussauds and Warwick Castle were taken over by Merlin Entertainments (and unfortunately, visitor numbers are now not publicly available).

We engaged in fieldwork at Warwick Castle in 2011. Having both visited it previously, we were interested to see the changes brought in by Merlin Entertainments. On the one hand, there was a much greater emphasis on tie-ins with media productions, including the television series *Merlin* (2008–2013) and *Horrible Histories* (2009 onwards). Intriguingly, *Merlin* was not filmed at Warwick Castle. Nonetheless, Merlin Entertainments grasped the opportunity presented by the show's popularity to open an attraction entitled 'Merlin: The Dragon Tower' (Figure 6.1). Adding to the sense of hyper-reality, they employed actor Warwick Davis to launch the new enterprise. Davis had appeared in only one episode of the television series, but presumably the connection with his name was behind the choice.

In contrast to these two media-themed exhibitions, Warwick Castle also featured a new history-based attraction in 'Kingmaker: The Eve of Battle'. This

Figure 6.1 Merlin: The Dragon Tower at Warwick Castle.

Source: Jennifer Frost.

focussed on Richard Neville, the fifteenth-century Earl of Warwick nicknamed the Kingmaker. As visitors walk along the battlements and through the medieval towers, a series of filmed dramatisations were projected regarding preparations before the Battle of Barnet in 1471. Some of the characters – including Warwick – are brash and confident, whereas others are haunted by a sense of doom. The latter is particularly powerful, for the Earl of Warwick will be defeated and killed and the chaotic spiral of the War of the Roses will continue. Indeed, over the next 14 years, England would have four kings, three of whom will be killed by their rivals.

Media connections continued to be strong at Warwick Castle. In 2014, a movie tour was staged (Warwick Castle, 2014). This was developed as an indoor tour, occurring through the winter, with a view to diversifying the offerings to tourists during this traditionally slower time of year. The main emphasis of the tour was on Charles Greville, the Seventh Earl of Warwick. In the 1930s, he headed for Hollywood, signing a contract with MGM and establishing himself as a celebrity socialite. As Michael Brooke, he appeared in seven movies, with his biggest role co-starring with Errol Flynn and David Niven in *Dawn Patrol* (1938). Returning to England, he hosted visits by a range of Hollywood stars at Warwick Castle, and the tour mainly focussed on this. The tour also featured the idea that J.R.R. Tolkien based the city of Minas Tirith in Gondor on Warwick Castle for *The Lord of the Rings*. He certainly lived nearby and was married at Warwick, so he was most likely quite familiar with the castle. In terms of films, the tour featured modern productions that visitors may have seen, such as *King Ralph* (1991) and *Nativity 2* (2011). Somewhat surprisingly, movies from the 1950s – such as *Prince Valiant* – were seemingly ignored.

Alnwick Castle

Like Warwick, Alnwick Castle was first built in the eleventh century and evolved into a combination of palace and castle (Pounds, 1990). Unlike Warwick, it is still owned and operated by the aristocratic Percy family and still partly serves as a residence for the Duke of Northumberland. In the 1950s, it was used as a location for *Prince Valiant* (1954) and the television series *The Adventures of Robin Hood* (1955–1960). Later, it featured in *Blackadder* (1982–1983) and *Robin Hood: Prince of Thieves* (1991). It was, however, through Harry Potter that it really came to the attention of the filmgoing public. In the first two films in the series – *Harry Potter and the Philosopher's Stone* (2001) and *Harry Potter and the Chamber of Secrets* (2002) – the exteriors of Hogwarts School were shot at Alnwick.

In the 1990s, visitation was around 60,000, leading to the idea to revitalise the castle through restoring the derelict garden. Coincidentally, the garden reopened just before the release of the first Harry Potter movie. The result of the two new developments was that visitation rose from 60,000 in 2001, to 140,000 in 2002 and 250,000–300,000 in 2003. Since then, annual visitor numbers have stabilised at around 250,000 to 290,000 (Bąkiewicz *et al.*, 2017; Sharpley, 2007). With the success of the Harry Potter films, a marketing campaign was developed to link the castle to the fictional wizard. In targeting fans of the books and films, this, 'created a new type of visitor who would not normally be interested in visiting heritage sites' (Bąkiewicz *et al.*, 2017). There was also a particular challenge in marketing Alnwick as Hogwarts, when it was used only for exteriors and not for interiors, particularly the grand dining hall. As the castle's marketing manager summarised it:

> I have heard a visitor saying, 'I came in and expected to see the Great Hall from Hogwarts' and, of course, that wasn't here. So I think some people, when they go inside, are surprised that it doesn't look like Hogwarts on the inside, but it's difficult to manage those expectations.
>
> (quoted in Bąkiewicz *et al.*, 2017: 557)

Similarly to Warwick Castle, issues arose in terms of achieving the right balance of the historic and fictional in the marketing and interpretation of Alnwick Castle. This difficulty came down to which 'Harry' narrative to emphasise. In the past, the emphasis tended to be on Harry Hotspur, a member of the Percy family who was a famed knight in the fourteenth century and features significantly in Shakespeare's *Henry IV*. With the advent of Harry Potter, the shift has been towards the fictional; though the juxtaposition of the 'Two Harrys' has an attractive resonance in marketing (Bąkiewicz *et al.*, 2017; Lee, 2012).

Chinon Castle

Situated in the Loire Valley of France, Chinon is a royal castle with narratives tied to both English and French kings (Figure 6.2). In 2000, the Loire Valley was World Heritage listed for its medieval landscape and chateaux. Following on from this listing, a major restoration program at Chinon was conducted between

Figure 6.2 Chinon Castle in the Loire Valley, France.
Source: Jennifer Frost.

2003 and 2010, including the development of new interpretation. We engaged in fieldwork in 2016. The two main historical narratives at Chinon revolve around the English King Henry II and the French King Charles VII. These are presented to visitors via video in the royal apartments. These rooms are quite bare. Owing to a lack of remaining furnishings and historical debates about how they would have looked, a decision was made during the restoration not to include reproductions. These rooms are accordingly activated by the video projections on the bare walls (Figure 6.3).

Henry II used Chinon as his main residence from 1156 to his death in 1189 (see also Chapter 3). The video projections focus on his uneasy relationships with his four sons and wife Eleanor of Aquitaine. With the ageing Henry unwilling to confirm inheritances, this at times led to armed rebellions by his frustrated sons (Asbridge, 2014; Jones, 2013). This conflict forms the basis of the film *The Lion in Winter* (1968), which, while set at Chinon, was not filmed there (see Chapter 4). In an adjoining room, the story of Charles VII is told. In 1429, as the Dauphin (heir to the French throne), he was hard pressed by the English. A meeting was arranged at Chinon with Joan of Arc, a young girl who was claiming to experience visions. As Charles was somewhat sceptical, he arranged for her to be admitted to a crowded room in which he was not wearing any special royal insignia. Faced with such a test, Joan successfully picked out Charles and continued to insist that he was the Dauphin, even though he denied it. After that, Charles was convinced of the veracity of Joan's claims, and the tide of battle was turned against the English (Laing and Frost, 2018). As with *The Lion in Winter*, film versions of Joan's life feature the meeting at Chinon but were not filmed there.

Figure 6.3 Projections in Chinon Castle in the Loire Valley, France.
Source: Jennifer Frost.

Walled towns

Walled towns work for tourists in different ways to castles and are accordingly worth separate examination. Across Europe, there are numerous examples of cities and towns that have retained some of their medieval fortifications and have utilised them to attract tourists. In the main, these are smaller cities and towns, where modernisation has been constrained. Their city walls not only provided defence but defined an urban identity of a separate and distinctive community and culture (Reyerson, 2000). Conversely the physical fabric of larger cities has changed over time, partly through continued growth and partly through the replacement of stone walls with embankments and star forts designed to withstand artillery. In turn, those early modern defences were often swept away in the nineteenth century for boulevards and parks (Lawrence, 2006).

In contrast, some smaller cities and towns have remained as 'historic gems'. These occur where the built heritage:

> is both so dramatic, extensive and complete and also so valued as to dominate their urban morphology, their identity and their policy options. They are frequently dominated by structures from a single historical period and contain, at least in their central areas, few discordant elements. In Europe they are typically medieval or renaissance survivals.
>
> (Ashworth and Tunbridge, 2000: 155)

The survival of relatively intact historic gem cities is through a series of phases in urban evolution. The initial creation phase is one of rapid growth, resulting in a variety of buildings from a particular period. In normal circumstances, these would gradually be mostly replaced as a result of continuing development, so that only a few scattered medieval buildings would remain in the modern era. This process, however, is subverted by a period of stagnation that restricts further development. A common cause of this was changes in transport technology. For example, at Bergamo in Italy, when the railway was built in the nineteenth century, the city walls and hilly topography meant that the station and railyards were situated on flat ground some distance from the 'old town', leading to a new development node, or 'new town', growing around the new transport link. In other cases, the causes of atrophy included the loss of administrative functions, ports being too small to handle larger vessels and changes in consumer demand leading to declines in certain industries. With little ongoing development, older structures might be neglected but not subject to wholesale demolition, The final phase is one of rediscovery, renewed appreciation and preservation (Ashworth and Tunbridge, 2000).

Within the city walls, the historic gem of an 'old town' – often of medieval origin and fabric – provides extensive opportunities for tourists to stroll, sightsee and shop. Impressive stone city gates function as entrance portals, delineating the past and the present (Figure 6.4). The modern everyday world – including cars, buses and parking lots – is left behind once one passes through the gate. Inside, there is an urbanscape that can be imagined as medieval. Indeed, walls and gates

Figure 6.4 Entering the Walled Town of San Gimignano, Italy.
Source: Jennifer Frost.

are often effective traffic barriers, so that the old town is characterised by pedestrian precincts (Figure 6.5), with many alleyways and lanes to explore and discover (Ashworth and Bruce, 2009).

The walls themselves provide a strong visual presence, as in the view of Dubrovnik in Croatia as seen by tourists arriving along the coastal road or by boat (see Chapter 1). In some cases, such as York and Dubrovnik, walking the walls has become popularised as the iconic tourist activity (Figure 6.6). As Ashworth and Bruce have argued:

> This is an almost ideal tourist experience. It provides, usually without cost to the tourist or much supervision from the managers, a flexible product consumable at the pace and duration determined by the visitor ... It allows heritage to be actively used, indeed almost automatically re-enacted as the strolling visitor imitates the patrolling watch man, rather than passively viewed.
>
> (2009: 303)

An appealing variant is the walled hill-town or fortress, as epitomised by Bergamo and San Gimignano (Italy) and Sighişoara (Romania). Here – as in larger towns and cities – the historical reality that the walls were a military necessity has been overtaken by tourists' romantic imaginaries that these places are quaint and cute (Ashworth and Bruce, 2009). Being smaller, they are more easily consumed by tourists. There are also instances in which medieval precincts have been constructed through the resiting of buildings, a practice often frowned upon as it may

Figure 6.5 Strolling the Shambles in York.

Source: Jennifer Frost.

Figure 6.6 Tourists Walking on the City Walls of York.
Source: Jennifer Frost.

take heritage buildings outside of their historical context. An example of this is Spon Street in Coventry (Figure 6.7). In the 1960s, the development of a ring road cut access to Spon Street. To regenerate the street, it was decided to remove and restore a range of medieval buildings – some damaged during World War II – bringing them all together in one place with the aim of attracting tourists and providing a distinct retail area (Sandford, 2018).

Whilst walled cities provide great opportunities for heritage tourism, they have their challenges. Overtourism is a common problem. The immense volume of tourists, particularly during the summer holidays, places great strain on the facilities and fabric of a small area. In Chapter 1, we discussed this problem in the context of Dubrovnik, where cruise tourism deposits vast numbers of visitors in the town. Many tourism businesses suffer from a sameness, as in the ubiquitous generic cafés and ice-cream shops clustered around central squares. Though the numbers of tourists have risen in these cities, yield has often fallen, for the proportion of day-trippers has grown and the crowds and high prices force out those who potentially may stay longer. Success then leads to a vicious circle that threatens sustainability (Richards and Wilson, 2006; Russo, 2002). The impact of crowds on amenity is apparent at some of the most well-known city wall walks. In Dubrovnik, walking the wall has become a pay-for-entry attraction, with timed ticketing, in order to control high demand. In York, the walls are still free but are often very crowded in the peak season with resultant foot traffic jams.

Figure 6.7 Spon Street, Coventry.
Source: Jennifer Frost.

Conclusion

Castles and walled towns are the most popular of medieval heritage attractions. Their stone walls are universally recognisable as structures from the medieval period. As centres of authority and power, they were built both to last and to impress and so remain today as important markers, often dominating landscapes. In cinema, they often set the scene for medieval narratives and are spaces for actions and conflict. In many instances, the expense of constructing castle sets required film-makers to utilise them for spectacular set-pieces, such as battles, sieges and rescues. This dominance of visual imagery has reinforced a widely held view that castles define the medieval period. Sturtevant (2012) asked young British people to list the things that they most associated with the Middle Ages, in a 'stream-of-consciousness exercise' (p. 83) and found that castles were among the most frequently mentioned responses.

This role in media imaginaries flows through to tourism. Castles and walled towns offer tangibility. They provide the physical setting for visitors to better understand such intangibles as chivalry, courtly love, feudalism and absolute monarchy. Military concepts – including armoured knights, men-at-arms and weaponry – can come to life within an authentic context of a castle complex. Functioning as bounded attractions, they offer satisfying experiences to broad tourism markets and economic opportunities to host communities. This popularity, however, sets up challenges. A limited number of medieval castles and walled towns attract huge tourism flows. In the face of overtourism, the sustainable management of these tangible heritage sites will continue to be an ongoing issue for destinations.

References

Asbridge, T. (2014) *The greatest knight: The remarkable life of William Marshal, the power behind five English thrones*, New York: Harper Collins.

Ashworth, G. and Bruce, D. (2009) 'Town walls, walled towns and tourism: Paradoxes and paradigms', *Journal of Heritage Tourism*, 4(4), 299–313.

Ashworth, G. and Tunbridge, J. (2000) *The tourist-historic city: Retrospect and prospect of managing the heritage city*, Amsterdam: Pergamon.

Bąkiewicz, J., Leask, A., Barron, P. and Rakić, T. (2017) 'Management challenges at film-induced heritage attractions', *Tourism Planning & Development*, 14(4), 548–566.

Creighton, O. (2002) *Castles and landscapes*, London and New York: Continuum.

Crichton, M. (1999) *Timeline*, London: Century.

Follett, K. (1989) *The pillars of the earth*, London: Pan, 2007 reprint.

Frost, W. (2009) 'From backlot to runaway production: Exploring location and authenticity in film-induced tourism', *Tourism Review International*, 13(2), 85–92.

Jones, D. (2013) *The Plantagenets: The kings who made England*, London: William Collins.

Laing, J. and Frost, W. (2018) *Royal events: Rituals, innovations, meanings*, London and New York: Routledge.

Lawrence, H. (2006) *City trees: A history from the Renaissance through to the nineteenth century*, Charlottesville and London: University of Virginia.

Lee, C. (2012) '"Have magic, will travel": Tourism and Harry Potter's united (magical) kingdom', *Tourist Studies*, 12(1), 52–69.

Ortenberg, V. (2006) *In search of the Holy Grail: The quest for the Middle Ages*, London and New York: Hambledon Continuum.

Pounds, N. (1990) *The medieval castle in England and Wales: A social and political history*, Cambridge: Cambridge University Press.

Reyerson, K. (2000) 'Medieval walled space: Urban development v defense', in J. Tracy (Ed.), *City walls: The urban enceinte in global perspective* (pp. 88–116), Cambridge: Cambridge Univesrity Press.

Richards, G. and Wilson, J. (2006) 'Developing creativity in tourist experiences: a solution to the serial reproduction of culture?' *Tourism Management, 27*, 1209–1223.

Russo, A.P. (2002) 'The 'vicious circle' of tourism development in heritage cities', *Annals of Tourism Research, 29*(1), 165–182.

Sandford, E. (2018) 'Secret Coventry: The incredible long-forgotten tale of Spon Street', *Coventry Telegraph*, 18 November, https://www.coventrytelegraph.net/news/coventry-news/gallery/spon-street-coventry-secret-coventry-15387434 (accessed November 21, 2020).

Saul, N. (2011) *For honour and fame: Chivalry in England, 1066–1500*, London: The Bodley Head.

Sharpley, R. (2007) 'Flagship attractions and sustainable rural tourism development: The case of Alnwick Garden, England', *Journal of Sustainable Tourism, 15*(2), 125–143.

Sturtevant, P. (2012) '"You don't learn it deliberately, but you just know it from what you've seen": British understandings of the medieval past gleaned from Disney's fairy tales', in T. Pugh and S. Aronstein (Eds.), *The Disney Middle Ages: A fairy-tale and fantasy past* (pp. 77–96), New York: Palgrave Macmillan.

Tuchman, B. (1978) *A distant mirror: The calamitous 14th century*, London: Papermac, 1992 reprint.

Twain, M. (1889) *A Connecticut Yankee in King Arthur's court*, New York: The Library of America, 1994 reprint in *Mark Twain Historical Romances* omnibus.

Vance, J. and Maietta, T. (2008) *Douglas Fairbanks*, Berkeley: University of California Press.

Warwick Castle (2014) *Warwick Castle at the movies*, https://www.warwick-castle.com/downloads/press-releases/2014/14-01-09-Warwick-Castle-Movie-Tours.pdf (accessed July 12, 2019).

Westwood, M. (1989) 'Warwick Castle: Preparing for the future by building on the past', *Tourism Management, 10*(3), 235–239.

7 Positioning medieval cathedrals in the modern era

Introduction

Aside from their religious and state significance, the vast splendour of cathedrals, with their soaring architecture, paintings, stained glass and sculptures, make them popular with tourists. It is difficult to imagine touring London without a visit to Westminster Abbey, or Paris without visiting Notre Dame, and many smaller destinations such as Salisbury or Chartres promote their cathedrals as their chief tourism drawcard. While they both tower over skylines and dominate cityscapes, the appeal of cathedrals is arguably greater than their mere monumentality. As one of the characters in Joanna Trollope's novel *The Choir* observes, 'the fact that the Cathedral was a spiritual building set it apart, gave it a significance and a stature that it would not have had if it were a castle or a moated manor crowning the Close's green dome' (Trollope, 1988: 38). Their longevity and the solemnity of their purpose bestow a gravitas on them that forms part of our shared heritage, even for those who do not subscribe to the Christian faith. They are also an integral part of our cultural heritage, such as Hugo's novel *The Hunchback of Notre Dame* (1831); plays like *Murder In the Cathedral* (1935) by T.S. Eliot; and visual art, with the paintings of Turner, Constable and Monet particularly notable for their depictions of cathedrals in different lights and seasons.

It was for this reason that the 2019 fire that destroyed large parts of Notre Dame Cathedral, to the point where it was almost completely lost, was such a shock (Lyons, 2019). This was a cathedral that attracted over 12 million tourists a year (Ballantyne, Hughes and Bond, 2016). Locals and tourists watching the flames head towards the famous Gothic bell towers were visibly in tears, and news headlines around the world were saturated with coverage of the inferno and what had been lost, as well as saved through the dedicated work of the firefighters. French President Emmanuel Macron observed emotionally that the fire had 'burned part of us', and thus needed to 'be rebuilt by all of us together', adding, 'Notre Dame is our history, our literature, part of our psyche, the place of all our great events, our epidemics, our wars, our liberations, the epicentre of our lives' (quoted in Chrisafis and Henley, 2019). French analyst François Heisbourg agreed, 'it's universal, Western, religious, literary and cultural, and that's what makes it different from any other object. It's the whole spectrum from the trivial to the transcendent, the sacred to the profane' (quoted in Erlanger, 2019).

Restoration work will, however, afford scholars the rare opportunity to get up close with one of the great achievements of the medieval world. According to Emma Wells, a specialist in English architectural history,

> the silver lining, if we can call it that, is this allows for historians and archae-ologists to come in and uncover more of its history than we ever knew before. It is a palimpsest of layers of history, and we can come in and understand the craft of our medieval forebears.
>
> (quoted in Lyons, 2019)

At this stage, there is conjecture as to how the restoration will be approached. Contemporary practice in heritage restoration is generally to clearly delineate any new additions to the original (Yazdani Mehr, 2019). Whether this approach would be acceptable or appropriate for a medieval icon such as Notre Dame is open to debate.

The fashion for constructing large-scale cathedrals, formed 'part of a large social movement that swept across western and central Europe beginning in the third decade of the twelfth century and continuing in fits and starts for the next four hundred years' (Scott, 2011: 10). This sustained series of large-scale con-struction projects created tangible symbols of the power of the church, and thus made a political statement to all who saw them, emphasising the importance of religion to medieval lives. It reached its zenith in what Scott (2011) conceptual-ises as the *Gothic enterprise*.

The longevity and visibility of cathedrals at the centre of large contemporary urban tourist precincts make them central to the way in which we imagine the medieval period. Examples that we have visited on our fieldwork are Canterbury, York, Salisbury, Exeter, Norwich, Durham and Lincoln Cathedrals in the UK, Paris and Reims in France, Córdoba and Santiago in Spain, Monreale and Ravenna in Italy and Hagia Sophia in Istanbul, Turkey. Some of these are barely built within the time period we are studying in this book, but we see them as rel-evant to a discussion of medieval cathedrals more broadly. Research on the role of the cathedral has helped us to understand more fully the reasons why they were built, but an understanding of their function within tourism is less developed. This chapter will therefore try to unpack the appeal of the cathedral throughout the ages for tourists, but it will also consider the ongoing challenge for the church in maintaining and conserving these buildings, at a time when government sup-port is dwindling or being questioned. Many of these cathedrals are looking for ways to raise revenue, often involving the attraction of tourists, with a number of these initiatives involving the media, notably film, television or literature.

The media therefore provides a lens for experiencing and interpreting the medieval cathedral, but this may also lead to dissonance where the usage is seen as antithetical with the traditional role of cathedrals. For example, in 2017, Durham Cathedral allowed interior filming to take place for *Avengers: Infinity War* (2018). It was used to represent Asgard, the realm of Thor, and the dwelling place of the gods in Norse mythology. This required sets to be constructed in the main nave and the temporary closure of the Galilee Chapel, while the interior of the cathedral in its entirety was closed to visitors for three and a half days (Hutchinson, 2017). It is unlikely that this filming has led to film-induced tourism, given that on screen it was difficult to tell that scenes had been filmed within Durham Cathedral. The decision to allow the filming seems to be out of step with their formal policy, which disallows photography in the cathedral, in part because of, 'concern for the conservation of the collections', but also to ensure that the cathedral is 'creating the best visitor experience for exhibitions that include items of religious significance' (Durham Cathedral, 2019). Some may argue that it is inappropriate given that the film has no connection to the Christian faith or the cathedral in which the scenes were filmed. Visitors to Durham during the period of closure might also have been disgruntled at not being able to enter one of the region's premier tourist attractions. It is important to explore this phenomenon, including the perception that in some cases, the church has commodified the sacred, and the ethics of charging entrance fees to religious sites.

This chapter begins with a brief discussion of the history of cathedrals in the medieval period, including the rationale for their development, before moving on to examine their attraction for tourists. We consider the use of the cathedral as a film set, the cathedral as an integral part of the storyline of a film, television series or book, and the role of cathedrals in hosting events; exploring the way in which these phenomena shape our imaginings of the medieval cathedral, as well as the ramifications of decisions made to make these buildings commercially available. In doing so, we touch upon the conflict between the cathedral as a place of sanctuary and its potential links with dark, violent or sexualised subject matter.

The medieval cathedral

The medieval period saw a huge upsurge in ecclesiastical construction, with an estimate of roughly one church per 200 people in France and England (Scott, 2011). Surprisingly, despite the deleterious effects of the passage of time and the pressures of population growth, more than 9,000 of the 19,000 churches in England and Wales date from the Middle Ages (Morris, 1979). Our focus in this chapter is on the *medieval cathedral*. In the Christian tradition, a cathedral is normally the seat of a bishop, which distinguishes it from an abbey, convent or local parish church, and its area of influence is known as a diocese (Westminster Abbey is, strictly speaking, not a cathedral, as it is subject to the sovereign rather than to a bishop; however, we are regarding it as equivalent to one). There are 28 cathedrals in England and Wales that originate before Elizabethan times (Morris, 1979). Two of these – Durham and Canterbury – are on the World Heritage List, with Canterbury being the oldest English cathedral, dedicated in 602 (Lehmberg, 2014), although the present building is high medieval. A number of medieval cathedrals outside the United Kingdom have also achieved World Heritage status. Some of these cathedrals are listed in their own right, such as Speyer Cathedral in Germany and Chartres in France, while others are listed as part of an historic centre, old town or city, such as Santiago de Compostela in Spain.

While cathedrals pre-date the Gothic period, the style is often seen as quintessentially medieval. It is said to have its roots in the work carried out by Abbot

Suger at St. Denis near Paris, with hallmarks including large windows, often filled with stained glass, sometimes in the form of the famous rose window; pointed arches; ribbed vaults; and flying buttresses which helped to spread the load of the gargantuan structure. All these innovations were directed towards opening up the building to the light (Prak, 2011; Scott, 2011). This was a revelation to churchgoers who had been used to worshipping in semi-gloom. As Suger commented, 'the dull mind rises to the truth through material things; And is resurrected from its former submersion when the light is seen' (c1144–1148). The speed at which the Gothic cathedral spread across Europe, starting with modifications of existing Romanesque cathedrals in France such as Reims (Figure 7.1) and Notre Dame, and then becoming its own full-blown style, was startling (Scott, 2011).

The process of understanding the reasons why this movement occurred is still ongoing, and it is linked to the motivations behind the construction of modern architectural icons such as skyscrapers. The Gothic cathedral was a statement – both of the power of God and of the monarch as his representative on Earth (Prak, 2011). Their size and grandeur were designed to overawe, and to inspire a healthy respect in the general populace. Sudjic traces the historical link between architecture and power, arguing that, 'we build for emotional and psychological purposes, as well as for ideological and practical reasons' (2005: 9). In the case of religious architecture, he argues that it can be a tool to shape a common identity with others of the same faith, and to allow messages to be transmitted, but it also must facilitate a spiritual ambience or atmosphere where the visitor feels closer to their deity or deities and in communion with the sacred. This must feel authentic, even though it may be consciously manipulated through such devices as the alignment of the building with the sun and the use of light, which, 'is a symbolic call to consider the heavens; it puts the individual at a physical disadvantage, it turns an intellectual understanding into a visceral physical experience' (Sudjic, 2005: 360).

Prak characterised Gothic cathedrals as 'triumphs of human ingenuity, culturally as well as technologically' (2011: 382), but they are also triumphs of persistence and tremendous political will. They necessitated the expenditure of enormous sums of money and resources during periods of famine, war and disease. Scott observed that building Westminster Abbey represented '5 per cent of the total wealth available to the king [Henry III] for a quarter-century' (2003: 36). The symbolic importance of having a cathedral often kept the project going long beyond the lifespan of one man, with the average construction time of a Gothic cathedral lasting between 250 and 300 years (Scott, 2011). They required a large labour force, some of whom were itinerant workers who followed the building projects around, which is the story arc of Tom Builder in the novel *The Pillars of the Earth* (Follett, 1989). The work was collective, often involving the transfer of knowledge on the job. This interchange of ideas and cultures made medieval Europe far more cosmopolitan than it had been, but also made the construction of a cathedral 'a social as much as a technological challenge' (Prak, 2011: 405).

The feats of engineering and breadth of vision that produced the medieval cathedral still generate a sense of awe. Unlike the many monasteries that were destroyed during the Reformation, cathedrals survived, although some of their art

Figure 7.1 Reims Cathedral.
Source: Jennifer Frost.

treasures were lost in various waves of iconoclasm (Lehmberg, 2014; Shaw, 2013), and many have required major rebuilding or conservation efforts at different stages in their history. They are perhaps the most visible remnant of the medieval period apart from castles, and certainly in terms of the urban fabric, they may be all that is left of a medieval cityscape.

Cathedral tourism

There is a long history of cathedral tourism, whose origins are associated with medieval pilgrimages. Visits to Canterbury Cathedral to honour Thomas Becket started after his murder in 1170 and continued even after his shrine was destroyed during the Reformation in the fifteenth century (Hughes, Bond and Ballantyne, 2013), with the cathedral still an important tourist attraction (Figure 7.2). Pilgrimages along the Camino de Santiago in Spain started in the ninth century, with pilgrims visiting cathedrals in major cities such as Burgos and León, before finishing at the cathedral in Santiago de Compostela and its shrine of St James (Murray and Graham, 1997) (Figure 7.3).

The Camino Way was revived as a pilgrimage route in the late twentieth century, and it is arguably the best known and most popular Christian pilgrimage in the modern era. The numbers who walk the Camino increase in holy years, even though the main motivations for completing the Camino do not tend to be religious (Amaro, Antunes and Henriques, 2018; González and Medina, 2003).

Figure 7.2 A Candle Marks the Spot Where St Thomas Becket Was Murdered in Canterbury Cathedral.

Source: Jennifer Frost.

Figure 7.3 Pilgrims Visiting the Cathedral at Santiago de Compostela, Spain.
Source: Jennifer Frost.

Pilgrims who reach Santiago de Compostela congregate in one of the squares outside its cathedral, taking photographs of themselves and fellow travellers beside their backpacks and walking sticks to celebrate their achievement. An estimated 3.5 million people a year visit the cathedral at Santiago de Compostela (Ballantyne *et al.*, 2016), which includes those pilgrims who attend a mass to give thanks for their safe arrival and queue to visit the relics of St James. They may also see its famous Botafumeiro; involving an incense burner known as a *censer*, hung on ropes, which is swung theatrically across the nave almost to the roof and back again. This action is a metaphor for the cleansing that the pilgrimage experience is said to offer, where the sinner is absolved of their sins or given the opportunity to heal (Frost and Laing, 2018). Walking the Camino for reasons of redemption was dramatised in the film *The Way* (2010), where a grieving father (Martin Sheen) buries his son's ashes along the route and is forced to confront the lack of meaning and purpose in his life back home (Frost and Laing, 2018).

In the eighteenth and nineteenth centuries, many tourists visited medieval cathedrals during their Grand Tour (Barke and Towner, 1996), which were viewed as important sites of cultural and religious heritage, although there is some evidence of a lack of respect or even vandalism with respect to sacred objects dating from the medieval period. Jenkyns (2004: 65) observes that 'eighteenth century schoolboys carved their names on tombs [in Westminster Abbey] and on the Coronation Chair, scandalising later visitors'. This perhaps reflected a view that Gothic architecture was not as intricate or flamboyant as other architectural styles, and thus less admired.

The Victorian era, however, saw a new appreciation for all things medieval, with visionaries such as Augustus Pugin who wrote on medieval architecture, the art critic and patron John Ruskin and the designer William Morris, all supporting the Gothic revival (see Chapter 2). In places like Australia, Gothic architecture was adopted as the latest style from Great Britain, and 'for many of us who live outside Europe, our first experience of walking in a Gothic cathedral took place in nineteenth-century buildings' (Trigg, 2005: 12). Shaw (2013) also notes the resurgence of the importance of cathedrals in the late nineteenth century but attributes this to 'a series of reforming deans' who, 'took seriously the duty of a cathedral to provide regular and beautiful worship, improving the music ... preaching and liturgy ... [and] seeking to become popular and accessible' (p. 139). Crowds flooded the great cathedrals on tours, and printed guides were created that were aimed at tourists (Coleman and Bowman, 2019). This led Pugin to bemoan 'a mere flock of holiday people who come to London to see sights, and take the Abbey on their way to the Surrey Zoological Gardens' (quoted in Jenkyns, 2004: 114). On Easter Monday in 1870, an estimated 9,000 visitors progressed through Westminster Abbey (Shaw, 2013).

In the modern era, there is often a tension between maintaining the cathedral as a place of worship and opening it up to tourism, even though the medieval cathedral was traditionally used for a multitude of purposes, with only specific spaces dedicated to the sacred. Winter and Gasson (1996: 172) stated, 'throughout the world, churches, cathedrals, mosques and temples are being converted from religious to touristic functions', yet this division between the sacred and the profane is artificial, given the history of most medieval cathedrals. Certainly, there is a growing need for cathedrals to work with the tourism industry, given that some of them are amongst the most high-profile visitor attractions in their region and tourist dollars are one of the most popular ways to fund the day-to-day operations of the cathedral. This may create its own problems, as, 'tourist boards, local authorities and businesses seek to include cathedrals in their marketing in ways which may give little emphasis to religious ideals of service and the provision of sites of pilgrimage' (Winter and Gasson, 1996: 174). Tourists visiting cathedrals may be unaware of inappropriate behaviour or clothing that offends local customs or beliefs and may inadvertently affect the spiritual dimension of the experience for others (Griffiths, 2011; Woodward, 2004).

Most cathedrals were not built with such large volumes of visitors in mind. Hughes *et al.* (2013) observe that visitor numbers to Canterbury Cathedral are currently estimated at one million per annum. As Morris (1979: 3) points out, 'more people now file through the nave of Canterbury Cathedral in a year than were alive in all the land when the nave was built late in the fourteenth century'. This has led to concerns about the deleterious effect this level of tourism can have on cathedrals if it is not managed appropriately (Woodward, 2004). For example, the Camino Way's popularity with tourists has led to strategies to reduce the impact of visitors to the Cathedral at Santiago de Compostela, including:

> The installation of electronic mechanisms for visitor counting to monitor the limits of capacity, the creation of routes to facilitate circulation, and an

information and interpretation center to make visitors aware of the need to minimize their impact before entering the cathedral.

(Pérez Guilarte and Lois González, 2018: 501)

The dilemma for most cathedrals is that they need these tourists; not just for the revenue that they bring, but also because they are a potential source of growth in the numbers of worshippers, whether for the cathedral being visited or for other churches across the country and around the world, in what might be seen as 'subtle forms of mission' (Coleman and Bowman, 2019: 12). They may also represent 'a gathering place for a whole community' (Shaw, 2013: 142). We will return to these points later in the chapter when discussing the purpose behind staging events within a cathedral.

Previous studies have suggested that contemporary cathedral visitors are attracted by a diversity of pull and push motivations, and the dividing line between tourism and pilgrimage in this context is somewhat blurred (Hughes *et al.*, 2013; MacCannell, 1976; Shackley, 2002). A religious experience may not necessarily be the object of a visit, even for those who subsequently state that they have had a spiritual experience or have felt a sense that God was present during their visit (Winter and Gasson, 1996). For example, cathedrals may be seen as a symbol of national identity, such as Notre Dame in Paris. Their visit might be the outcome of an impulse or motivated by connections to one's family or famous people (Woodward, 2004). Cathedrals might also be popular to tourists because of their artistic and cultural heritage, such as the history of the cathedral or the beauty of its architecture. Interestingly, this appears to enhance the spiritual experience during a visit to a cathedral, and vice versa. Their artistic and cultural heritage has a particular resonance from being presented in an ecclesiastical setting, and 'those who enter a cathedral as tourists are sometimes beguiled by place, mood and size into a mode of wonder' (Winter and Gasson, 1996: 182). Voase (2007) refers to this as a *romantic gaze*, where the focus is on contemplation and wonder, akin to the benefits and outcomes of spending time in nature. Spending time in prayer or quiet reflection might also evoke fantasies of connection to or continuity with the medieval world (Eco, 1986; Trigg, 2005). The anonymity of a cathedral makes it easier for visitors to 'try' organised religion without obligation, but may also attract those who simply want to find a safe space within a city in which they can disappear or hide for a while (Shaw, 2013). Thus, the division between sacred and secular motivations may be artificial and unhelpful, and 'to move beyond the tourist-pilgrim divide we may [need to] look for commonalities' such as the intersection and linkages between 'travel, place and meaning-making' (Ackerman, 2019: 409).

Some cathedrals, in particular, are blessed with cultural artefacts of tremendous significance dating back to medieval times (Department for Communities and Local Government, 2017). For example, Jenkyns observes that Westminster Abbey 'has been called the finest sculpture gallery in Britain – or even in Europe' (2004: 1), and some of these treasures dating from the thirteenth and fourteenth centuries are particularly noteworthy. At Hereford Cathedral, one can see the thirteenth-century Mappa Mundi, believed to be the largest surviving medieval map, while Wells Cathedral is famous for its medieval astronomical clock, c 1390. Of the four remaining copies of the Magna Carta – a charter of rights signed by King John in 1215 which acknowledged important safeguards such as the right to a fair trial – one copy can be found at Salisbury Cathedral and another at Lincoln Cathedral, with the other two contained in the British Library. We visited the Magna Carta at Salisbury in 2018 (Figure 7.4). Its display in a closed chamber, which reduces light and protects the artefact, with a guard stationed outside and only a few tourists allowed into the display at a time, also had the effect of increasing the sense of awe felt by the visitor at what almost seemed to be a 'holy' book. The secular has become the sacred. This is appropriate, given that 'the Magna Carta has acquired the status of a cultural text that embodies, and guides, a perceived social order. Its principles have acquired the status of the sacrosanct' (Ardley and Voase, 2013: 350).

A more recent and high-profile example of a cathedral being developed for tourism involves Leicester, leveraging off the fortuitous discovery of the remains of King Richard III in a local carpark. They were interred in Leicester Cathedral in 2015 and now attract many visitors, who combine a visit to his tomb (Figure 7.5) with the nearby King Richard III Visitor Centre. The strength in visitor numbers has allowed Leicester Cathedral to fund building work, and it has developed an events program to take advantage of the interest in one of the most notorious of Britain's monarchs (Department for Communities and Local Government, 2017).

Figure 7.4 Magna Carta on display at Salisbury Cathedral.

Source: Jennifer Frost.

Figure 7.5 Tomb of Richard III at Leicester Cathedral
Source: Jennifer Frost.

Keeping the doors open

The daily running costs of a major cathedral have been estimated to be in the order of £18,000 in the case of Canterbury Cathedral (Canterbury Cathedral, 2019), and £23,000 for York Minster (York Minster, 2019). This covers items such as staffing, security, lighting and heating. Maintenance and repairs are an ongoing responsibility, given that many of these buildings are hundreds of years old and subject to heritage protection. All 42 Anglican cathedrals in England are heritage listed, with 39 at Grade 1 (Department for Communities and Local Government, 2017), which equates to 'buildings of exceptional interest'. This means that special listed building approval must be obtained before such a structure can be changed, adding to the cost of repairs.

Cathedrals in the UK are eligible to apply for funding from the Listed Places of Worship Grant Scheme, which covers the VAT (sales tax) paid on these conservation costs. They can also access the Heritage Lottery Fund (Coleman, 2019). Seeking access to the Lottery Fund may, however, be unpalatable to some cathedrals, being at variance with their anti-gambling stance. There are also one-off resources such as the First World War Centenary Fund, which was used by 57 Anglican and Catholic cathedrals to complete repairs in time for the centenary of the end of World War I in 2018 (Department for Communities and Local Government, 2017). As is a common problem with heritage stewardship around the world, applying for these grants may require expertise which some cathedrals do not possess (Coleman, 2019). Another challenge Winter and Gasson (1996: 176) point out is that 'there is no systematic public sector grant aid [in the UK] for day to day running costs'. State subsidisation of cathedrals also does not necessarily address concerns about the potential for commercialisation to outweigh the sacred (Coleman, 2019). The novel *The Cleaner of Chartres* observed that the French state's responsibility for the repair and maintenance of a cathedral that is then used by the Catholic Church has led to a contradiction, 'it is therefore subject to two ancient masters, God and Mammon who reputedly have differing aims' (Vickers, 2012: 21).

The need for an ongoing revenue stream has led some cathedrals to charge for admission, which has been controversial. This practice may run counter to visitors' sense of spirituality, spoiling its mystery and the sense of awe a visit inspires, in a place that is removed from 'time constraints and commerce' (Shackley, 2002: 351). Voase (2007) suggested a different reason behind dislike of paying an admission fee. His study participants, visitors to Lincoln Cathedral, saw the cathedral as *public space* and objected to paying for something which they felt already belonged to them, even though these are not publicly owned-and-operated buildings.

Most of the cathedrals that charge admission currently are the largest, most prominent cathedrals that attract high numbers of tourists, such as York Minster and Canterbury Cathedral, and represent only 9 of the 42 Anglican cathedrals (Department for Communities and Local Government, 2017). Lord Bourne, Minister for Faith, in fact noted that this practice might be needed to deal with high visitation rates (Department for Communities and Local Government, 2017); effectively a form of de-marketing. He also observed that some cathedrals who started charging an admission fee found that their overall income declined, as a result of smaller visitor numbers. Chester Cathedral, for example, decided to deploy a team of volunteers who sought to persuade visitors to donate, rather than charging for admission, and developed a program of events that brought people into the doors. They found that this was a more effective way to maintain income levels (Department for Communities and Local Government, 2017). Others sought out opportunities to sell gifts, guidebooks or religious artefacts (Griffiths, 2011). Despite these efforts at raising revenue, it appeared that 'visitors seldom pay the actual cost of their visit' (Wiltshier, 2015: 69), although Winter and Gasson (1996), in a study of English cathedrals 20 years earlier, found that those who spent the longest in a cathedral tended to spend more and make a donation. They argued that 'any suggestion that commodification is by definition at odds with a religious orientation appears not to be borne out by the data' (p. 179). Despite this, cathedrals are generally keen to find alternative sources of revenue to visitor admission, most notably in recent years through the use of the space for filming.

The cathedral as a film set

There are numerous examples of cathedrals being used for filming. A fee is generally paid for these services, with Lincoln Cathedral believed to have been paid

£100,000 for its use in the film *The Da Vinci Code* (The Guardian, 2005). Many of these cathedrals then develop interpretation for visitors connected to the films in which they have appeared. Lincoln Cathedral provides information for visitors about its use in the filming of *The Da Vinci Code*, including movie props (Griffiths, 2011), while Gloucester Cathedral, whose cloisters were used as the corridors of Hogwarts School in the *Harry Potter* films, has developed a trail for visitors about filming within the Cathedral (Shackley, 2006).

Many Cathedrals host *runaway productions*, where 'films may represent one place but be made at another' (Frost, 2009: 85). Aside from the *Harry Potter* connection, Gloucester Cathedral has been used for television productions such as *Doctor Who* (2008 and 2019), *Sherlock* (2016) and *Wolf Hall* (2015). Only the scenes from *Doctor Who* (2019) are actually set at Gloucester Cathedral. The rest of these productions use it as a proxy for other locations, such as Calais Castle in *Wolf Hall*. Lincoln Cathedral was used to represent Westminster Abbey in *The Da Vinci Code* and *The Young Victoria* (2009). In contrast, Lincoln Cathedral was the setting for two episodes of *Antiques Roadshow* (2009) and (2013), which included segments on the cathedral's historical background. This sort of programme heightens awareness of the cathedral in its own right, rather than merely as a decorative period setting for drama.

Another issue for cathedrals contemplating filming on site is the content of what is proposed. In Spain, the Cathedral in Girona was used as the location for filming part of *Game of Thrones*, including the scene where Jaime Lannister (Nikolaj Coster-Waldau) rides up the steps of the Great Sept to rescue Queen Margaery (Natalie Dormer) from the requirement to undertake a walk of shame. She is pardoned, yet her mother-in-law Queen Cersei (Lena Headey) is not so fortunate and is forced to walk naked through the streets of King's Landing to atone for adultery, enduring the taunts and missiles of the crowd. This more controversial scene was filmed in the streets of Dubrovnik rather than Girona. It nearly didn't happen, as the Croatian Film Commission and the Church of St Nicholas in Dubrovnik initially objected to its graphic nature; they subsequently changed their minds, so long as none of the footage involved Cersei being in the nude in the church itself (Acuna, 2015). Author George R. R. Martin has said that this scene was inspired by the real-life example of King Edward IV's mistress Jane Shore, who after his death in 1483, was made by Richard III to walk through London clad only in a kirtle (a medieval loose over-dress). Unlike Cersei, Jane was treated with respect by a sympathetic crowd, who knew that she was being used for propaganda purposes (Seward, 1995).

This potential for the subject matter of the production to be in conflict with religious values or beliefs has resulted in some cathedrals refusing to entertain this form of funding. The cloisters of Durham Cathedral were used as the quadrangle of Hogwarts School for all of the *Harry Potter* films; reportedly because the producers' first choice, Canterbury Cathedral, felt that the 'pagan theme' was not something with which they wanted to be associated (The Guardian, 2000). Westminster Abbey similarly declined the request from producers of *The Da Vinci Code* to film scenes using the Abbey as a backdrop, which led to Lincoln

Cathedral being used instead. The Dean and Chapter of Westminster Abbey made a statement to explain their rationale for making this decision:

> Although a real page turner, The Da Vinci Code is theologically unsound and we cannot commend or endorse the contentious and wayward religious and historic suggestions made in the book – nor its views of Christianity and the New Testament. It would therefore be inappropriate to film scenes from the book here.
>
> (The Guardian, 2005)

The Abbey subsequently developed information sheets for tour guides that were designed to 'correct the factual errors' of the book on which the film was based, after they found that 'guides have been inundated with questions from curious tourists' (The Guardian, 2005). This was a way of dealing with visitor interest and also presumably provides an opportunity for education and outreach. On the other hand, the Dean's Verger at Lincoln Cathedral, John Campbell, felt there were tangible benefits to agreeing to the film shoot, which led to a 22% increase in their visitor numbers:

> It sort of introduced people to this massive building – this great icon of Lincoln and people started to look at the building as they had never looked at it before ... We would certainly consider more applications from film makers, as long as they fit in with the diary and without compromising the core values of the cathedral.
>
> (BBC, 2012)

There is therefore a balancing act at play here, with Campbell making it clear that there were limits as to what was acceptable. Some cathedrals may look at the likes of *Harry Potter* as merely an example of the medievalism of '*so-called tradition*' (Eco, 1986) or a form of magical realism (Faris, 2004); the harmless representation of an imaginary world, primarily aimed at children.

Cathedrals in fictional media

If cathedrals wanted to limit their use in films to those with religious subjects, they could look to the preponderance of cathedrals that are portrayed in fictional media. A recent example of this phenomenon is Ken Follett's best-selling novel, *The Pillars of the Earth* (1989), along with its sequel *World Without End* (2007) and prequel *The Evening and the Morning* (2020), all set in the same fictional English cathedral town of Kingsbridge. The novels dramatise the construction of a cathedral in the twelfth century (1123–1155), and they were inspired by Follett's fascination with the beauty of cathedrals, but more importantly by his desire to understand the reasons why they were constructed in the first place and how they have managed to survive into the current day (Follett, 2010). The first novel introduces Tom Builder, a master builder who is obsessed with the idea of working on a cathedral, which he regards as the pinnacle of the work in his profession. His stepson Jack becomes his apprentice, and after time spent in France and Spain, Jack brings back ideas for England's first Gothic Cathedral.

Follett is painstaking in the detail he provides on the technical demands of designing and building a cathedral, as well as the beauty that results from the regularity of the proportions. The challenges faced by the craftspeople of the day are manifold, such as the difficulty of drawing designs without paper (Tom etches his drawings in mortar, using a needle); understanding the load-bearing system required to make it stand up; and the complexity of marshalling contract human labour over decades. The monumentality of these structures is emphasised repeatedly by various characters. Prior Philip visits Winchester Cathedral and observes, 'it was an eighth of a mile long: Philip had seen villages that could fit inside it' (p. 327), while Tom notes the impact that these buildings had on ordinary people of his time (p. 311):

> The nave he had drawn was high, impossibly high. But a cathedral had to be a dramatic building, awe-inspiring in its size, pulling the eye heavenward with its loftiness. One reason people came to them was that cathedrals were the largest buildings in the world: a man who never went to a cathedral could go through life without seeing a building much bigger than the hovel he lived in.

The other revelation for medieval cathedral-goers was the effect of the stained-glass windows. Familiar with architecture that minimised windows, or framed them in linen rather than glass, the pouring of sunshine through translucent colour was literally dazzling, illuminating stories of the Bible to the general populace, the vast majority of which could not read. At the consecration of Kingsbridge Cathedral, 'the church was full of people craning their necks to stare up at the windows' (p. 1001). The exquisiteness of the vistas soaring into the sky is contrasted with the earthy commercial goings-on in the shadows of the cathedral floor, 'walking up the nave William was offered cold beer, hot gingerbread and a quick fuck up against the wall for threepence' (p. 1000).

The Pillars of the Earth was made into a television series in 2010, starring Rufus Sewell as Tom the Builder, Matthew Macfadyen as Philip and a young Eddie Redmayne prior to his Oscar success as Jack. Its sequel, *World Without End*, was filmed two years later, with a less high-profile cast. Exterior shots of the cathedral in the second series were partly filmed at Salisbury Cathedral and featured in visitor interpretation that we viewed there during fieldwork in 2017. Follett has clarified the reason for the connection with Salisbury:

> When I was creating Kingsbridge for my book, I had Wells Cathedral in mind ... But the finished building that I described in my book looks like Salisbury Cathedral – and this is how the producers of the Channel 4 series made the Kingsbridge cathedral look.
>
> (Follett, 2010)

In 2014, Follett carried out a speaking tour of five English cathedrals (Lincoln, Salisbury, Canterbury, Peterborough and Winchester) on the topic of 'Why

Cathedrals?' and, in the publicity, discussed his explanation for the enduring appeal of his Kingsbridge books:

> Many times I have been asked why *Pillars* has such a big impact. There is no simple answer, because a novel is so complex. But I come back again and again to the people who built the cathedrals. Those men and women were by modern standards, poor and ignorant. They lived in wooden huts and slept on the floor. Yet they created the most beautiful and awesome buildings the world has ever known. Human beings have the capacity to rise above mundane circumstances and touch the eternal. That is what *Pillars* is about and, in the end, I think that may be why it has so profoundly touched the hearts of so many readers for so many years.
>
> (quoted in Shaffi, 2014)

Speaking tours connected to books are a means for cathedrals to attract broader audiences by emphasising these links with popular culture. Another example occurred in 2013, when Salley Vickers visited various British cathedrals to publicise her novel *The Cleaner of Chartres* (2012), which features a lead character with a mysterious past who helps to look after Chartres Cathedral. Like in *The Pillars of the Earth*, a cathedral is both the backdrop and an important element of the plot; a place of refuge for a young woman seeking to live down her previous notoriety, but which paradoxically brings her to the attention of various residents of the town, including priests, gossipy old women and artists. The current cathedral is the sixth to be built on the site; all destroyed by fire, including the last iteration in 1194, and that the townsfolk were more upset by the cathedral being razed to the ground than their own homes:

> Perhaps this was in part because, as today, their livelihoods depended on the many parties of pilgrims visiting the town to pay reverence to its most venerated relic, the birthing gown of the Virgin Mary, a gift to the cathedral by the grandson of Charlemagne, Charles the Bald.
>
> (Vickers, 2012: 2–3)

Many passages in the book extol the beauty of the work that makes the current cathedral such a tourist drawcard, but also the mystery of some of its spaces and decorative elements, such as the labyrinth inset into the floor, with its ancient Greek motifs. There is a sense of a building which is inextricably linked to its predecessors, including those built by other civilisations, thus giving the town an identity that is both parochial and universal at the same time. This idea of a *global inheritance* is perhaps one of the reasons why many of the world's cathedrals have been nominated for and received World Heritage protection.

Another novel is *The Choir* (Trollope, 1988), which was made into a TV series in 1995 starring James Fox and concerns the political machinations behind the fictional cathedral of Aldminster in England. As with *The Cleaner of Chartres*, there are references to the beauty of the cathedral setting: 'in the soft light the Cathedral seemed to float a little on [the Close's] vast green cushion' (p. 221).

The plot, however, revolves around plans to disband Aldminster's famous choir, in order to fund restoration of the cathedral roof and install new lighting. The Dean is adamant that preservation of the fabric of the building is worth more than the rich music within, while others see them as intertwined. Nicholas, a former chorister, reflects on the symbiosis between the two, 'the faces all down the nave, row upon row, were reflecting, whether their owners meant them to or not, the effects of the building, the music and the occasion, all at once full of power and excitement and peace' (p. 65). For some, the music to be heard within the cathedral brings the place alive, making this type of building, as Jenkyns (2004: 5) argues in relation to Westminster Abbey, more than just a 'beautiful shell'.

A number of the characters in *The Choir* also ruminate on the cathedral as a place for tranquil reflection or contemplation. Frank, a socialist councillor, while not religious, has a deep-seated need to visit the cathedral, 'because he needed calm and quiet and time in a place where the outside world didn't obtrude' (p. 263). He realises, however, that many of the people he serves would feel intimidated in venturing inside its doors, for 'he felt a huge moral indignation, as well as a great sadness, that they should be daunted by something that had been put up by men like them for men like them' (p. 38). The ideal of a cathedral as a quiet refuge is potentially threatened by their use as event spaces or venues, although the latter may have other benefits, outlined in the next section.

The cathedral as an event space

Cathedrals are increasingly looking to events as a way to increase their outreach to people who are not regular churchgoers or who otherwise would not think to set foot in a cathedral. Curtis (2016) has created a typology of these events, consisting of ecclesiastical/liturgical events, cultural and community events and openly commercial event activity. It could be argued that most cultural/community events and some commercial events may have a dimension of outreach, in that they help to introduce new audiences to the work, religious or otherwise, that is done in and by cathedrals and thus help to counteract the view of cathedrals as 'gated communities' (Curtis, 2016: 9). This has been conceptualised as fostering *spiritual capital* in the community (Coleman, 2019; Curtis, 2016). Events may also have an important role to play in the portfolio of fund-raising initiatives. For example, Lincoln Cathedral 'costs £3m-a-year to run, with about £1m being raised from visitors and events' (BBC, 2012).

Ecclesiastical or liturgical events comprise the everyday services of a cathedral but also special liturgies of reflection, commemoration or thanksgiving – for example, at times of natural disaster or tragedy – which may attract a broader community audience. Instances include the Field of Remembrance created by the Royal British Legion in the grounds of Westminster Abbey in London each November; a series of crosses with poppies that represent people who have died in conflict (Laing and Frost, 2018); the use of St Paul's Cathedral in London in 2017 for the memorial service for those who died in the Grenfell Tower fire; and the memorial service held one year after the 2009 Victorian bushfires in Australia at St Paul's Cathedral in Melbourne. This links to their traditional role in pastoral care, as well as providing a dignified setting for commemoration. The willingness of many cathedrals to engage in inter-faith dialogue also means that these events can bring together representatives of many religious communities, potentially facilitating the development of bonding and bridging social capital and a more inclusive society. For example, on the first anniversary of the terrorist bombing attacks at a pop concert in Manchester in 2017, a memorial service was held at Manchester Cathedral, involving the leaders of various faiths such as Christianity, Judaism, Muslim, Hinduism and Buddhism, as well as a humanist, Dr Kevin Malone of the University of Manchester (BBC, 2018).

Cathedrals are also used as the backdrop for ceremonial or state occasions, such as royal weddings, coronations or national memorial services (Jenkyns, 2004; Trigg, 2005). Examples in recent times include the funeral of Princess Diana in 1997 and the marriage of Prince William to Kate Middleton in 2011, both taking place in Westminster Abbey; and, in 2018, the state funeral for former President George H. W. Bush in Washington National Cathedral and the Armistice Day Centenary memorial concert in Strasbourg Cathedral. An unusual example was the new mayor of London in 2016 choosing Southwark Cathedral for the swearing-in ceremony. Sadiq Khan, a Muslim, felt that the selection of the Christian place of worship for this purpose would show that he would be a mayor for the diverse populace that is London; thus demonstrating, 'the continued and evolving salience of cathedrals in civic space' (Coleman and Bowman, 2019: 2).

The Gothic style of cathedral in particular, with its longevity and grandeur, provides a tangible dignity to proceedings and is often selected for events that demand national if not global commemoration. Diana's funeral was held at Westminster Abbey in acknowledgement of the importance of this service, with the venue also earmarked for the funerals of Prince Philip and Queen Elizabeth (Jenkyns, 2004). Diana's wedding to Prince Charles had been held at St Paul's Cathedral, and choosing a different venue for her funeral also made sense in that it did not revive memories of that earlier event. The choice of Westminster Abbey symbolised the respect in which she was held, even if some doubted the veracity of the outpourings of grief (Laing and Frost, 2018). Taking the casket of the princess through the streets of London, and holding a service that combined pop culture and ritual tradition, provided a form of *catharsis* (Jenkyns, 2004) for millions, who mostly watched the telecast at home, or on big screens or televisions in public spaces such as pubs, parks and squares. The advent of television has thus allowed audiences an intimate view of proceedings within these cathedrals that would be impossible even for many of those attending in person to achieve.

There had been resistance to this level of access to royal events within cathedrals, with much discussion preceding the decision to allow Queen Elizabeth II's coronation to be televised in 1953 (Laing and Frost, 2018). Parts of the ceremony were protected from the cameras, such as the anointing of the new queen by the Archbishop of Canterbury (Haseler, 2012), in recognition of Bagehot's (1867) famous warning in *The English Constitution* that the mystery of monarchy needs to be respected and preserved: 'we must not let in daylight upon magic'. Nevertheless, it was a turning point in making cathedrals more inclusive spaces as well as whetting the appetite for a personal visit. Queen Elizabeth's coronation was said to have attracted a worldwide audience of 300 million people (Laing and Frost, 2018). Contemporary audiences are even higher, with the 2011 wedding of the Duke and Duchess of Cambridge seen by an estimated 2 billion viewers around the globe (Winnett, 2011).

The second type of event, *cultural and community*, is defined by Curtis (2016: 6) as 'events held as part of wider city festival programmes; to celebrate a significant anniversary or moment in history; to enhance the visitor experience; to develop new audiences and/or contribute to community causes and initiatives'. There is therefore a crossover with ecclesiastical events, where a church service is the focal point of what is offered but goes beyond this to include activities that are of broad community interest, such as the staging of theatre or musical productions, talks and exhibitions. Such events, however, have the potential for internal conflict with tourism and other activities. We found this when visiting one of the English cathedrals. While paying our admission fee, the cashier said to us, 'I have to apologise, but there is a choir of retired men singing at the moment, but don't worry, they will finish soon'. From our perspective, their performance added considerably to the atmosphere of our visit and was highly enjoyable, but clearly not everybody thought that way.

Increasingly, such events are broadening what occurs within a cathedral. In 2017, York Minster staged a *Tourist, Traveller, Pilgrim?* exhibition, using artefacts that belonged to the cathedral to present the idea of sacred travel and highlight the pilgrimages of St William of York. Coleman observed, 'what is striking about the exhibition is the way in which it also deploys such material culture to represent pilgrimage as an entirely modern phenomenon' (2019: 136); which connects the heritage of the past with current-day practices and beliefs. Intriguingly, Curtis (2016: 8) noted that, 'rock concerts, comedy performances, wine fairs, film showings, and "son et lumieres" have all been held at [his] case study cathedrals, without attracting controversy' and refers to 'fashion shows (St Paul's) and street art/hip hop music nights (York)'.

The third type of event, the *commercial event*, is less overtly connected to the core activity of the cathedral, where the site is essentially a 'venue for hire' (Curtis, 2016: 6) for a private organisation or purpose. Their Gothic beauty makes them a magnificent frame for private gatherings such as dinners, conferences or student graduations. Martikainen (2006) referred to these types of events as potential examples of commodification of a religious site, where, 'the churches have consciously or unconsciously adopted the logic of the marketplace, which already guides a part of their activities' (p. 142). One could, however, argue that this form of event, similar to the cultural and community event, provides scope for introducing a new type of visitor to the cathedral.

There is potential for dissonance, however, where locals or parishioners seek to overturn decisions about events in cathedrals that they regard as being inappropriate. A petition was initiated in 2017 and signed by 615 supporters to prevent the screening of *Harry Potter and the Philosopher's Stone* in Durham Cathedral during the Durham Book Festival, even though the movie had been partly filmed in its environs. The petition noted that using the cathedral as a cinema was 'totally antithetical to the purpose and essence of the place'. It stated, 'this church, a site of pilgrimage for many over the centuries is about to embark on a new episode of self-desecration' (quoted in White, 2017). The screening went ahead, with 1,500 tickets sold in 12 hours, a record for the festival. The Senior Programme Manager for the Festival, Rebecca Wilkie, was proud to announce:

> Durham Cathedral is a regular partner in the book festival, so it made sense for us to commemorate the 20th anniversary of the publication of Harry Potter, in this iconic building, which served as a filming location for the first two instalments of the series. We hope that this year's Durham Book Festival, which takes place between 7th and 15th October, will see more people attending than ever before.
>
> (quoted in Wood, 2017)

According to Conner (2017), 'many of those attending accepted the invitation to "immerse yourself in the story as never before" by wearing Hogwarts-themed fancy dress', and her article in the local newspaper *The Northern Echo* features a photograph of a woman dressed in a witch's hat like Professor McGonagall (Maggie Smith) in the *Harry Potter* films. Clearly, Durham Cathedral saw this as harmless fun and embraced their links with *Harry Potter* as an opportunity to forge relationships with the community. Events are the perfect vehicle to achieve this goal. As Curtis (2016: 10) observed, 'events, at their core, are designed around the spirit of hospitality and sharing, a founding feature of the cathedral ethos and one to which they adhere very naturally'.

Conclusion

Medieval cathedrals inspire awe and wonder, in part because of their longevity and monumentality. They can be said to link the modern and the medieval worlds through their survival into the current era. Unlike many abbeys or monasteries, they are not ruins but intact heritage that can be enjoyed by contemporary worshippers and visitors. They are colossal in scale, yet often delicate in their tracery, and their light-filled spaces and the brightness of their stained glass are a magnificent foil for the treasures that lie within. Their solidity, however, is deceptive. While they have lasted centuries in some cases, these are fragile buildings, and their upkeep is a constant burden for church authorities. Maintaining cathedrals as viable spaces within which hundreds of visitors a day can congregate requires huge sums to be raised. There is also a need to reach out to the local community and a broader worshipping base, without which cathedrals run the risk of being seen as insular and irrelevant in contemporary society.

Many medieval cathedrals maintain their importance in modern times through a 'juxtaposition of "sacred space and common ground"' (Coleman and Bowman, 2019: 11). They seek out and welcome new audiences and are open to innovative new ways to raise the enormous levels of funding that they need to continue operating as a cathedral. This may include hosting events, agreeing to the use of the cathedral for film and television production and highlighting their cultural heritage and links to popular culture to visitors. The challenge, however, for cathedrals is not to move so far away from their core values that they become simply an event venue, film set or tourist attraction. Even though charging admission fees has its critics, it may in fact be a less controversial route to take than some of the other strategies discussed in this chapter for raising funds. There may be a reduction in opportunity cost, in that rather than devoting management resources to innovative fund-raising, the relatively simpler strategy of charging admission fees allows the cathedral to focus on worship, outreach and its role as a place for community bonding and healing, especially in troubled times.

References

Ackerman, J. (2019) 'Meaning-making in the course of action: Affordance theory at the pilgrim/tourist nexus', *Tourism Geographies*, *21*(3), 405–421.

Acuna, K. (2015) '"Game of Thrones" producers had to get to permission to film the finale's controversial nude scene', *Business Insider Australia*, 15 June, https://www.businessinsider.com.au/game-of-thrones-finale-permission-film-nude-scene-2015-6 (accessed February 21, 2020).

Amaro, S., Antunes, A. and Henriques, C. (2018) 'A closer look at Santiago de Compostela's pilgrims through the lens of motivations', *Tourism Management*, *64*, 271–280.

Ardley, B., and Voase, R. (2013) 'Magna Carta: Repositioning the secular as "sacred"', *International Journal of Heritage Studies*, *19*(4), 341–352.

Bagehot, W. (1867) *The English constitution*, London: Kegan Paul, 1905 reprint.

Ballantyne, R., Hughes, K. and Bond, N. (2016) 'Using a Delphi approach to identify managers' preferences for visitor interpretation at Canterbury Cathedral World Heritage Site', *Tourism Management*, *54*, 72–80.

Barke, M. and Towner, J. (1996) 'The tourist-historic city in Spain', in M. Barke, J. Towner and M. Newton (Eds.), *Tourism in Spain. Critical Issues* (pp. 343–371), Wallingford, UK: CABI.

BBC (2012) 'Da Vinci Code filming 'boosted' Lincoln Cathedral's income', *BBC News*, 25 March, https://www.bbc.com/news/uk-england-lincolnshire-17457506 (accessed January 5, 2019).

BBC (2018) 'Manchester attack: Hundreds gather to remember victims', *BBC News*, 22 May, https://www.bbc.com/news/uk-england-manchester-44197949 (accessed January 5, 2019).

Canterbury Cathedral (2019) *Opening times and entry charges*, https://www.canterbury-cathedral.org/visit/information/opening-times-entry-charges/ (accessed February 20, 2019).

Chrisafis, A. and Henley, J. (2019) 'Notre Dame fire: Macron pledges to rebuild devastated Paris cathedral', *The Guardian*, 16 April, https://www.theguardian.com/world/2019/apr/15/notre-dame-fire-paris-france-cathedral (accessed April 22, 2019).

Coleman, S. (2019) 'On praying in an old country: Ritual, replication, heritage, and powers of adjacency in English cathedrals', *Religion*, *49*(1), 120–141.

Coleman, S. and Bowman, M. (2019) 'Religion in cathedrals: Pilgrimage, heritage, adjacency, and the politics of replication in Northern Europe', *Religion*, *49*(1), 1–23.

Conner, R. (2017) 'Harry Potter fans give Durham Book festival a magical launch', *The Northern Echo*, 7 October, https://www.thenorthernecho.co.uk/news/15582324.harry-potter-fans-give-durham-book-festival-magical-launch/ (accessed November 3, 2019).

Curtis, S. (2016) 'English cathedrals: Events and spiritual capital', *International Journal of Religious Tourism and Pilgrimage*, 4(2), 1–11.

Department for Communities and Local Government (2017) *Cathedrals and their communities: A report on the diverse roles of cathedrals in modern England*, London: Ministry of Housing, Communities and Local Government, https://www.gov.uk/government/publications/cathedrals-and-their-communities (accessed January 29, 2019).

Durham Cathedral (2019) *Photographic and filming policy*, https://www.durhamcathedral.co.uk/about-us/photographic-filming-policy (accessed January 29, 2019).

Eco, U. (1986) *Faith in fakes*, London: Seeker & Warburg.

Erlanger, S. (2019) 'What the Notre-Dame fire reveals about the soul of France', *The New York Times*, 16 April, https://www.nytimes.com/2019/04/16/world/europe/france-notre-dame-religion.html (accessed April 22, 2019).

Faris, W. (2004) *Ordinary enchantments: Magical realism and the remystification of narrative*, Nashville: Vanderbilt University Press.

Follett, K. (1989) *The pillars of the earth*, London: Pan Macmillan, 2007 reprint.

Follett, K. (2010) 'Britain's soaring spires that became Ken Follett's Pillars of the Earth', *Daily Mail*, 29 November, https://www.dailymail.co.uk/travel/article-1331731/Salisbury-Cathedral-Ken-Folletts-Pillars-Of-The-Earth.html (accessed January 21, 2019).

Frost, W. (2009) 'From backlot to runaway production: Exploring location and authenticity in film-induced tourism', *Tourism Review International*, 13(2), 85–92.

Frost, W. and Laing, J. (2018) 'Long-distance walking in films: Promises of healing and redemption on the trail', in C.M. Hall, Y. Ram and N. Shoval (Eds.), *The Routledge handbook of walking studies* (pp. 46–54), London: Routledge.

González, R., and Medina, J. (2003) 'Cultural tourism and urban management in northwestern Spain: The pilgrimage to Santiago de Compostela', *Tourism Geographies*, 5(4), 446–460.

Griffiths, M. (2011) 'Those who come to pray and those who come to look: Interactions between visitors and congregations', *Journal of Heritage Tourism*, 6(1), 63–72.

The Guardian (2000) 'Harry Potter's magic fails to work in Canterbury', *The Guardian*, 30 June, https://www.theguardian.com/film/2000/jun/30/news2 (accessed September 9, 2020).

The Guardian (2005) 'Westminster Abbey counters Da Vinci Code', *The Guardian*, 1 June, https://www.theguardian.com/uk/2005/may/31/religion.books (accessed June 5, 2020).

Haseler, S. (2012) *The grand delusion: Britain after sixty years of Elizabeth*, London and New York: I.B. Tauris.

Hughes, K., Bond, N., and Ballantyne, R. (2013) 'Designing and managing interpretive experiences at religious sites: Visitors' perceptions of Canterbury Cathedral', *Tourism Management*, 36, 210–220.

Hutchinson, L. (2017) 'Avengers filming begins as Durham Cathedral confirms 'major project' is under way', *ChronicleLive*, 4 May, https://www.chroniclelive.co.uk/whats-on/film-news/avengers-filming-begins-durham-cathedral-12984401 (accessed January 29, 2019).

Jenkyns, R. (2004) *Westminster Abbey*, London: Profile, 2011 reprint.

Laing, J. and Frost, W. (2018) *Royal events: Rituals, innovations, meanings*, London: Routledge.

Lehmberg, S.E. (2014) *The reformation of cathedrals: Cathedrals in English society*, Princeton, NJ: Princeton University Press.

Lyons, K. (2019) 'Notre Dame fire: Macron promises to rebuild cathedral within five years', *The Guardian*, 17 April, https://www.theguardian.com/world/2019/apr/17/

notre-dame-fire-macron-promises-to-make-cathedral-more-beautiful-than-before (accessed April 22, 2019).

MacCannell, D. (1976) *The tourist: A new theory of the leisure class*, New York: Schoken Books.

Martikainen, T. (2006) 'Consuming a cathedral: Commodification of religious places in late modernity', *Fieldwork in Religion*, *2*(2), 127–145.

Morris, R. (1979) *Cathedrals and abbeys of England and Wales: The building church, 600–1540*, New York: Norton.

Murray, M. and Graham, B. (1997) 'Exploring the dialectics of route-based tourism: The Camino de Santiago', *Tourism Management*, *18*(8), 513–524.

Pérez Guilarte, Y. and Lois González, R. (2018) 'Sustainability and visitor management in tourist historic cities: The case of Santiago de Compostela, Spain', *Journal of Heritage Tourism*, *13*(6), 489–505.

Prak, M. (2011) 'Mega-structures of the Middle Ages: The construction of religious buildings in Europe and Asia, c. 1000–1500', *Journal of Global History*, *6*(3), 381–406.

Scott, R.A. (2003) *The Gothic enterprise. A guide to understanding the medieval cathedral*, Berkeley, CA: University of California Press.

Scott, R.A. (2011) *The Gothic enterprise. A guide to understanding the medieval cathedral*, 2nd edition, Berkeley, CA: University of California Press.

Seward, D. (1995) *The Wars of the Roses: Through the lives of five men and women of the fifteenth century*, London: Penguin.

Shackley, M. (2002) 'Space, sanctity and service; The English cathedral as heterotopia', *International Journal of Tourism Research*, *4*(5), 345–352.

Shackley, M. (2006) 'Costs and benefits: The impact of cathedral tourism in England', *Journal of Heritage Tourism*, *1*(2), 133–141.

Shaffi, S. (2014) 'Follett goes on cathedral tour', *The Bookseller*, 3 February, https://www.thebookseller.com/news/follett-goes-cathedral-tour (accessed January 21, 2019).

Shaw, J. (2013) 'The potential of cathedrals', *Anglican Theological Review*, *95*(1), 137–147.

Sudjic, D. (2005) *The edifice complex: The architecture of power*, London: Penguin.

Suger, A. (c 1144–1148) *On what was done during his administration*, https://sourcebooks.fordham.edu/source/sugar.asp (accessed January 23, 2021).

Trigg, S. (2005) 'Walking through cathedrals: Scholars, pilgrims, and medieval tourists', in W. Scase, R. Copeland and D. Lawton (Eds.), *New medieval literatures* (pp. 9–33), Oxford: Oxford University Press.

Trollope, J. (1988) *The choir*, London: Black Swan, 1993 reprint.

Vickers, S. (2012) *The cleaner of Chartres*, New York: Viking.

Voase, R. (2007) 'Visiting a cathedral: The consumer psychology of a "rich experience"', *International Journal of Heritage Studies*, *13*(1), 41–55.

White, R. (2017) 'Muggles rise up over Potter film', *The Sunday Times*, 13 August, https://www.thetimes.co.uk/article/muggles-rise-up-over-potter-film-h2xlqp3t7 (accessed October 1, 2020).

Wiltshier, P. (2015) 'Derby cathedral as a beacon: The role of the Church of England in tourism management', *International Journal of Religious Tourism & Pilgrimage*, *3*(2), 65–76.

Winnett, R. (2011) 'Royal wedding watched around the world', *The Telegraph*, 30 April, https://www.telegraph.co.uk/news/uknews/royal-wedding/8484257/Royal-wedding-watched-around-the-world.html (accessed January 29, 2019).

Winter, M. and Gasson, R. (1996) 'Pilgrimage and tourism: Cathedral visiting in contemporary England', *International Journal of Heritage Studies*, *2*(3), 172–182.

Wood, H. (2017) 'Harry Potter screenings break Durham Book Festival records', *The Bookseller*, 23 August, https://www.thebookseller.com/news/cathedral-screenings-harry-potter-break-durham-book-festivals-records-620946 (accessed January 29, 2019).

Woodward, S. (2004) 'Faith and tourism: Planning tourism in relation to places of worship', *Tourism and Hospitality Planning & Development*, *1*(2), 173–186.

Yazdani Mehr, S. (2019) 'Analysis of 19th and 20th century conservation key theories in relation to contemporary adaptive reuse of heritage buildings', *Heritage*, *2*(1), 920–937.

York Minster (2019) *Plan your visit*, https://yorkminster.org/visit/plan-your-visit/ (accessed March 1, 2019).

8   Robin Hood
Reinterpreting the medieval outlaw

Introduction

Sherwood Forest and Nottingham are the settings for Robin Hood, one of the greatest of medieval legends. However, despite the importance of a sense of place to the story of the English outlaw, neither Sherwood Forest nor Nottingham are major heritage tourist attractions. Instead, their links with the iconic narrative seem underdeveloped and uneven. Nottingham remains primarily a medium-sized English city, with just a scattering of sites linked to its medieval past. In no way is its tourism economy comparable to a York, Winchester or Glastonbury. Sherwood Forest is a county park, difficult to access unless by car and primarily attracting local visitors. Nonetheless, the potential exists for greater leveraging of the Robin Hood legend, particularly as new media versions are released. There have been a number of interesting attempts over time – which we will consider later in this chapter – but little has come to fruition in terms of sustainable tourism development.

This lack of tourism development is paradoxical when compared to the enduring power and reach of media portrayals of the Robin Hood story. Constantly reinvented for new audiences, the various retellings of the legend provide new interpretations reflecting contemporary issues and concerns; an example of inter-textuality (Månsson, 2011). Accordingly, these imaginaries come across as fresh and relevant to each new generation. Furthermore, older versions of the story may stimulate strong feelings of nostalgia. Multiple versions for multiple generations should be a powerful combination for tourism operators to take advantage of, which makes the lost opportunities for Robin Hood tourism development even more surprising.

The Outlaw Myth

Robin Hood epitomises the Outlaw Myth. Found across many time periods and countries, stories of the good outlaw are another variant on the universal myth of the hero's journey (Campbell, 1949). Whilst the outlaw archetype may be present in many different places and time periods, Robin Hood is the outstanding exemplar, providing a template to be copied by others. This, accordingly, raises an important question. Why does our model of the heroic outlaw arise so strongly from the medieval period? There are three possible explanations. The first is that the medieval period is widely seen as a Golden Age, a time of heroes. Robin Hood is like Arthur, Charlemagne, Joan of Arc or Ragnar Lothbrok; a hero from deep in history who has endured. The second is that Robin Hood is one of the cornerstones of the medieval revival in the nineteenth century. Third, like King Arthur (see Chapter 3), Robin has been reinvented time and time again, being reshaped to remain appealing and relevant.

The outlaw archetype is remarkably consistent across time and place. It is easy to draw parallels between Robin Hood and later outlaws such as Ned Kelly, Joaquin Murrieta, Jesse James, Billy the Kid, and Bonnie Parker and Clyde Barrow (Wheeler *et al.*, 2011). Indeed, many of these later outlaws were quite keen to justify themselves through references to the legend of Robin Hood, and Murrieta was the subject of a film titled *Robin Hood of El Dorado* (1936). Commonly emerging when there is corruption and oppression and the rule of law has failed, the archetypal outlaw takes the paradoxical path of going outside the law to bring a return to justice and order (Frost, 2006; Frost and Laing, 2015; Knight, 2003; Kooistra, 1989; Seal, 1996. Wheeler *et al.*, 2011). Drawing on the extensive literature into outlaws, a number of common elements are identifiable, and all of these are apparent within the Robin Hood narrative:

1. The outlaw hero either comes from humble origins or chooses to reject their privileged upbringing and join a dispossessed or marginalised underclass.
2. Injustice and oppression rules. The government fails to remedy this and is often an active agent in this inequity. Law and order has either broken down or has become complicit in this injustice.
3. The hero is young and is a natural leader. Their ability to stand out may be epitomised in their physical prowess, ability with weaponry or the wearing of distinctive clothing.
4. The hero has been away and returns home to find that society has dramatically changed. Their absence may be due to serving in a war, which has sharpened their military and leadership skills.
5. There is an incident that forces the hero to change. Often, it is a cruel injustice that forces them to intervene. This is akin to Campbell's (1949) *Call to Adventure*, which unwittingly forces the hero to embark on a journey.
6. In a corrupt and decadent society, the hero must go outside the law to achieve justice.
7. Action is taken only against the oppressors, and this aids others who are suffering ('robbing from the rich to give to the poor'). The common people are sympathetic and provide assistance.
8. The outlaw is bold and fearless – sometimes a cunning trickster – and their daring exploits expose the inadequacies and impotence of the authorities.
9. The heroic outlaw is 'a symbol of social and political discontent, and this is what separates them from common robbers and murderers' (Kooistra, 1989: 37–38). A legend develops, disseminated through stories and songs (Seal, 1996).
10. The outlaw is betrayed and destroyed. The traitor is often someone from

their trusted group of supporters (a strong Christian allegory). Despite his destruction, the outlaw has succeeded in drawing attention to the injustices. Their oppressors are exposed and defeated, so that their sacrifice was worthwhile. Their death is necessary to close the story. The outlaw has led a violent life and cannot return happily to a normal life in society. Such an ending is modified in the Robin Hood stories, in which Robin does not die but is forced to remain an outlaw in Sherwood Forest.

Initially disseminated in medieval times through ballads and performance, the Robin Hood story was revived in the nineteenth century, before becoming popular in cinema and television. The various media representations of the Robin Hood myth present different interpretations and meanings, reflecting the issues of the time in which they were produced. Through an examination of a range of these media productions over time, we can observe these variations in the key features of the story and their relevance.

Ballads and festivals

Robin Hood is both a story *set* and *created* in the medieval period. The outlaw evolved as 'a creature of syncretism, part woodland spirit, part a confused recollection of some historical figure' (McLynn, 2007: 243). Throughout medieval England, he was manifested through a series of popular ballads and various festivals, particularly mid-summer celebrations in which he was the Lord of Misrule and people took part in Robin Hood 'games' themed around the popular figure. Knight (2003) found that before 1600, there were around 200 historical references to Robin Hood, with about half of these relating to festivals. Anarchic and carnivalesque, these festivities had an important role in allowing society to let off steam through ritual inversion. Robin Hood, as the Lord of Misrule, 'poses no threat to the established order, for he is the arbiter of a world turned temporarily upside down, the better to consolidate it right side up' (Schama, 1995: 152). Even at the highest levels of society, playing at the story of the outlaw was enjoyed. In 1510, King Henry VIII pretended to be Robin Hood. In costume and with 12 noble companions portraying his Merrie Men, he burst into Queen Anne's bedchamber, jokingly frightening her before they all indulged in dancing and games (Knight, 2003).

Whether or not there really was a Robin Hood has long been debated. On the one hand, the connection with forests, dressing in green and having supernatural qualities make him appear to be purely a mythical figure. On the other hand, the political elements, his use of the longbow as a distinctive fourteenth-century weapon and various court records referring to Robin Hoods point to some historical substance. The evidence for his existence is widespread and accordingly confusing. Many of the references to him are focussed in the period 1215–1381, intriguingly putting him later in time than King Richard I or Prince John. Geographically, he is associated with a number of forests: Sherwood, Barnsdale Forest in Yorkshire or the Forest of Barnsdale in Rutland. Huntingdon, of which he is sometimes named as being the earl, is in Cambridgeshire. Loxley (sometimes rendered as Locksley), is his traditional birthplace and is in south Yorkshire. History could have met myth on 29 March 1195. Richard, having returned to England and captured Nottingham Castle, rode through Sherwood Forest. There was, however, no record of any meeting with the outlaw (McLynn, 2007).

Ivanhoe (Sir Walter Scott, 1819)

Up until the nineteenth century, Robin Hood was placed generally in medieval times. Sir Walter Scott changed that with his successful novel *Ivanhoe* (1819); which consolidated the story and introduced a range of features that would be repeated in later retellings (Knight, 2003). The action takes place specifically in the late twelfth century, pushing the outlaw story back in time at least a century and accordingly creating future confusion. Scott paints a picture of profound tensions between the Normans and the Saxons, which in reality had disappeared by this period. Robin Hood is a Saxon commoner rather than a noble. He is a loyal supporter of King Richard the Lionheart, working with Ivanhoe to defeat the usurper Prince John and the Norman oppressors (Laing and Frost, 2012; Phillips, 2008).

Whilst Robin is a loyal foot-soldier deputy to the aristocratic Ivanhoe, Scott's outlaw demonstrates some exceptional abilities. He is highly adept with the long-bow and wins an archery tournament by the 'impossible shot' of splitting his competitor's arrow. This skill with the longbow – such a major part of how Robin is imagined in the modern world – is an invention of Scott's, one of many anachronisms throughout the novel. The longbow was not in use at this time and was not widespread until introduced by Welsh soldiers in the fourteenth century. The longbow, however, takes on a symbolic power in Scott's narrative. It is constructed as an indigenous Saxon weapon, which both empowers the conquered Saxons and provides a contrast between the more 'natural' Saxons and the armour of the Norman knights (Phillips, 2008).

Interestingly, this is the one version in which the everyman Robin is the first to realise that Richard is flawed – being both brave and foolhardy – and his reign will be effective only if he is carefully guided by wise advisors. Robin thus becomes an advocate of constitutional monarchy (Laing and Frost, 2012). It is a perspective that is rarely touched upon again. Generally, Richard is portrayed as a worthy monarch, brave, wise and honourable; thereby justifying the unswerving loyalty of Robin and his followers. It is only in recent versions, such as *Robin Hood* (2010), that Richard is shown as flawed in the mould of the Scott portrayal.

Robin Hood (1922)

The athletic Douglas Fairbanks was highly successful in costume dramas, and *Robin Hood* was a perfect vehicle for him. It was a film of two parts. In the first, the Earl of Huntingdon (Fairbanks) departs for the Crusades with his friend King Richard (Wallace Beery). As with many crusader narratives (see Chapter 10), there are hidden traitors amongst the army. Richard's brother John (Sam de Grasse) plots to seize power and has an assassin at work. By chance, it is the jester who is murdered, when he pretends to be the king. Fearful that Marian (Australian Enid Bennett) is in danger, Huntingdon returns home. In the second half, Huntingdon has adopted the persona of the outlaw Robin Hood and resists Prince John's tyrannical rule (Aberth, 2003; Nollen, 1999; Vance and Maietta, 2008; see also Chapter 6).

The film draws heavily on the nineteenth-century romances that flourished after the success of Scott's novel. Robin is heroic and dynamic (though for audiences today, Fairbanks is just too hammy). Bennett is a beautiful and feisty Marian – aided by stunning costumes that are inspired by the art of the nineteenth-century Pre-Raphaelite Brotherhood – and is Robin's equal (see Chapter 4 on Marian as an archetypal character). De Grasse is a suitably oily and sadistic villain, and Alan Hale is a worthy Little John. The action scenes shine, particularly where Robin must infiltrate the dark and foreboding Nottingham Castle. For Fairbanks, the film was a commercial and critical triumph (Hahn and Knight, 2008).

The Adventures of Robin Hood (1938)

In the late 1930s, Warner Brothers developed the idea of remaking Fairbanks's *Robin Hood*. The concept of reshooting silent films was common at the time, applying the technology of sound to stories that had already been proven to be successful. For example, Paramount remade the 1926 version of *Beau Geste* in 1939. *The Adventures of Robin Hood* (1938) was a big-budget Warner Brothers epic, filmed with the new medium of Technicolor. Its star was a young Errol Flynn, fresh from tremendous success as a pirate in *Captain Blood* (1935). As such, Warner Brothers were keen to star him in a similar dashing role. Apart from Flynn as Robin, it featured a perfect supporting cast, with Olivia de Havilland as Marian, Claude Rains as Prince John, Basil Rathbone as the villainous Sir Guy and Alan Hale as Little John (who had played the same role in the 1922 film). The result was a huge success, eclipsing Fairbanks's silent effort and setting the standard as one of the best medieval films of all time (Nollen, 1999).

Whilst filmed in California by a major Hollywood studio, *The Adventures of Robin Hood* has a strong British flavour. Of the 11 main characters, 9 were played by British actors. Flynn was Australian (though often mistaken as Irish due to his name), de Havilland was born in Japan of British parents, Rains was a Londoner and South African-born Rathbone had grown up in England. Such casting was common in 1930s Hollywood and was due to the popularity of *Empire Films* (Slotkin, 1992). These were historical action films focussing on England and the British Empire and were curiously successful at a time when films about American history were often viewed as box office poison. Due to their success, the studios recruited many British actors, though – for economic and logistical reasons – all these films were made in the USA.

The Adventures of Robin Hood differs in many ways from the 1920s film. The story starts with the news that King Richard has been captured returning from the

Crusades and is being held for ransom. Prince John takes control of the government and raises taxes to pay for the ransom. However, as he confides to his henchmen, the Sheriff of Nottingham and Guy of Gisborne, he has no intention of freeing his brother and will keep the money for himself. The Norman tax collectors unleash a reign of terror. Robin is a Saxon nobleman, though of Locksley rather than Huntingdon. When he comes across some Norman soldiers attempting to execute a peasant, Robin intervenes and saves him. Now an outlaw, Robin organises a resistance movement from within Sherwood Forest. In comic vignettes based on traditional ballads and stories, Little John and Friar Tuck are recruited to the merry band. In an ambush, a Norman convoy is captured and Robin meets Lady Marian. A fierce rivalry develops between Robin and Guy, which is in part sexual jealousy, as they both seek to win Marian (Symons, 2016). In disguise, Robin takes part in an archery contest, winning through splitting his competitor's arrow, a storyline from Scott's *Ivanhoe*. When Richard escapes from captivity and returns home, he and Robin storm Nottingham Castle. In an epic swordfight, Robin kills Guy. John and his cronies surrender, and King Richard pardons Robin and his men.

Ostensibly a light action romance, *The Adventures of Robin Hood* had two strong sub-textual messages reflecting the political interests of Warner Brothers and aimed at the American public of the day. The first is that the violent and oppressive regime instigated by Prince John and his henchmen is suggestive of the rise of the Nazis and other fascist groups in Europe. In resisting, Robin Hood provides a call to arms – particularly against isolationist sentiment in the USA. The second is that the dispossessed peasants who seek protection in Sherwood Forest are similar to Midwest farmers forced off their land during the Great Depression. That Robin provides aid calls to mind Roosevelt's New Deal. Interestingly, this film predates John Steinbeck's *The Grapes of Wrath* (novel 1939, film 1940) and its representation of starving and dispossessed Americans. It is also important to note that this film was released in the same decade that real-life outlaws like Bonnie and Clyde and Pretty Boy Floyd were active in the rural USA.

The Adventures of Robin Hood and Errol Flynn's portrayal of the outlaw came to be seen as the definitive versions of the story. For the next 30 or so years, most media productions drew on it heavily (Knight, 2003). The British *Robin Hood Annual 1959*, for example, contained a 20-page cartoon version of the film, and all the illustrations were modelled on Errol Flynn (Amalgamated Press, 1958). Indeed, a cross-generational influence was at work, as the pre-war generation championed the Errol Flynn film of their youth to their baby boom children. That *The Adventures of Robin Hood* was in Technicolor helped its longevity, and it is still shown regularly on television.

The children's Robin Hood of the 1950s and 1960s

For film-makers in the following decades, there was little hope of competing with such a successful blockbuster as *The Adventures of Robin Hood* and its charismatic cast. This was particularly so as the Warner Brothers film was kept in circulation, first in cinema re-releases and later through being regularly shown on television. Accordingly, films in the 1950s and 1960s tended to be low-budget and aimed at children. The Robin Hood story was also ripe for comedy, as in the animated Daffy Duck short *Robin Hood Daffy* (1958).

While new versions of Robin Hood could not compete in the cinema, the outlaw story could be transferred to the small screen. The first television production starring the outlaw was the BBC's *Robin Hood* (1953), with Patrick Troughton as Robin. A live version, only 28 seconds of footage and some stills remain, whetting the appetite of fans of Troughton who later appeared as a quirky *Doctor Who*. This was followed by the successful *Adventures of Robin Hood* (1955–1960), with Richard Greene in the lead role. For children brought up on Errol Flynn, it tended to be a bit wooden and set-bound. However, it did contain a major plot diversion in depicting Robin Hood as returning from the Crusades. It was also notable for its popular and catchy theme song ('Robin Hood, Robin Hood, Riding through the glen').

A by-product of the television series was the *Robin Hood Annual* (Amalgamated Press, 1959). As with many British annuals of the period, this was a compilation of magazine stories packaged up for the lucrative Christmas market. In this case, Amalgamated Press drew on its monthly magazine *Robin Hood: The Lord of Sherwood* for content. The 1959 annual contains a selection of colour comics and prose stories about Robin Hood, mixed in with some other medieval tales, including Hereward the Wake, Roland and William Rufus. Dressed in green and red, Robin battles the Normans, often using trickery to outwit them. Robin is consistently centre stage in these stories; Little John is the only one of his men to feature and Marian appears only once, with long yellow hair, a short tunic and very little dialogue. The inspiration for the artwork seems to be the actor Errol Flynn rather than the 1950s English television series, and this may be due to copyright issues. The longest story in the annual is a reworking of some episodes in *The Adventures of Robin Hood* (1938), with clear representations of that film's cast.

A completely different children's version of Robin Hood arose in the novel *The Sword in the Stone* (White, 1938). It is a magical-realist tale of King Arthur's childhood. Strangely, King Uther Pendragon is depicted as a Norman, and this accounts for the plot device of Saxon outlaws hiding in the forest. Robin is the Saxon leader of these outlaws, a disjointed addition to this fresh retelling of the Arthurian legend. Not surprisingly, Robin and his band were missing from the 1963 Disney film version. Disney subsequently produced its own animated version of Robin Hood in 1973 and used animals as the characters, with the wily Robin portrayed as a fox.

Brave and wise, Robin leads children Arthur and Kay on an adventure through the forest. Unusually, Marian is a far more developed character than Robin. Unlike other versions of her narrative, she is presented as Robin's equal in leadership, weaponry and forest skills (see Chapter 4). Leading the future king through the forest, she provides an instructive lesson in stealth:

> they were supposed to go in silence. Marian showed them how to go sideways ... how to stop at once when a bramble caught them, and take it patiently

out; how to put their feet down sensitively and roll their weight to that leg as soon as they were certain that no twig was under the foot … it was impossible to keep up with her unless she waited for them.

(White, 1938: 114)

Robin and Marian (1976)

The dominance of the Flynn film allowed scope for a revisionist version. *Robin and Marian*, however, probably went too far and accordingly was not a success at the box office (Nollen, 1999). Originally with the working title of *The Death of Robin Hood*, it was conceived as a thoughtful elegiac piece (Aberth, 2003). The action takes place 20 years after the conventional Robin Hood story. Robin (Sean Connery) and Little John (Nicol Williamson) have been on the Crusades and return only after the death of King Richard (Richard Harris). Robin finds that Marian (Audrey Hepburn) has become a nun. Now that Richard is dead, his brother John (Ian Holm) becomes king and the Sheriff of Nottingham (Robert Shaw) recommences his tyranny. In response, Robin leads the resistance.

Marketed as an action piece, the film did not connect with audiences. Connery, though only aged 46 at the time, played Robin as an old man, constantly complaining of aches and pains. A script that had both Robin and Marian killed provided a very downbeat ending. A quirky supporting casting – including Ronnie Barker as Friar Tuck and Denholm Elliott as Will Scarlett – also made the film confusing. Connery summarised the film's problems as:

> people were disappointed because from the new title they expected some stirring adventures. The whole thing was very much anti-mythic … they hated the idea in the [United] States. They can't take the idea that their hero might be over the hill and falling apart … Maybe you just can't tamper with myths that way.

(quoted in Nollen, 1999: 164)

Robin Hood: Prince of Thieves (1991)

Whereas Errol Flynn's version of Robin Hood was widely regarded as the best, Kevin Costner's came to be seen as the worst. Since it was over 50 years since the iconic film, it seemed that the time was ripe for a new heroic version. The result was lame. Costner was miscast, which at the time was a surprise, given his generally acclaimed performance in the Oscar-winning film *Dances with Wolves* (1990), and his American accent grated on audiences. The addition of a Moorish friend, Azeem (Morgan Freeman), seemed contrived, as was Sean Connery's cameo as King Richard. Alan Rickman's over-the-top portrayal of the Sheriff of Nottingham was memorable but also came across as a desperate effort to inject some life into the film. A subplot of sibling rivalry between Robin and Will Scarlett (Christian Slater) was tedious and unnecessary.

Yet for all its faults, there were some interesting developments in how the narrative was retold. Robin returns from the Crusades, cynical and war-weary. He becomes an outlaw after the Sheriff kills his father, Lord Locksley (Brian Blessed). Providing Robin with the sole motivation of personal revenge is distinct from other versions of the story. This new plot direction did, however, follow more closely with the narratives of New World outlaws who have family members killed or attacked, which gives them a rationale for their deeds. Examples include Joaquin Murrieta (brother), Jesse James (mother), Ned Kelly (mother and sister) and Billy the Kid (father figure). The role of the Moorish companion was also new for films and was copied from a British television series *Robin of Sherwood* (1984–1986), while the use of the camera following the arrow to its target (the point of view shot) was innovative and striking. The adverse publicity generated by Costner's effort led to a comic spoof in Mel Brooks's *Robin Hood: Men in Tights* (1993).

Robin Hood (2010)

Robin Longstride (Russell Crowe) is an ordinary soldier, rather than a noble. He fights in King Richard's army in France, and before that he spent years as a crusader. When Richard is killed in battle, he grabs the opportunity to return home. The trope of Robin as a returning soldier has become very common in recent versions, and it is interesting to see a similar angle with Doctor John Watson returning from Afghanistan in *Sherlock* (2010–2017). Giving the hero such a background allows an exploration of modern concerns of soldiers reintegrating into society and buys into populist rhetoric that ordinary patriotic soldiers have been let down by their uncaring leaders.

England is slipping into chaos. John, the new king, is vain and foolish. He dismisses the wise counsellor William Marshal (John Hurt) and replaces him with his friend Godfrey (Mark Strong). Godfrey, however, is a double agent employed by the French king. Bearing the king's warrant, but leading an army of French troops, he stirs up previously loyal lords to revolt. That villainous foreigners have infiltrated England in disguise and are attacking civilians suggests modern concerns with terrorism. As Haydock (2002) argues, modern cinema representations of the medieval period have been firmly aimed at the lucrative US market and have incorporated American world views. Accordingly, villains are usually foreigners, are working surreptitiously and have fooled or co-opted the authorities. Such deception can only be defeated by a vigilant everyman, a role perfectly cast for Robin. It is a provocative addition to the Robin Hood narrative. Rather than being evil, John is only weak, leading to his being so easily fooled.

This version also borrows heavily from *The Wife of Martin Guerre* (Lewis, 1941). In order to gain passage on a ship home, Robin Longstride takes on the identity of dead noble Robin of Locksley. Venturing to Nottingham, he is accepted as the nobleman's estranged son returning from the Crusades. Locksley's wife Marian (Cate Blanchett) knows he is not the real Locksley, but is happy to play along, eventually falling in love with him. A novel subplot is that William Marshal reveals Longstride's true identity as the son of one of the leaders of an earlier peasants' revolt. This allows for the modern trend of historical epics characterised by highly generalised calls for freedom and *Robin Hood* – with the star of *Gladiator* (2000) in the title role – is no exception.

Eventually, Robin and John join forces (certainly a first!) and defeat Godfrey and the French invasion force. Then comes the twist that takes us back to the earlier legends and ballads. Having seen off the French, John reneges on his agreement and declares Robin an outlaw. Robin and Marian quite happily retreat into Sherwood Forest, setting up the traditional conflict between outlaw and king.

Robin Hood (2018)

With both Sean Connery and Russell Crowe playing Robin Hood at 46 years of age, it opened up the likelihood that other productions would distinguish themselves by utilising younger casts. Accordingly, the television series *Robin Hood* (2006–2009) cast actors in their twenties to play Robin and his band; only slightly older than those used in the television series *Merlin* (see Chapter 3). Similarly, the film *Robin Hood* (2018) self-consciously set out to provide a radically new interpretation, very much in the spirit of the 2017 *King Arthur: Legend of the Sword* (see also Chapter 3). For its Robin and Marian, it cast Taron Egerton and Eve Hewson, both in their twenties. In style, the film strongly evoked the look of video games and there is a vibe – common to many recent films – that this is an alternative universe. The result was disappointing, and the film was neither a critical nor a commercial success.

Robin is Lord Loxley (using the spelling of the Yorkshire town). He returns from the Crusades after five years to find that he has been declared dead, his lands have been confiscated and Marian has married politician Will (Jamie Dornan). Eager for revenge, he teams up with Arab Little John (Jamie Foxx) to steal the tax money. Leading a double life – a plot point used in many films – as Lord Loxley, he pretends to support the Sheriff (Ben Mendelsohn) while undertaking daring robberies as the disguised Hood. The alternative Nottingham is a combination of CGI technology and Dubrovnik, making it confusingly resemble King's Landing in *Game of Thrones*.

The message of this modern riff on the Robin Hood story is that Brexit is a good idea. Life is hard in this northern city, and the cripplingly high taxes are being sent south. The untrustworthy authorities are working together to oppress the people, and even their local representative in Will is untrustworthy. Robin Hood accordingly arises as a populist hero who encourages the locals to try to take back control. Under his leadership, they retreat into Sherwood Forest, where they will govern themselves. In an interesting twist, the Sheriff is killed by Robin, only for a new Sheriff to be appointed in the vengeful Will.

Locational dissonance and Robin Hood movies

The medieval outlaw's adventures took place in Sherwood Forest and nearby Nottingham. However, that is not the case with the film and television versions of the story. As Shackley observed, 'visitors to Nottingham have an image of place derived from Robin Hood feature films, which have always been shot elsewhere' (2001: 315). That 'elsewhere' covers a wide geographical range, and three patterns for locations are apparent. First, they are filmed in Hollywood, second, in other parts of England and Wales and third, in continental Europe.

Robin Hood (1922) and *The Adventures of Robin Hood* (1938) were made in California. Like nearly every other Hollywood film up to the 1950s, they were shot there for commercial and logistical reasons, which precluded filming outside of the USA. *Robin Hood* was mainly filmed on sets and backlots. The set for Nottingham Castle was five storeys high and towered over downtown Hollywood. Not only did this generate good publicity for the film but, according to legend, also captured the imagination of a young film-maker called Walt Disney. Thirty years later, the scale of this centrepiece of the *Robin Hood* set was said to have served as the inspiration for the castle that is the centrepiece of Disneyland. Whilst a compelling story, there is no evidence that Disney was influenced as such, though he was in the right place at the right time. A short distance away, a forest was utilised around a reservoir later named Lake Sherwood. *The Adventures of Robin Hood* was filmed in a combination of parks around Los Angeles (including Lake Sherwood) and Bidwell Park in Chico in northern California that was a substitute for Sherwood Forest. The decision to travel up north was made because Bidwell Park had a good number of mature trees. This included the Hooker Oak, named after the naturalist and claimed to be the largest oak in the world at the time, which featured as Gallows Oak, the outlaw's rendezvous point. To green the California landscape – and hide some of the eucalypts – green paint and fake vines left over from a Tarzan movie were liberally utilised on set (Frost, 2009).

The second option for locations has been to shoot in England, using a combination of sets and existing historical sites. None, however, were in Sherwood or Nottinghamshire. The long-running 1950s television series *The Adventures of Robin Hood* was mainly filmed in a studio but moved outside for castle shots, utilising Alnwick Castle in Northumberland and Bodiam Castle in Sussex. The 1980s series *Robin of Sherwood* used a wide range of locations in England and Wales and also used Alnwick as the stand-in for Nottingham Castle. *Robin Hood: Prince of Thieves* (1991), followed suit with a variety of English locations, and the ubiquitous Alnwick Castle. *Robin Hood* (2010) similarly used English and Welsh locations.

The third pattern is filming in Europe. As with *Braveheart* (1995) – set in Scotland, but shot in Ireland – this is in order to take advantage of cheaper filming costs. Increasingly, this strategy of 'runaway productions' is being initiated by active national film boards seeking productions. In addition to cheaper costs, part of the offering is attractive locations, including forests and castles. *Robin and Marian* (1976) was filmed in Spain, the television series *Robin Hood* (2006–2009) in Hungary and *Robin Hood* (2018) in Croatia and Hungary. These three models are examples of *locational dissonance*, where the audience thinks they are seeing a certain place, but it is actually a completely different country. Does this affect tourism patterns? The evidence is: hardly ever. Tourists generally go to the places depicted on the screen (Frost, 2009).

The tourism geography of Robin Hood

Tourists inspired by the media head to Nottingham for their Robin Hood experiences. In that city, place marketing tied to Robin Hood tends to be episodic, with film releases providing the catalyst for new campaigns. In turn, these tend to fall away as the memory of the film fades. It is a dynamic and problematic example of the nexus between film and tourism, illustrating the difficulty of fashioning a sustainable leverage of a film. In the 1990s, the release of Kevin Costner's *Robin Hood: Prince of Thieves* led to a sharp – though temporary – increase in visitor numbers and the development of new visitor interpretation (Shackley, 2001). Two decades later, the release of Russell Crowe's *Robin Hood* prompted the city's destination marketing organisation to produce a guide, trail and discount card for attractions on the trail (Experience Nottingham, 2010). However, this too had only a limited lifespan and, by 2018, the internet site and marketing material were no longer in existence.

Geographically, tourism connected to Robin Hood is found in two distinct and separate nodes. The first is just on the outskirts of the central business district, clustered around Nottingham Castle. The castle itself tends to be a bit disappointing, as it was remodelled in modern times as a seat of regional government and looks little like the popular conception of a medieval castle. Interestingly, hardly anything is made of what should be a very compelling story concerning the castle and Edward III. In 1330, a small group of armed men crept into the castle through the tunnels in the cliff at its base (see Chapter 4). Working on behalf of the 17-year-old Edward, they captured Queen Isabella and her lover Roger Mortimer, allowing the king to commence ruling in his own right (Jones, 2013). Right next to these tunnels at the foot of Nottingham Castle is a statue of Robin Hood dating from the 1950s. When we were undertaking fieldwork in 2014, we observed that this was very popular with tourists, who climbed upon the statue to pose for individual and group photos (Figure 8.1). A short distance away is the popular tourist pub Ye Olde Trip to Jerusalem, which claims to date from 1189 and is associated with the Crusades and pilgrimages (Figure 8.2).

Between 1989 and 2009, there was also a tourist attraction called The Tales of Robin Hood (Henesey, 2009). This followed the trend of the day of having visitors in a moveable chair-ride, Disney-style, travelling past changing dioramas; an approach which is still to be seen at the Jorvik Viking Centre in York (see Chapter 9). Unlike the Richard III Visitor Centre in Leicester (see Chapter 3), which engages its audience through interactive interpretation and presents mysteries to be solved by science (archaeology), this type of tourist attraction is passive and more about entertainment. Another Robin Hood-themed attraction opened its doors in 2016. Originally known as the Robin Hood Legacy, it was renamed The Robin Hood Experience and uses hologram technology in its storytelling; it also has a small museum, which includes some film and television memorabilia, and a gift shop. The owner, Adam Greenwood, dresses up as Robin Hood to greet visitors (Wright, 2017).

This concentration of tourism attractions and associated souvenir shops in Nottingham raises an interesting issue about place and heritage tourism. Robin

Figure 8.1 Young Tourists Posing for Photographs at the Robin Hood Statue, Nottingham.
Source: Jennifer Frost.

Figure 8.2 Ye OldeTrip to Jerusalem.
Source: Jennifer Frost.

Hood's home is Sherwood Forest. He is a rural outlaw, helping the peasants and robbing the rich on isolated roads within the forest. Nottingham is the base of his enemies – the Sheriff of Nottingham and his garrison. Yet, it is Nottingham, a growing regional city with transport connections, hotels and restaurants, which draws in the tourists. A similar situation occurs with the Australian outlaw Ned Kelly, with the main tourist attractions focussed on the base of his adversaries in Melbourne rather than in his rural heartland. Indeed, it is striking that the most popular tourism attraction associated with that outlaw is the gaol in which he was executed (Frost, 2006).

Robin's legendary home is Sherwood Forest. This has led to a second node about 20 miles north of Nottingham at the Sherwood Forest National Nature Reserve. This nature reserve contains the largest remnant of the ancient forest. It attracts approximately 350,000 visitors per year, though only a part of them are drawn by the Robin Hood story. This area is protected as a nature reserve as it contains over a thousand mature oak trees, including the iconic Major's Oak (Nottingham City Council, 2017) (Figure 8.3). As such, many of the visitors to this free attraction are simply seeking a walk in nature.

The visitor centre at the nature reserve provides a central point for providing interpretation regarding Robin Hood. What is fascinating is how that has changed over time, as the story and its connection to Sherwood Forest have evolved. In 1989, Warwick visited Sherwood Forest, and it was a very curious experience. The visitor centre interpretation at that time firmly explained that Robin never

Figure 8.3 Major's Oak, Sherwood Forest.
Source: Jennifer Frost.

existed and that popular media representations were romanticised rubbish. Instead – as the interpretation narrative lectured the hapless tourists – it was important to focus on the oppression of medieval peasants. This crude attempt at 'myth-busting' was similar to the video about King Arthur at Tintagel discussed in Chapter 3. Certainly, comments by Nottingham residents to Warwick at the time were that they found this display embarrassing and counterproductive in terms of trying to encourage tourism to the city.

In the early 1990s, the release of the Kevin Costner film was the catalyst to change this interpretation to recognise that tourists were interested in the Robin Hood story (Shackley, 2001). In 2014, we both visited Sherwood Forest and viewed the permanent exhibition 'Robyn Hode's Sherwode'. This provided an entertaining and insightful experience. Rather than attempting to preach a *master narrative*, it provided historical evidence from the medieval period that the story was well-known then and that an outlaw might have existed. These were juxtaposed with brightly coloured representations of medieval castles and banners; traditional images that the public would associate with the period. Reinforcing the light approach taken was a large banner proclaiming 'Hooray for Robin Hood!' (Figure 8.4). The exhibition concluded with a large panel containing a montage of film and television images and book covers of Robin Hood (Figure 8.5). As a nostalgic display, this strongly appealed to visitors, many of whom lingered as they identified and reminisced about their favourite productions. Similarly, the visitor centre cafe was decorated with posters from Robin Hood films.

The visitor centre at Sherwood Forest was built in the 1970s and in 2014 we commented to each other that it was starting to look tired. It was no surprise that in 2017, the Nottingham City Council announced that it was to be demolished and replaced with a new facility (Nottingham City Council, 2017). The impetus for this came from a greater focus on the natural values of the reserve and the need to cater for strong visitor flows. Tellingly, the announcement makes no mention of any Robin Hood film narratives being featured in the new development. Whilst the 2010 film *Robin Hood* had been used for destination marketing at that time, it is noticeable that the marketing material generated has now disappeared from the council's website. It seems that the new visitor centre demonstrates a negative aspect of film tourism, in that the absence of any productions at the time it was conceived will flow through to an absence of interpretation. That said, it is noticeable that in 2018, the annual Robin Hood Festival was staged at the new visitor centre (Sherwood Forest, 2018)

The Robin Hood Festival has been held annually at Sherwood Forest since the 1980s. It involves people dressing up as and adopting the persona of medieval characters. This is essentially a *freestyle* historic re-enactment, unencumbered by the need to closely follow a historic narrative, 'because there are no agreed and documented truths and historical facts' (Everett and Parakoottahill, 2018: 31). Held over five days, it is suggestive of the medieval carnivalesque. As with many re-enactment events, it attracts those who are passionately committed to such performances as a form of *serious leisure*, which offers emotional and psychological benefits (Hunt, 2004). Taking on these costumed roles, provides an

Figure 8.4 Displays at the Visitor Centre at Sherwood Forest in 2014.

Source: Jennifer Frost.

Figure 8.5 Robin Hood Montage at the Visitor Centre at Sherwood Forest in 2014.
Source: Jennifer Frost.

'opportunity to develop a better (and truer) sense of oneself … through a process of character adoption and identity to generate a form of existential authenticity' (Everett and Parakoottahill, 2018: 31).

Adjacent to the nature reserve is the small village of Edwinstowe. As a service centre for tourists, the village manifests certain connections to the Robin Hood story. These are primarily constructed around the twelfth-century St Mary's Church, in which legend has Robin marrying Marian. St Mary's is one of seven Nottingham churches linked by the Robin Hood Churches Trail (Church History Project, 2018). Edwinstowe markets itself as 'Robin Hood's Village', and on the main street there is a recent statue of Robin proposing to Marian (Figure 8.6). For this village, the Robin Hood legend provides a strong sense of identity and economic benefits for hospitality and retail operators.

Conclusion

Robin Hood remains an enigma on many levels. A legend with elements of truth, the decisive historical evidence is tantalisingly just out of reach. A story that became popular in the late medieval period, it has been reinterpreted time after time, often with new inflexions and inventions reflecting contemporary concerns. It is strongly linked with Nottingham, yet tourism related to Robin Hood remains relatively undeveloped in its place of origin. The 1938 *Adventures of Robin Hood* is one of the greatest historical action films of all time; however, its huge success

Figure 8.6 Robin and Marian Statue at Edwinstowe.
Source: Jennifer Frost.

has worked against the various remakes. In the late twentieth century, *Robin and Marian* failed at the box office with an elegiac tale of ageing heroes. *Robin Hood: Prince of Thieves* was a success but quickly gained a reputation as a bad film. *Robin Hood* (2010) underperformed, and *Robin Hood* (2018) was an ill-conceived flop. Given such a cinematic history, it is tempting to feel that this story has run its course and that there is very little new for film-makers to say. Perhaps there is an opportunity to turn the narrative on its head, in the way that the television series *Merlin* did for King Arthur. There are possibilities for a reboot, and two recent efforts are worth noting. The first is a production that was underway as of 2020. Titled *Hood: A Legend Reborn*, it has stuntman/actor Adam Collins directing and in the title role, and its publicity promised a gritty and violent style unlike all previous Robin Hood movies. The second takes a radical approach in having a Black Robin Hood. This is *Robbie Hood* (2019). Updated to modern Alice Springs in Outback Australia, Robbie Hood (Pedrea Jackson) is a 13-year-old Aboriginal boy. It seems that the temptation to reinvent Robin for a new audience remains strong.

References

Aberth, J. (2003) *A knight at the movies: Medieval history on film*, London and New York: Routledge.
Amalgamated Press (1958) *Robin Hood annual 1959*, London: Amalgamated Press.

Campbell, J. (1949) *The hero with a thousand faces*, London: Fontana, 1993 reprint.

Church History Project (2018) *Robin Hood Churches Trail*, http://www.nottsopen-churches.org.uk/RobinHoodLeaflet%20FINAL.pdf (accessed October 1, 2018).

Everett, S. and Parakoottahill, D. (2018) 'Transformation, meaning-making and identity creation through folklore tourism: The case of the Robin Hood Festival', *Journal of Heritage Tourism*, *13*(1), 30–45.

Experience Nottingham (2010) *Experience the home of Robin Hood: Map & guide*, www. experiencenottinghamshire.com/xsdbimgs/in_the_footsteps_of_rh_web.pdf (accessed July 21, 2014).

Frost, W. (2006) 'Braveheart-ed Ned Kelly: Historic films, heritage tourism and destination image', *Tourism Management*, *27*(2), 247–254.

Frost, W. (2009) 'From backlot to runaway production: Exploring location and authenticity in film-induced tourism', *Tourism Review International*, *13*(2), 85–92.

Frost, W. and Laing, J. (2015) *Imagining the American West through film and tourism*, London and New York: Routledge.

Hahn, T. and Knight, S. (2008) "Exempt me, Sire, for I am afeard of women': Gendering Robin Hood', in H. Phillips (Ed.), *Bandit territories: British outlaws and their traditions* (pp. 24–43), Cardiff: University of Wales Press.

Haydock, N. (2002) 'Arthurian melodrama, Chaucerian spectacle, and the waywardness of cinema pastiche in *First Knight* and *A Knight's Tale*', in T. Shippey and M. Arnold (Eds.), *Film and fiction: Reviewing the Middle Ages* (pp. 5–38), Cambridge: D.S. Brewer.

Henesey, B. (2009) 'Nottingham will "fall off tourist map" after closure of Tales of Robin Hood', *Nottingham Post*, 15 January, www.nottinghampost.com/Nottingham-fall-tourist-map-closure-Tales-Robin-Hood/story-12271988-detail/story.html

Hunt, S. (2004) 'Acting the part: Living history as a serious leisure pursuit', *Leisure Studies*, *23*(4), 387–403.

Jones, D. (2013) *The Plantagenets: The kings who made England*, London: William Collins.

Knight, S. (2003) *Robin Hood: A mythic biography*, Ithaca, NY: Cornell University Press.

Kooistra, P. (1989) *Criminals as heroes: Structure, power & identity*, Bowling Green, KY: Bowling Green State University Press.

Laing, J. and Frost, W. (2012) *Books and travel: Inspiration, quests and transformation*, Bristol: Channel View.

Lewis, J. (1941) *The wife of Martin Guerre*, London: Penguin, 1977 reprint.

Månsson, M. (2011) 'Mediatized tourism', *Annals of Tourism Research* 38(4), 1634–1652.

McLynn, F. (2007) *Lionheart & Lackland: King Richard, King John and the wars of conquest*, London: Vintage.

Nollen, S. (1999) *Robin Hood: A cinematic history of the English outlaw and his Scottish counterparts*, Jefferson, NC: McFarland.

Nottingham City Council (2017) 'A firm foundation for a new era at Sherwood Forest', *Newsroom*, www.nottinghamshire.gov.uk/newsroom/news/a-firm-foundation-for-a-new-era-at-sherwood-forest (accessed August 22, 2018).

Phillips, H. (2008) 'Scott and the outlaws', in H. Phillips (Ed.), *Bandit territories: British outlaws and their traditions* (pp. 119–142), Cardiff: University of Wales Press.

Seal, G. (1996) *The outlaw legend: A cultural tradition in Britain, America and Australia*, Cambridge: Cambridge University Press.

Scott, W. (1819) *Ivanhoe*, London: Dent, 1965 reprint.

Schama, S. (1995) *Landscape and memory*, London: Fontana.

Shackley, M. (2001) 'The legend of Robin Hood: Myth, inauthenticity, and tourism development in Nottingham England', in V.L. Smith and M. Brent (Eds.), *Hosts and Guests Revisited: Tourism Issues in the 21st Century* (pp. 315–322). New York: Cognizant.

Sherwood Forest (2018) *Robin Hood Festival*, https://www.visitsherwood.co.uk/things-to-do/robin-hood-festival/ (accessed October 1, 2018).

Slotkin, R. (1992) *Gunfighter nation: The myth of the frontier in twentieth-century America*, Norman: University of Oklahoma Press.

Symons, D. (2016) 'Relishing the kill, becoming a man: Robin Hood's rivalry with Guy of Gisborne', in L. Coote and V. Johnson (Eds.), *Robin Hood in Outlaw/ed Spaces: Media, performance and other new directions* (pp. 147–162), London and New York: Routledge.

Vance, J. and Maietta, T. (2008) *Douglas Fairbanks*, Berkeley: University of California Press.

Wheeler, F., Laing, J., Frost, L., Reeves, K. and Frost, W. (2011) Outlaw nations: Tourism, the frontier and national identities, in E. Frew and L. White (Eds.), *Tourism and national identities: An international perspective* (pp. 151–163). London and New York: Routledge.

White, T.H. (1938) *The sword in the stone*, London: Harper Voyager, published in *The Once and Future King* omnibus 2015.

Wright, A.W. (2017) 'Adam Greenwood from the Robin Hood experience', *Robin Hood: Bold Outlaw of Barnsdale and Sherwood*, https://www.boldoutlaw.com/robint/robin-hood-legacy.html (accessed January 19, 2021).

9 The hammer of the gods?

Contested and changing imaginaries of the Vikings

Introduction

There is a song that sums up the popular image of the Vikings. It is Led Zeppelin's 'Immigrant Song' (1970). Loud and anthemic, it, 'cast the band in the role of Viking invaders raping, burning and pillaging, and whispering tales of glory … the song was hard to take seriously because its premise was so goofy, but Zeppelin fans adored it' (Davis, 1985: 120–121). Nearly half a century later, it is still hugely popular, lighting up the soundtrack of the Marvel movie *Thor: Ragnarok* (2017) – where it was used twice for key battle scenes – and heard at sporting contests such as T20 cricket.

At the heart of the appeal for 'Immigrant Song' is that it taps into such a deep-rooted fantasy regarding the Vikings. The song was written by band members Jimmy Page and Robert Plant in a cottage in Snowdonia in rural Wales. Lyricist Plant was especially immersed in Celtic mythology and mysticism, and this was evident in a number of their songs, particularly their biggest hit, 'Stairway to Heaven'. Raised in middle-class suburbia in Kidderminster on the outskirts of Birmingham, Plant was similar to many baby boomer teenagers in the 1960s in being attracted to the medieval aesthetic of Tolkienism and Arthurian romance. Somehow, this all translated to Plant, the former trainee accountant, happily imagining himself as a berserk Viking. Such a fantastic imaginary was neither new nor confined to Britain. In the late nineteenth and twentieth centuries, the mythology of the Viking held a strong grip on the American imagination. Stimulated by books, operas, art and later cinema, a fascination with Vikings tapped into concerns about declining masculinity in an increasingly urban, safe and sedentary world. While the links were tenuous for many, the Vikings were widely imagined as providing a foundation heritage narrative that was reassuringly masculine, White and non-Catholic. In the USA, this was reinforced by increasing historical evidence that the Vikings had reached the Americas and that Leif Erikson could be constructed as a sort of Norse Columbus (Lunde, 2010; Williams, 2017).

How the Vikings are perceived is one of the most contested issues in regard to the modern imagining of the medieval. In much of popular culture – including a range of Hollywood films and television series – the line taken is very similar to that of Led Zeppelin: that the Vikings are destructive and blood-crazed invaders who send Europe once again into the Dark Ages. They are the epitome of the view that the medieval period was a *Barbaric Age* (Eco, 1986) While some historians now emphasise their skill as traders, seafarers and explorers, for many, the Viking legacy lies in being the destructive *Other* that plunged Europe into chaos.

This dissonance was highlighted by the 2014 British Museum exhibition Vikings: Life and Legend, which we visited as part of our fieldwork. Curator Thomas Williams recounted how the *Guardian* newspaper reviewed the exhibition as not placing enough emphasis on warfare, being too much about art and culture and offering 'little for the fans of *Horrible Histories*'. In response, Williams bemoaned that there was a popular view that Vikings:

> are a cheerful, bloody diversion for the kids ... Brooches? Women? Trade? BORING! Vikings are big men with swords, crushing skulls ... [they] have been fetishized and infantalized, set apart from wider history alongside pirates, gladiators, knights-in-armour ... The Vikings are presented as cartoon savages.
>
> (Williams, 2017: xv–xvi)

The two contrasting imaginaries of the Vikings are both apparent in heritage tourism, dependent on one's geographical perspective:

> The Anglo-American stereotypical representation of Viking heritage is of seafaring, sexist, and blood thirsty men raping and pillaging. ... In contrast, in Scandinavia the image of Vikings in popular culture finds fewer references to war and warriors. Here the Viking representation is very much concerned with the people [at home] ... European Viking heritage tourism has largely attempted to give greater credence to the latter representation.
>
> (Halewood and Hannam, 2001: 566)

Halewood and Hannam explored this more peaceful representation of the Vikings through a number of case studies of heritage attractions. These tended towards a social or living history approach, focussing on the everyday lives of ordinary people as traders and farmers rather than warriors. Their typology of Viking heritage attractions comprised:

1. Conventional museums (such as the Roskilde Viking Ships Museum in Denmark).
2. Viking heritage centres (particularly Jorvik in York, UK).
3. Viking theme parks (Viking Land in Norway).
4. Village reconstructions (Lejre in Denmark, Hög in Sweden and Foteviken in Sweden).

Despite the common desire to focus more on social history, all of these attractions were found to engage in the negotiation of authenticity, recognising that it was 'often still the more bloodthirsty image that initially inspires tourists to visit sites'

(Halewood and Hannam, 2001: 566). Accordingly, curators and interpretation staff were faced with the challenge of introducing counter-narratives that hopefully re-educated visitors without alienating them. As seen with heritage attractions themed on King Arthur (Chapter 3) and Robin Hood (Chapter 8), such approaches may be ineffective, as tourists immersed in the mythology are often dissatisfied with the preaching of a contrary interpretation.

Our aim in this chapter is to further explore this dichotomy between the two views of the Vikings. In the first half of the chapter, we examine a range of media representations of the Vikings, highlighting key themes about their characteristics and historical influences. In the second half, we focus on heritage tourism attractions, particularly the Jorvik Viking Centre. Here, we are interested in how they represent the Vikings and how they attempt to explain differences between their social history-orientated approach and that portrayed in much of popular culture.

Vikings in the popular media

To illustrate how Vikings are typically represented, six examples from popular media are considered in detail. These are four films from the 1950s through to the 1970s and from the twenty-first century, a novel and two television series.

Prince Valiant (1954)

In the 1950s, Hollywood discovered the medieval period, leading to this confection, which closely followed the popular cartoon strip of the same name. This was created in 1937 by Hal Foster, who had previously drawn a strip based on the novel *Tarzan* by Edgar Rice Burroughs. The comic strip told the story of Valiant, a Viking prince in exile, who joins the Knights of the Round Table. The film version followed the conventions of the comic strip and the film *The Knights of the Round Table* released the previous year, with the armour and fortifications portrayed being from the late Middle Ages, approximately 500–700 years later than the time period in which the story was set.

As befits a film based on a comic strip, the depiction of the Vikings is cartoonish. Nearly every Viking is bare-chested and muscle bound and wears a helmet with enormous horns. Ludicrous, impractical and historically incorrect, in the nineteenth century such headwear became indelibly linked with the Vikings (Trow, 2005, Williams, 2017). Valiant does not wear a helmet but sports a striking page-boy haircut, which greatly embarrassed the young actor Robert Wagner. Supporting Valiant is the pig-tailed Viking Boltar, played by Academy Award winner Victor McLaglen, who was nearly 70 at the time. Though exciting and entertaining, the film tells us little about the Vikings. The great set piece regarding the Vikings is the assault on their castle. This is well-staged, but Vikings did not build immense stone castles in the Norman style. In contrast, there is almost nothing in the film about Vikings as raiders, traders or seafarers. Apart from being true to the source material of the comic strip, there is no real reason for this film to be about Vikings at all.

The Vikings (1958)

Whilst made only four years after *Prince Valiant*, this is much more of a realist attempt at depicting the Vikings. Aberth described it as 'Hollywood's best attempt to portray the Viking age' (2003: 42). Produced as an intensely personal project by star Kirk Douglas, all references to King Arthur were jettisoned. Visually, this is a much more spectacular film, with filming taking place on location at Hardanger Norway and at the thirteenth century Castle La Latte in Brittany in France. The film commences with a narration voiced by Orson Welles, setting the stage for the medieval as the Age of Barbarism (Eco, 1986):

> The Vikings, in Europe of the 8th and 9th century, were dedicated to a pagan god of war, Odin. Trapped by the confines of their barren ice-bound north-lands, they exploited their skill as shipbuilders to spread a reign of terror, then unequalled in violence and brutality in all the records of history.

The film searches for authenticity in how the Vikings are dressed and behave. As Halewood and Hannam (2001) noted, their representation as marauders may not be acceptable nowadays, but for a 1950s Hollywood film, it is quite exceptional in how it depicts an exotic culture. There is much emphasis, for example, on the Vikings' religious beliefs. The portrayal of three beliefs is worth noting. The first is that the Vikings are in awe of fortune-tellers, who through casting the runes-sticks or dreams are able to interpret the will of the gods. This trope is repeated in nearly every fictional Viking narrative and is based on traditional Viking practices. The second, specifically stated in the opening narration, is that 'the greatest wish of every Viking was to die, sword in hand, and enter Valhalla, where a hero's welcome awaited them from the god Odin'. Again, this is now a common convention in popular culture, but is an exaggeration of Viking beliefs. Third, a Viking king must be honoured with a fiery funeral, involving a boat set ablaze by a flaming arrow. This conflates traditions of cremating a body on a pyre or burying a Viking with their boat. This trope is most likely influenced by the novel *Beau Geste* (Wren, 1924), which features two English brothers in the French Foreign Legion who make a pact that they will provide each other with a Viking funeral, just like the stories they read in childhood. Further reinforcing the links with Viking religion is that the main character in Einar (Kirk Douglas) is associated with Odin throughout the film, represented visually through his only having one eye, just like the Norse god.

There is no attempt to ridicule these beliefs in *The Vikings*. Even when the Vikings' religion is juxtaposed against the Christianity of the English, there is no narrative that the Christians are right and the Vikings are wrong to believe as they do (Aberth, 2003). Furthermore, Viking society is represented as essentially democratic, with decisions made by village meetings rather than just following the orders of the chieftain. In the scenes of the Viking village filmed in Hardangerfjord in Norway, the imagery is of farmers, artisans, women, children and old people. These visuals are helped by the recruitment of Norwegian locals as extras, so that the Viking villagers are uniformly blonde, weather-beaten and Nordic. It is only in the interior scenes of the great hall that the film returns to the stereotypes of the Vikings as drunken ruffians.

The plot follows 1950s cinematic conventions of the love triangle, as half-brothers Einar (Kirk Douglas) and Eric (Tony Curtis) compete for the captured English princess Morgana (Janet Leigh). Einar and Eric hate each other, but they join forces to avenge their father Ragnar (Ernest Borgnine), who has been executed by the English king Aella (Frank Thring). Both Ragnar and Aella were real historical characters. The ninth-century Ragnar Lothbrok (or Lodbrok) was one of the most famous Vikings, whose exploits were recorded in various Norse sagas and Frankish accounts. In 865, Ragnar was captured by King Aella of Northumbria, who had him tossed into a pit of snakes. In revenge, the sons of Ragnar led a great invasion force against the English, killing Aella. This is essentially what happens in this film, with the exception that Ragnar is thrown into a pit of wolves rather than snakes.

Between 1952 and 1955, Hollywood studios had produced a 'chivalric cycle' of medieval films, focussed on courteous and clean-cut knights (see Chapter 5). For Richards (2008), *The Vikings* represented a major change in direction away from the emphasis on knightly chivalry. The old studio system was rapidly declining, and individual stars and their production companies were coming to the fore. *The Vikings* was Kirk Douglas's vision, rather than a product of the studio factory system (Aberth, 2003). As Richards argues, *The Vikings* reflected a growing societal trend towards 'hedonistic individualism', resulting in a film 'in which the heroes were hard-fighting, hard-drinking, lusty, pagan Viking warriors, with a code of instant gratification, violence and self-assertion' (2008: 192). Whilst neither the Vikings nor their Saxon opponents have any sense of chivalry as portrayed in the earlier 'chivalric cycle' of films, it is important to recognise that this film does represent the Vikings as both religious and as having their own strong code of honour and justice.

The Long Ships (1964)

This British–Yugoslavian production is an entertaining romp. Whilst having some similarities to *The Vikings* in the representation of the Viking village and masculine drinking culture, it is not at the same level of quality or complexity. The story revolves around the search for the lost Golden Bell of Byzantium – three men high and made of solid gold – 'the Mother of Voices'. One group seeking the bell is a boatload of Vikings led by brothers Rolf and Orm (Richard Widmark and Russ Tamblyn). Their search takes them into the Mediterranean, allowing much of the film to be shot around the coastal resort of Budva in Montenegro. Opposed to the Vikings are the Moors, led by Ali Mansuh (Sidney Poitier), who are also seeking the bell.

The film is squarely aimed at a juvenile market, with the highlights in terms of the strong visual imagery being the story of the making of the bell (told in an innovative montage of Byzantine mosaics) and the battles. The acting is at the level of a pantomime. Widmark, in particular, does nothing to hide his midwestern drawl and has no subtlety at all. The Vikings have a wide variety of accents, being played by actors from the USA, Serbia, Austria, England, Scotland, Wales and Northern Ireland (but not from Scandinavia). Such issues with quality are common to many historical adventure films of the 1950s and 1960s.

Nonetheless, *The Long Ships* adds some interesting dimensions to how the Vikings were portrayed. Whereas earlier films focussed on conflict with England, here the conflict is with the Moors, as another group on the fringes of Western Europe. The action takes place in the Mediterranean, illustrating how far the Vikings journeyed, and there is also a focus on Byzantium (where Vikings were prominent in the Varangian Guard, the personal bodyguard of the Emperor). Rolfe is constructed as a teller of tall tales and a 'Trickster' rather than a straightforward hero. In Viking culture, such characteristics were esteemed and personified in the god Loki.

The Norseman (1978)

In fictional travel narratives, there is a particular trope of going well beyond the limits of the known world in searching for lost explorers or travellers. Examples include *In Search of the Castaways* (Jules Verne, 1867), *King Solomon's Mines* (Henry Rider Haggard, 1885) and *Heart of Darkness* (Joseph Conrad, 1899) (Laing and Frost, 2014). *The Norseman* applies this concept to the Viking journeys to North America in the eleventh century. King Eurich (Mel Ferrer) has been lost on an earlier expedition, and so his son Thorvald (Lee Majors) leads a party to find him. Landing in America, they encounter a tribe of hostile Native Americans who have captured Eurich. The film's plot is little more than a series of battles as Eurich is rescued; this serving to emphasise the clash between two warrior societies.

Once again, the mainstays of cinematic Viking culture are represented. They are fierce warriors, they are loyal to a charismatic leader, they must die with a sword in their hand to enter Valhalla, the dead must be honoured with a traditional funeral and their number includes an old wizard and they are guided by his predictions. As in earlier films, their mobility is stressed. Through the use of their longship and superior seacraft, they are able to reach distant lands. Indeed, in this film there are no scenes set in Scandinavia, and all the action takes place far from home. This is similarly the case in *The Thirteenth Warrior* (1999), which takes the Vikings eastwards rather than westwards to the other extremity of their influence, being set in what is now Russia and the Ukraine.

The film does contain some oddities. Whereas the Vikings called their new discovery Vinland, after the wild grapes they found, when that story is played out in *The Norseman*, Thorvald decides to call it Vine-Land. One of the Vikings is Thrall, a Black warrior they captured in the past and who is now one of their company (played by American footballer Owen Deacon). The Vikings all wear enormous horned helmets. Finally, the credits list the actual Viking ship used in the film as being supplied by the town of New Bern in North Carolina. This seems most probably to have been the ship donated to the town's museum by the Lorilliad Tobacco Company in the 1930s. That ship had been used in advertising campaigns, but it does raise the question as to why a cigarette company owned a functioning Viking longship. The answer possibly lies with Catherine Lorilliad Wolfe, an heiress who owned the company in the late nineteenth century. She was obsessed with Vikings in the Americas and built a mansion called 'Vinland', decorated by William Morris at Newport, Rhode Island (Sharpe and Kuchta, 2007; see also Chapter 2). Was she responsible for her tobacco company's Viking longship?

The Last Kingdom (Bernard Cornwell, 2004)

In 866, the sons of Ragnar Lodbrok invaded England in revenge for their father's death at the hands of King Aella of Northumbria. They killed Aella and captured York. As with a number of medieval heroes, separating myth and fact in regard to Ragnar is difficult. It may be that he is just a later invention, created to provide a justification for an invasion (Williams, 2017). Nonetheless, the story of Ragnar and his sons is a popular one, being also the central plot of the film *The Vikings* (1958) and television series *Vikings* (2013–2021). Cornwell's novel – and the book and television series that it spawned – follows the Vikings as they progressively conquer each of England's kingdoms, heading south towards the last kingdom of Wessex.

The narrator is Uhtred, a young Saxon boy captured by the Viking leader Ragnar during the battle at York. Uhtred lives with the Vikings, learning their ways and eventually becoming a warrior. He is also conscious that he is a Saxon, and at times his loyalties are conflicted. Being divided between the two cultures is a useful literary device, allowing Cornwell to observe and comment upon both sides. His captor is confusingly not Ragnar Lodbrok, but shares both the name and a great deal of the same characteristics as the legendary leader. Uhtred quickly comes to idolise the charismatic Ragnar, who treats him as a surrogate son. Ragnar initially appears to be the fictional Viking *par excellence*; his father tells Uhtred how, 'my son's ambitions are very few; merely to hear jokes, solve riddles, get drunk, give rings [to vassals], lie belly to belly with women, eat well and go to Odin' (Cornwell, 2004: 163). That is, however, not all that there is to Ragnar. He explains to Uhtred that he comes from Denmark, where the land is poor and crowded. Rather than just being a raider after plunder, Ragnar wants to permanently settle in England.

Ragnar is renowned as a trickster, particularly adept at luring overconfident enemies into ambushes. At York, the Saxons decide to attack what seems to be a weak palisade. The Vikings fall back under their onslaught, and the Saxons are jubilant that they are on the verge of victory. However, they have fallen into Ragnar's trap and are surrounded and overwhelmed, with King Aella and Uhtred's father killed. The disaster at York highlights a weakness of Saxon military tactics. Their general approach for internal warfare was that an open battleground was selected, often near ancient monuments that were seen as holding special power. Siege warfare and castles were relatively unknown to them. The Vikings, in contrast, were more flexible, were comfortable in fighting from defensive positions and – as at York – using ambushes (Williams, 2017).

Uhtred learns later that the Viking invasion has come because they see that the kingdom of Northumbria is weakly defended, due to divisions arising from two claimants to the throne. Indeed, throughout the book series, the Saxons are often weakened by internal divisions. Uhtred recalls:

> One thing I learned about the Danes was that they knew how to spy. The monks who write the chronicles tell us that they came from nowhere, their dragon-prowed ships suddenly appearing from a blue vacancy, but it was rarely like that … the war fleets, went where they knew there was already trouble.
>
> (Cornwell, 2004: 17)

The Vikings are confident in their military superiority over the Saxons. Ravn, one of their warriors, explains to Uhtred:

> Mercia is frightened of us … I think that only one man in three is a warrior, and sometimes not even that many, but in our army, Uhtred, every man is a fighter. If you do not want to be a warrior, you stay home in Denmark. You till the soil, herd sheep, fish the sea, but you do not take to the ships and become a fighter. But here in England? Every man is forced to fight, yet only one in three, or maybe only one in four has the belly for it. The rest are farmers who just want to run. We are wolves fighting sheep.
>
> (Cornwell, 2004: 64–65)

However, as the novel progresses, the situation changes. Alfred, the King of Wessex, starts to organise more effective defences. Ragnar is killed by a rival Viking and Uhtred flees south, joining the Saxon cause. As such, the book series becomes a narrative of King Alfred leading the resistance to Viking invasions, which becomes an example of Eco's medievalism of creating 'National Identities' (Collins, 2013; Eco, 1986; Williams, 2017). Alfred's aim is to unite the kingdoms into one England. Uhtred does not like Alfred personally, seeing him as pompous and hypocritical, and Uhtred particularly resents being manipulated by the King to fight for Wessex against the Vikings. His position is complicated by his divided loyalties, yet Uhtred ultimately becomes an important weapon in Alfred's strategic plan to defeat the Danes. When the Vikings invade Wessex, Uhtred utilises what Ragnar has taught him, leading a sneak attack that burns the Vikings' boats. For the first time, it is the Vikings who have been outwitted. As the book series develops, Uhtred becomes a feared warrior. Trained by Ragnar, he knows the value of ambushes and trickery. Leading a surprise attack on the Vikings at London, Uhtred reveals an approach that mirrors what Ragnar must have thought at York:

> the joy of battle was tricking the other side. Of knowing what they will do before they do it, and having the response ready so that, when they make the move that is supposed to kill you, they die instead.
>
> (Cornwell, 2007: 132)

The Last Kingdom book and television series have shone a spotlight on the so-called Dark Ages, which has traditionally been overlooked in popular culture. Ken Follett's recent novel *The Evening and the Morning* (2020) follows the same pattern, going back to the tenth century in a medieval cathedral town to cover its origins in England's early history. This growing interest in the early medieval period can also be traced to the popularity of *Vikings*, discussed in the next sub-section. Collectively, these media have helped to reshape our ideas about a period of time of which little was known compared to other eras in our history. While barbarism is frequently depicted, one of Eco's (1986) medievalisms, there is a counterpoint in the lives of ordinary people that are shown, and we are provided with examples of a rich heritage, spanning religion, cultural practices and beliefs, and technological developments.

Vikings (2013–2021)

With the success of *Game of Thrones*, the History Channel made a strategic decision that for the first time they would commission a similar action drama based on history. The result was *Vikings*, which told the story of legendary Viking hero Ragnar Lodbrok. As detailed earlier, Ragnar and his sons had previously featured in earlier fictional media productions, such as *The Vikings* and *The Last Kingdom*. For the History Channel, focussing on Ragnar had advantages in that while he was a real historical character, only the bare outline of his story was known; this allowed for a degree of fictional invention whilst retaining the verisimilitude that this television series was based on history. Similar to *Game of Thrones*, *Vikings* was a high-budget production with spectacular battle scenes and a strong attention to detail in depicting the clothing, hairstyles, weaponry and social life of the time period. Filming took place in Ireland, Canada and, in a later series, Iceland. The cast was multicultural, though not typical of Hollywood, with many of the actors drawn from Canada, Australia, Ireland and Scandinavia. Interestingly, this series came after a long hiatus in Viking action films, which had seemed to indicate that representations of the Vikings as violent raiders were no longer in favour (Aberth, 2003). *Vikings* certainly reversed that trend.

The series started with Ragnar (Travis Fimmel) as a minor lord, who gradually works his way up to king through defeating his overlords in Earl Haraldson (Gabriel Byrne) and King Horik (Donal Logue). Ragnar is supported by his wife Lagertha (Kathryn Winnick), brother Rollo (Clive Standen) and shipbuilder Floki (Gustaf Skarsgård). Lagertha provides a new dimension to the Viking narrative in that she is also a mighty warrior, leading a group of females known as the 'shield-maidens'. This is another aspect of Viking history which has entered popular culture, with females now depicted as fierce fighters (see Chapter 4). Brida (Emily Cox) in *The Last Kingdom*, a Saxon woman brought up as a Viking, who leads many battles for her adopted people, also fits within this narrative. Ragnar's rise to power is aided by his success in leading the first raids on Saxon England, which increases his wealth and status. While most of his companions are interested only in loot, Ragnar sees the opportunity for permanent settlement in England, another idea which is also prominent in *The Last Kingdom*.

Ragnar and Rollo are both mighty warriors, but Ragnar is also a leader. His attributes include wisdom and tactical thinking, allowing him to outwit his adversaries, and he increases his legendary renown through audacious deceptions. For example, when the Vikings are besieging Paris, Ragnar pretends to have died. His followers tell the jubilant Parisians that their chief has converted to Christianity on his deathbed and wants to be buried in a church. When they carry his coffin in, Ragnar bursts out and starts attacking the off-guard French. This is actually a story usually attributed to another charismatic leader in the eleventh century, Norman lord Robert Guiscard (Robert the Crafty).

As in earlier media imaginaries, the Vikings have strong religious beliefs. Soothsayers can see the future, and Odin walks amongst them in the guise of a mortal. Ragnar is, however, an exception, for when they encounter the Saxons, he takes an interest in Christianity. Athelstan (George Blagden), a captured monk from Lindisfarne, becomes his friend. Indeed, while Athelstan starts to doubt his religion, Ragnar becomes more open to it. Ecbert (Linus Roache), the King of Wessex, seeks Ragnar as a possible ally and aspires to convert him. In truth, once the Vikings settled in England, their leaders did convert to Christianity. King Cnut, for example, even made a pilgrimage to Rome in 1027 (Trow, 2005). For the Viking leaders, the attraction of Christianity was most likely practical. It helped them to rule the conquered Saxons and was hierarchical, concentrating power in the king and lords. In contrast, Viking religions – as epitomised by Floki in this series – were highly individualistic (Williams, 2017).

After Ragnar is killed by King Aella, the series focussed more on his sons. While they are successful in capturing York, their sibling feuding – fuelled by poisonous infighting amongst other Viking lords – leads to their failure to conquer England. The youngest is Ivar the Boneless (Alex Høgh Andersen), who, while having the cunning of his father, is portrayed as paranoid, bloodthirsty and mentally unstable. Paralleling the destructive fighting between the brothers, a settlement on Iceland led by Floki descends into hateful vendettas. Somewhat like its progenitor *Game of Thrones*, there were difficulties in bringing the series to a worthy conclusion. Nonetheless, it was highly popular and reinforced many of the key cinematic conventions regarding the Vikings, while also continuing the move towards a more rounded picture of their culture.

Medieval York, Jorvik and the commodification of the Vikings

A number of places have developed heritage tourism based on their Viking past. In the second part of this chapter, we focus on the English city of York, which is probably the most successful of these. In York, tourism has always been heavily focussed on the medieval period, with attractions in the cathedral, city walls, castle motte, various urban buildings and the iconic laneway known as the Shambles. In recent decades, however, the focus of tourism has diversified from the later medieval period to incorporate the short period of just under a hundred years in which York was ruled by the Vikings. This began in 866 when the city was captured by Ivar the Boneless, seeking revenge for the killing of his father Ragnar Lothbrok; events covered in the fictionalized novel *The Last Kingdom*

(Cornwell, 2004) and television drama *Vikings* discussed earlier in this chapter.

The catalyst for Viking tourism at York was an archaeological dig conducted between 1976 and 1981 at a former industrial site in the area known as Coppergate. The site was due to be redeveloped as a shopping centre, but the richness of finds from the Viking period opened up the possibility of some sort of cultural heritage display being incorporated in the project. What eventually opened in 1984 went well beyond this original conception, with the Jorvik Viking Centre being sited underneath the shops in a busy part of York. In their rationale for developing the Jorvik Centre, the York Archaeological Trust explained how they were influenced by both cinema and the possibilities of doing something different:

> Many ideas were floated around but one thing was clear, they wanted to create a heritage experience as unique as the artefacts that would be on show and as exciting as the period it would be showcasing. The result was a historic attraction that was more like a film set than a museum. Instead of walking around looking at exhibits, the visitor would sit in specially designed time-cars, and move around the 'set' of a Viking village, taking it in from all angles, and witnessing Viking life up-close.
>
> (York Archaeological Trust, 2018a)

The approach taken at Jorvik was very different to the more commonly used *living history* mode of presenting and interpreting cultural heritage for visitors. Living history was developed as an alternative to what was seen as the inflexibility and stuffiness of conventional museum displays. Instead, living history focussed on outdoor museums – usually representing historical villages – in which heritage was demonstrated by having costumed actors or volunteers play the roles of people from the past and engage in everyday activities. Interestingly, living history at outdoor museums originated in Scandinavia. The first instance was the 1873 establishment of the Museum of Scandinavian Folklore in Sweden (now the Nordic Museum). This was followed by the Skansen Museum in 1891 and similar operations in Norway and Denmark (Timothy and Boyd, 2003). Other countries around the world followed, and living history was further manifested through events re-enacting historical episodes such as battles. In line with these trends in museology, the decision was made to create Jorvik as an indoor museum – somewhat suggestive of the dark or closed rides in theme parks – in which visitors were conveyed past a range of recreated scenes. As noted earlier, this indoor re-creation was conceptualised in terms of being similar to a film production.

Furthermore, the York Archaeological Trust aimed for a strong sense of authenticity through the placement of the Jorvik Viking Centre on the site – and at the actual historic ground level – of the archaeological dig. A 2001 redevelopment of the centre continued the concept of mediatised time travel through fixed-rail autonomous vehicles:

> Guided by TV historian, Michael Wood, visitors to JORVIK journeyed past the home of the antler worker, the blacksmith, the wood turner, the home and

workshop of the butcher and finally arrived at Coppergate, a market street with the stalls of a leather worker and a moneyer. For the first time, Jorvik was populated by animatronic Vikings, which gave visitors a sense of the activity in the 10th-century city. Away from the hustle and bustle of Coppergate, the time travellers turned the corner to where a house was being repaired for fire damage, in the exact spot that it burned down more than 1,000 years ago.

(York Archaeological Trust, 2018a)

This use of animatronics has led to researchers debating the level of authenticity at Jorvik and its effect on visitor satisfaction (D'Arcens, 2011; Halewood and Hannam, 2001; Meethan, 1996; Voase, 1999). Such debates are common in regard to many heritage attractions, including a number of those associated with the medieval period. A particular issue for the representation of Viking heritage at places like Jorvik is that the visitors' expectations are strongly shaped by the larger-than-life imagery of the Vikings which have been created through media productions, such as those discussed earlier in the chapter. A major part of that imagery is that Vikings are violent, loud and large. Following popular imagery opens up heritage attractions to the charge that they are pandering to broad and possibly inauthentic tastes. To represent the Vikings otherwise is to potentially disappoint visitors, given that Jorvik is a tableau of the everyday lives of the populace during Viking times, not its warriors. It is indicative, however, of a greater emphasis on social history by medieval scholars and aligns with the most recent representations of the Vikings in popular media (Figure 9.1).

Figure 9.1 Animatronics Used at Jorvik to Represent the Everyday Life of Artisans.
Source: Jennifer Frost.

Figure 9.2 Billboard for New Exhibition at Jorvik.
Source: Jennifer Frost.

In 2010, Jorvik placed a greater emphasis on the archaeological dig, and this was continued with a 2017 redevelopment after the site was closed due to severe floods (Figure 9.2). The backdrop was increasing public interest in archaeology, fuelled in part by the television series *Time Team* (1994–2014). This redevelopment reorientated the centre so that visitors started with the story of the dig:

> At JORVIK Viking Centre you are standing on the site which revealed some of the most famous and astounding discoveries in modern archaeology, so, it is fitting that your first experience at JORVIK is an exploration of the Coppergate dig, with a fully immersive display taking you back to the 1970s. Here you will hear the stories of the archaeologists who were involved in this revolutionary excavation and helped piece together the story of the Vikings of Jorvik, where they came from, how they lived, died and where they travelled to.
>
> (York Archaeological Trust, 2018a)

This was the situation when we conducted fieldwork at York in 2017. Jorvik was a highly visible and major part of York's heritage tourism offering. Complementing its role as a museum, a range of Viking and medieval-themed activations has been developed, including buskers and events (Meethan, 1996). Of particular note are a range of ghost tours, arguably the most of any town in England (Hanks, 2015: 64–69) and the annual Viking Festival. The latter includes a march of costumed Viking warriors through the city streets, a re-enactment of the 1043 battle between

Vikings and Saxons and a night-time burning of a Viking longboat (Meethan, 1996; York Archaeological Trust, 2018b). During our fieldwork in the summer of 2017, a large open-air night market drew on Vikings and the medieval period for its themes and ambience.

Viking events have become popular at a range of places with Viking heritage, including Scandinavia and Germany (Hannam and Halewood, 2006) and the Shetland Islands (Callahan, 1998; Finkel, 2010). Sometimes promoted as authentic and having a long history, these events are actually modern and may be seen as examples of the 'invention of tradition' (Hobsbawm, 1983). It is notable that the annual festivals at York and in the Shetland Islands culminate in the spectacular night-time burning of a Viking funerary longboat, a finale very much based on modern media productions. The other major feature of these events is that participants dress in Viking costume. This is an example of both 'serious leisure' and participation in exclusive 'social worlds', in which status and cultural capital may be gained by the perceived authenticity and quality of replica clothing and accoutrements (Frost and Laing, 2013).

The evolution of Viking heritage tourism in York has raised the issue of the commodification of the past. Researchers have focussed on the economic impact of tourism, the growth of shops targeted at tourists, the role of strategic partnerships and the problems of displacement and exclusion (Augustyn and Knowles, 2000; Halewood and Hannam, 2001; Meethan, 1996; Mordue, 2005; Snaith and Haley, 1999; Voase, 1999). It is notable that much of this research was centred on the turn of the last century, a period in which traditional industries had recently departed the city core and tourism had rapidly expanded in its place. In facing such challenges, York was similar to many other cities and towns throughout England and Europe. As Meethan argued:

> York can be seen as a microcosm of recent changes in the urban environment … in which the processes of history are commodified and organized as narratives of objects and spaces for leisure consumption … a reflection of national trends, in particular the growth of heritage as entertainment, spectacle and mass consumption.
>
> (1996: 336)

Recent years have seen the development of niche heritage consumption and commodification in York. While the medieval Shambles has become the centre of Harry Potter-themed retailing – due to its resemblance to Diagon Alley (Figure 9.3) – other retailers have focussed more strongly on Viking iconography. The documentary *Britain's Most Historic Towns: Viking York* (2018) highlighted that the city was attracting people immersed in alternative sub-cultures, who drew on media representations of Viking heritage for developing a modern culture, including Viking-inspired hairstyles, beards, tattoos, clothing and music. With the embrace of this alternative vision of Viking heritage, it is noticeable that women were also attracted, a divergence from the common view that enacting Viking heritage is typically both male-dominated and overtly 'macho' (Finkel,

Figure 9.3 York's Medieval Shambles Reimagined as Diagon Alley with Harry Potter-Themed Shops.

Source: Jennifer Frost.

2010). The 2019 Jorvik Viking Festival was sponsored by a clothing company called Descended from Odin, whose website featured a range called the Ragnar Saga, which drew on the television series *Vikings* and included apparel named after that show's characters in Ragnar, Lagertha and Bjorn. Under the heading 'We Are Descended from Odin', its website explains that this is:

> A sustainable clothing company for wanderers and warriors, based in the heart of the former Viking occupied England. Our mission is to tell the story of the germanic & norse peoples & gods and to educate on the impact of the viking age on world history.
>
> (Descended from Odin, 2018, capitalization unchanged)

Furthermore, to emphasise the importance of corporate social responsibility, the company's website continues:

> [Ten per cent] of our profits from all our sales go to environmental charities to honour the earth, our ancestors and the gods. Our connection to the natural world and each other gives us our strength, for the earth is fertilised with our blood.
>
> (Descended from Odin, 2018)

Conclusion

In the twentieth century, a popular imaginary was firmly established of the Vikings as bloodthirsty raiders. While questioned in Scandinavia, one-dimensional Hollywood depictions were highly influential in Britain and the USA (Halewood and Hannam, 2001; Williams, 2017). In the twenty-first century, that picture has changed, and there is wider acceptance of a complex and more nuanced history. A major factor in this change has been the television series *Vikings* (2013–2021) and *The Last Kingdom* (2015 onwards). With high cinema-quality production standards and complex plots and characters, these series drew viewers into an historical world that was previously little known and understood. The Vikings were still warriors, but they were also settlers, traders and artisans. As King Angantyr (Markjan Winnick) explained in a 2019 episode of *Vikings*, 'we are hard-working and prosperous people. In the past you have mistaken us for savages'. In addition to depicting the Vikings in a broader way, both series also firmly placed them within English history, linking them with King Alfred (see Chapter 3). This was a narrative that had perhaps previously not been widely known and only sketchily understood. In line with the school curriculum when we were younger, English history was normally depicted as only beginning in 1066.

The recent tourism developments at York are indicative of how perceptions of the medieval world are still constantly evolving. The long-term success of Jorvik

Figure 9.4 Viking Clothing and Handicrafts Sold at the Shield Maiden Shop, Glastonbury.
Source: Jennifer Frost.

Viking Centre has branded the city as a destination rich in Viking heritage. What we are seeing now is the growth of new variations of Viking imaginings, built on Jorvik and tourism, but also crafting a new and alternative imagery. Aligning with modern trends in youth culture, York is developing what we might call a 'New Age' take on its heritage; which is also visible in other tourist towns such as Glastonbury (Figure 9.4). This has resulted in an emphasis on artisanal products (particularly jewellery), handmade clothing, music, beer, hairstyles and tattoos. All of these may be viewed as heritage products reimagined for modern tastes. While much of this may be drawing on the recent popular television series *Vikings* and *The Last Kingdom*, this focus on Viking culture and lifestyle has dramatically changed the lens through which this medieval period is viewed.

References

Aberth, J. (2003) *A knight at the movies: Medieval history on film*, London and New York: Routledge.

Augustyn, M. and Knowles, T. (2000) 'Performance of tourism partnerships: A focus on York', *Tourism Management*, *21*(4), 341–351.

Callahan, R. (1998) 'Ethnic politics and tourism: A British case study', *Annals of Tourism Research*, *25*(4), 818–836.

Collins, P. (2013) *The birth of the West: Rome, Germany, France, and the creation of Europe in the tenth century*, New York: Public Affairs.

Cornwell, B. (2004) *The last kingdom*, London: Harper Collins.

Cornwell, B. (2007) *Sword song*, London: Harper Collins.

D'Arcens, L. (2011) 'Laughing in the face of the past: Satire and nostalgia in medieval heritage tourism', *Postmedieval*, *2*, 155–170.

Davis, S. (1985) *Hammer of the gods: The Led Zeppelin saga*, New York: Boulevard, 1987 reprint.

Descended from Odin (2018) *Descended from Odin*, https://descendedfromodin.co.uk/ (accessed January 2, 2019).

Eco, U. (1986) *Faith in fakes*, London: Seeker & Warburg.

Finkel, R. (2010) '"Dancing around the ring of fire": Social capital, tourism resistance and gender dichotomies at Up Helly Aa in Lerwick, Shetland', *Event Management*, *14*(4), 275–285.

Follett, K. (2020) *The evening and the morning*, London: Macmillan.

Frost, W. and Laing, J. (2013) *Commemorative events: Identity, memory, conflict*, London and New York: Routledge.

Halewood, C. and Hannam, K. (2001) 'Viking heritage tourism: Authenticity and commodification', *Annals of Tourism Research*, *28*(3), 565–580.

Hanks, M. (2015) *Haunted heritage: The cultural politics of ghost tourism, populism, and the past*, Walnut Creek, CA: Left Coast Press.

Hannam, K. and Halewood, C. (2006) 'European Viking themed festivals: An expression of identity', *Journal of Heritage Tourism*, *1*(1), 17–31.

Hobsbawm, E. (1983) 'Introduction: Inventing tradition', in E. Hobsbawm and T. Ranger (Eds.), *The invention of tradition* (pp. 1–14), Cambridge: Cambridge University Press.

Laing, J. and Frost, W. (2014) *Explorer travellers and adventure tourism*, Bristol: Channel View.

Lunde, A. (2010) *Nordic exposures: Scandinavian identities in classical Hollywood cinema*, Seattle and London: University of Washington Press.

Meethan, K. (1996) 'Consuming (in) the civilized city', *Annals of Tourism Research*, *23*(2), 322–340.

Mordue, T. (2005) 'Tourism, performance and social exclusion in "Olde York"', *Annals of Tourism Research*, *32*(1), 179–198.

Richards, J. (2008) 'Robin Hood, King Arthur and Cold War Chivalry', in H. Phillips (Ed.), *Bandit territories: British outlaws and their traditions* (pp. 167–195), Cardiff: University of Wales Press.

Sharpe, A. and Kuchta. S. (2007) 'Rediscovering Vinland', *The Pre-Raphaelite Society Newsletter of the United States*, *17*, pp. 1–2.

Snaith, T. and Haley, A. (1999) Residents' opinions of tourism developments in the historic city of York, England, *Tourism Management*, *20*(5), 595–603.

Trow, M. (2005) *Cnut: Emperor of the North*, Stroud, UK: Sutton.

Timothy, D. and Boyd, S. (2003) *Heritage tourism*, Harlow UK: Prentice Hall.

Voase, R. (1999) 'Consuming tourist sites/sights: A note on York', *Leisure Studies*, *18*(4), 289–296.

Williams, T. (2017) *Viking Britain: A history*, London: William Collins.

Wren, P.C. (1924) *Beau Geste*, London: John Murray.

York Archaeological Trust (2018a) *Jorvik story*, https://www.jorvikvikingcentre.co.uk/about/jorvik-story/#DmDqAddXswaXtDLD.97 (accessed January 2, 2019).

York Archaeological Trust (2018b) *Jorvik Viking Festival*, https://www.jorvikvikingfestival.co.uk/about/ (accessed January 2, 2019).

10 Encounters with the 'Other'

Crusaders and Muslims in medieval narratives

Medieval Córdoba

The medieval Mosque-Cathedral of Córdoba in Spain attracts approximately one million visitors per year. As its very distinctive – seemingly contradictory – name suggests, this is a structure that is both an Islamic mosque and a Christian cathedral. To be more accurate, it is a mosque *within* a cathedral. In its origins and evolution, the Mosque-Cathedral highlights the history of Córdoba and Spain as the frontier between Christianity and Islam for much of the medieval period, and it is the juxtaposition of these two cultures that attracts tourists to this city.

In the eighth century, the Islamic Umayyad Caliphate defeated the Visigothic Kingdom in Spain and gained control of much of the Iberian Peninsula. The Muslims became known to the Europeans as Moors, their state was Al Andalus and Córdoba its capital. Late in the ninth century, the mosque was built, with further expansions throughout the tenth century bringing it to its current state. Much of the mosque, including its most famous feature of 856 decorated columns (Figure 10.1), was built using material from Roman buildings within the city. In 1236, Córdoba was captured by King Ferdinand III of Castile as part of the Spanish *Reconquista* that would finally extinguish Moorish rule in Spain by the fifteenth century. King Ferdinand converted the mosque into a church and began the process of additions that would gradually encase the mosque within the cathedral.

As Monteiro argues, this site stands in contrast to many of the typical cathedrals of Western Europe (see Chapter 7) in that it evolved over time rather than being purpose-built to a specific and comprehensive design. As she describes it:

> the space appears non-hierarchical, lacking a clear itinerary for visitors. Freely wandering around the space, a visitor might encounter the Catholic chapels that have been built into the sides of the structure, the original [Islamic] mihrab, an ornate archway [which] … provides the directional focus for prayers, … a large hole in the floor, which reveals the excavated remains of the Visigothic cathedral that once stood on the site … a dizzying array of detailed Moorish decorations … [or] the portion built in the sixteenth century specifically for Catholic worship.
>
> (Monteiro, 2011: 317–318)

Figure 10.1 The Columns of the Mosque-Cathedral of Córdoba.
Source: Jennifer Frost.

Not surprisingly, given its history, the Mosque-Cathedral is a contested space. At times, there have been attempts to reclaim it as Islamic heritage, and these have led, in turn, to counter-claims. In 2010, for example, a group of Muslims knelt in front of the *mihrab* and began to pray. The police were called and the group removed, with six charged with crimes against public order and two jailed. In the face of such attempts, the Catholic Church has consistently argued that this is a consecrated Christian church which is still in use by the local community and accordingly, no non-Christian religious practices are allowed (Monteiro, 2011).

The reverse situation to this occurred in the case of Hagia Sophia in Istanbul, Turkey. Built by the Emperor Justinian between 532 and 537, it represented the pinnacle of Byzantine culture and reminds us that even during the period conventionally characterised as the Dark Ages, European culture continued to flourish in the Eastern Roman Empire. With the conquest of Constantinople in 1453 by the Muslim Ottoman Turks, the city was renamed Istanbul and the cathedral of Hagia Sophia (Holy Wisdom) was converted into a mosque. With the decline of the Ottoman Empire in the late nineteenth century, a movement began amongst Westerners to reclaim Hagia Sophia and reconsecrate it as a Christian church. This almost happened with British occupation at the end of World War I, and pressure continued with the establishment of a Turkish Republic. In 1935, President Mustafa Kemal Atatürk defused the situation by disestablishing it as a mosque and turning the building into a historical museum (Goldstein, 2011). It is in this form that arguably the greatest building of the early medieval period continues to operate as a tourist attraction.

These two instances highlight how conflicts rooted in medieval history are still very much alive today and continue to influence how heritage is perceived and operated through heritage attractions. They also demonstrate that while the medieval is conventionally defined in Western European terms, encounters and conflict with other cultures are also part of the story. This chapter particularly focusses on medieval interactions between Christian Europe and the Muslim world, both through the Crusades to the Middle East and with the Moors of Spain. Conventionally, Western media narratives depict these Muslim societies as a hostile Other, though at times there is a theme of portraying some of them in a more positive light. Such dual representations are particularly apparent in films, in instances as diverse as *The Crusades* (1935), *King Richard and the Crusaders* (1954), *El Cid* (1961) and *Kingdom of Heaven* (2005), with much attention devoted to portraying the twelfth-century Sultan Saladin as highly chivalrous. We also examine the representation of Westerners as the savage Other, through consideration of the invading Teutonic Knights in *Alexander Nevsky* (1938) and the Scottish experience of English invasion in *Braveheart* (1995). The final part of this chapter focuses on heritage tourism related to medieval Muslim–European interactions in two cities: Córdoba, and Palermo in Sicily.

The Crusades

The Crusades (1095–1221) refer to a series of military campaigns by various combinations of Western European armies to reconquer and establish Christian states in the Holy Land. Their genesis came from a call for help by the Byzantine Emperor Alexius I, who was seeking assistance to fight off Muslim expansion in Anatolia. The emperor was probably hoping to recruit a few bands of knights who would enter his service. Instead, his call was taken up by Pope Urban II, who urged Western princes to cease their infighting and redirect their military resources towards taking Jerusalem. The resultant multinational First Crusade succeeded in this goal in 1099, establishing a series of crusader states in the Middle East. Increasing pressure from Muslim forces led to a Second Crusade (1146–1148). A massive defeat of the crusader army by Saladin at Hattin (1187) led to the Third Crusade (1187–1197) which temporarily regained most of the lost ground. This was the crusaders' last major success. The Fourth Crusade (1198–1204) was subverted into an attack on the Byzantines and led to the sack of Constantinople. The Fifth Crusade (1217–1221) was directed at Egypt without success. The crusader states held on along the coast, but 1291 saw the fall of their last stronghold in Acre. While further crusades were contemplated from time to time, they came to nothing. The Ottoman Turks spread into Eastern Europe in the fourteenth century and captured Constantinople in 1453, ending the Byzantine Empire.

The preceding provides a basic history of the Crusades, but it is important to recognise their complexity and the multiple interpretations attached to them. Until late in the twentieth century, the Crusades were often presented in heroic terms, with a strong emphasis on kings, lords and knights engaged in epic conflicts. Well-known examples of these 'classic' narratives include the trilogies of Norwich (1988–1991) and Runciman (1951–1954). In more recent times, such interpretations have increasingly been seen as no longer tenable, not only for the Crusades, but for the medieval period in general. Modern scholarship tends towards social history, with far greater interest in those voices that have previously been overlooked. Accordingly, recent studies of the Crusades have focussed on the peasantry, women, religious orders, minority ethnic groups and the peoples who lived in the lands that the crusaders moved through or invaded (see for example Lock, 2006; Nicholson, 2005; Wickham, 2017). An increasingly strong body of work has considered the Crusades from Muslim perspectives (see Maalouf, 1984). This critical approach to the Crusades is greatly influenced by current events in the Middle East, including the Gulf Wars, hawkish American foreign policy, the Israel–Palestine question, the Arab Spring, the Syrian conflict, the Islamic State and the ongoing instability of the region. All of this sets up potential disconnections between current medieval historiography and popular Western views of the Crusades, particularly as they are expressed and reinforced through the media.

Media representation of the Crusades

Only a small number of films deal directly with the Crusades. This is most likely due to the difficulty of effectively representing landscapes that look authentically Middle Eastern. For film-makers required to stick to a budget, most medieval landscapes were simply shot in rural parts of California or England, which worked well as they were pleasantly green, idyllic and pre-modern. More arid environments tested logistics and budgets. The solution was often to suggest the Crusades, including them in a storyline that was still firmly placed in Western Europe. The common trope was of a returning crusader, a plot device directly borrowed from Sir Walter Scott's novel *Ivanhoe* (1819). In *Robin Hood* (1922), Locksley sets out for the Crusades full of martial ardour and jingoistic bombast. However, he does not get far before he has to return home to deal with issues there, becoming the eponymous outlaw. This decision to abandon the Crusade may be interpreted as suggesting the desirability of American non-involvement in World War I and the League of Nations. In *The Adventures of Robin Hood* (1938), Robin chides King Richard for gallivanting off overseas when there are problems at home that need the king's attention. In *Ivanhoe* (1952), there are a number of references to a tournament in Jerusalem in which Sir Brian was defeated by Sir Ivanhoe, and even though they are now back in England, he still thirsts for revenge. *The Seventh Seal* (1957) similarly features returning Swedish crusaders who are disillusioned and accordingly questioning their faith. *Robin Hood: Prince of Thieves* (1991) begins in a Jerusalem prison cell, from which Robin escapes and heads home. *Robin and Marian* (1976) and *Robin Hood* (2010) both commence with a world-weary hero returning from the Crusades, disillusioned by King Richard's actions in massacring prisoners after the capture of Acre in 1191. These conventions also appear in other forms of media. In *The Pillars of the Earth* (Follett, 1989), Earl Richard is accused of murder by his rival, Sir William. To avoid possible execution, Richard is convinced to undertake penance through joining a Crusade. For Richard, this is an ideal solution. He is bored by being an administrator and the Crusade offers the opportunity for fighting and adventure.

Faced with the logistics and costs of representing the spectacle of crusader military campaigns, only a few big-budget films have taken on the challenge. Three major film productions – *The Crusades* (1935), *El Cid* (1961) and *The Kingdom of Heaven* (2005) – are considered. In addition, we consider two recent efforts that covered the crusades in part, in the television series *Knightfall* (2017–2019) and the film *Robin Hood* (2018).

The Crusades (1935)

This expensive Cecil B. DeMille production was intended to appeal to conservative Christian markets in the USA. There was, however, a problem. If the Crusades were to be presented as a worthy religious undertaking, how could their ultimate failure be explained? DeMille's solution was to focus on how treachery and infighting amongst the crusaders worked against their success. Accordingly, he juxtaposes the clean-cut King Richard (Henry Wilcoxon) and the pure Berengaria (Loretta Young) against two oily and scheming villains who sabotage the Crusades in Conrad of Montferrat and King Philip II of France. To reinforce their dark natures, DeMille cast in these roles two character actors well-known for playing foreign malefactors, Joseph Schildkraut and C. Henry Gordon.

This historical epic illustrates a common cinema 'technique of compressing history' (Eyman, 2010: 316). The film is meant to cover the Third Crusade, but also includes the story of Peter the Hermit (former English cricketer C. Aubrey Smith) preaching a holy war amongst the masses, which occurred with the First Crusade. In addition, DeMille draws on literary sources, especially the novel *The Talisman* (Scott, 1825), for parts of the plot. As with many productions of the time, there was no thought of filming on location. Instead, the Paramount Ranch in California stood in as Palestine.

In the early scenes, 'Richard is played as a stalwart Robin Hood surrounded by Merry Men' (Eyman, 2010: 317). This part of the storyline seems heavily influenced by Douglas Fairbanks's *Robin Hood* (1922), and this is reinforced by having Alan Hale (Little John in the earlier film) playing Richard's drinking buddy in Blondel. When working on movies, DeMille commonly watched other films of the same genre with a view to picking up ideas. During the filming of *The Crusades*, he watched *Robin Hood* twice, so it is not surprising that there are such parallels between the heroes of both films (Eyman, 2010). When attempts are made to arrange a strategic marriage with Alice, the sister of King Philip of France, Richard wants no part of it. Accordingly, he chooses to go on the Crusades rather than get married. Such a representation highlights the long-standing debate over King Richard's sexuality and tries to interpret it for early twentieth-century audiences. As Stock argued:

In portraying Richard's character and his imputed sexual orientation, DeMille has it both ways. In the first third to half of the film, Richard's behaviour creates the impression that he finds women abhorrent, greatly prefers the company of men, and will do anything to extricate himself from an arranged engagement to Princess Alice of France ... in the second half of the film, DeMille hetero-normalizes Richard by romanticizing his union with Berengaria well beyond the historical reality of their practically sham marriage.

(2009: 65)

Opposing the crusaders is the Muslim leader Saladin (played by American actor Ian Keith in politically incorrect dark makeup). While far more cultured and sophisticated than Richard, Saladin is equally bent on war. His representation is very much based on that of Sir Walter Scott in *The Talisman*, which had been highly influential in creating a nineteenth-century image of Saladin as a chivalrous and virtuous hero. In the end, both Richard and Saladin undergo transformations, becoming more like their historical images. Berengaria is the catalyst for these changes, brokering a peace deal and leading these two characters to their historic destiny. At this time, DeMille was a strong supporter of the USA remaining neutral and not being involved in European affairs. Accordingly, his aim was to promote a message that peace was achievable, even between powers that were seemingly strongly opposed and intractable (Aberth, 2003).

El Cid (1961)

The medieval conflict between Christians and Muslims in Spain is often thought of in terms of it being a crusade, though it was technically quite separate from the series of expeditions to the Middle East described earlier. Indeed, the action in this film takes place just before Pope Urban II issued his call for a holy war in 1096. Nonetheless, what occurred in Spain has many similarities with the Crusades in being a bloody frontier on the edges of Europe.

In this big-budget epic, Charlton Heston played the title role of eleventh-century Spanish noble Rodrigo Diaz de Vivar, who becomes known as El Cid, after the Arabic term 'El Sayad', which means leader. The production spearheaded a new trend in the 1960s, being filmed on location in Spain, rather than on sets in Hollywood. Through the film was made in Spain, there were immense financial advantages in government support, including the use of soldiers as extras. The Spanish dictator, General Francisco Franco, was a major supporter of the project, as it allowed his regime to associate itself with the legendary Spanish hero. The story of El Cid had become popular in Spain at the beginning of the twentieth century. He was promoted as the Spanish equivalent to King Arthur, particularly during the burst of nationalism that occurred following defeat in the Spanish-American War of 1898, which had stripped Spain of colonial possessions like Cuba and the Philippines (Aberth, 2003). This focus on El Cid as Spain's legendary saviour aligns with the medieval period being a Golden Age in which a country's national identity was forged (Eco, 1986).

Shooting in Spain provided authenticity in the landscapes used, particularly through the filming of actual medieval towns and castles. Most notably, to represent the siege of Valencia, the nearby coastal town of Peñiscola was made available by the Spanish government. As Heston commented:

> Peñiscola was crucial to *El Cid*. It doubled for Valencia in the film because it was the only walled city in Spain … that hadn't yet extended outside the stone walls its medieval defenders built to protect it. The real Valencia is a modern city, looking not at all as it had in the eleventh century. Peñiscola did.
>
> (Heston, 1995: 253)

As with a number of films about the Crusades, there is a strong focus on how in-fighting and treachery weakens the Spanish effort to drive the Muslims out of Spain. The royal family is shown as wracked by sibling rivalry, leading the people of Valencia to offer the throne to El Cid. Conscious of the need for unity, he refuses to overthrow the ruling family, and the theme of noble sacrifice and loyalty runs throughout the film. As Heston summarised the character he played:

> Even if we strip away a thousand years of mythic excess, history still gives us a battered, striving man, stubbornly loyal to the king who exiled him and imprisoned his wife and daughters. I came to see Rodrigo as a biblical Job figure, defiant and enduring.
>
> (Heston, 1995: 242)

In this sense, *El Cid* is a throwback to the chivalric cycle of Hollywood films of the 1950s, and Heston's hero is perhaps not as complex and morally ambivalent as in his other historical epics later in the 1960s.

Once again, the chief Islamic protagonists are played by Western actors with skin darkened with makeup. The Muslim leader Ibn Yusuf is played as a cartoon villain by Herbert Lom. Curiously, Lom was a Jew who had fled Czechoslovakia after it was invaded by the Nazis. He specialised in playing the outsider in a long career. The other key Muslim leaders were played with greater subtlety by Australian Frank Thring and English actor Douglas Wilmer. Their roles required the representation of shifting alliances between the Spanish and the Muslims. When banished by the king, El Cid takes service with one of these Muslim rulers and at other times he has Muslim allies in the battle with Ibn Yusuf for Valencia. These complexities are historically correct and are kept in the film's narrative to suggest that El Cid's role is to unify these disparate groups within a Spanish people. While Franco wanted to lay claim to such a concept, it was also applicable on a global scale, suggesting that unity behind the Americans was needed during the Cold War.

Kingdom of Heaven (2005)

In 1187, Saladin annihilated a crusader army at the Battle of Hattin. He then proceeded to lay siege to Jerusalem. After a spirited defence, the crusader commander Balian of Ibelin negotiated terms, which allowed most of the defenders safe passage. In Europe, the shock of the news of the crusader defeat led to the Third Crusade. This film accordingly considers a lesser-known section of crusading history, setting the scene for the much wider-known and often-filmed contest between Richard the Lionheart and Saladin. As with many historical epics, some parts adhere to the historical narrative and other parts are invented for cinematic effect. The latter fictions include Balian's humble origins and love interest. In turn, the Battle of Hattin, Saladin's treatment of prisoners and much of the siege follow the history books (Lindley, 2007). In addition, there are two particular areas in which the film successfully marries dramatic content and historical accuracy.

The first concerns the infighting between the crusaders. King Baldwin (Edward Norton) has brokered a peace treaty with Saladin. The king, however, is dying of leprosy. His likely replacement is his brother-in-law Guy (Martin Csorkas). Guy is against the desire for peace and believes that there should be no negotiations with the infidel. He is encouraged in this by Raynault, the flamboyant Head of the Knights Templar (Brendon Gleeson) and a host of visiting knights. Balian (Orlando Bloom) and Tiberius (Jeremy Irons) support the king's quest for a peaceful accommodation with Islam. When King Baldwin finally dies, Guy is crowned and immediately launches the ill-fated attack that results in the crusaders' defeat at Hattin.

The second focusses on the sympathetic treatment of Muslims through the film. Balian's estate includes peasants who are Muslim, Jewish and Christian and under his wise leadership, they co-exist peacefully. Balian spares the life of Imad (Alexander Siddig), who he thinks is a servant. Later, he finds out that Imad is a general. Balian and Imad represent the moderates seeking some form of resolution between the two warring sides. Later, Imad mediates between Balian and Saladin (Ghassan Massoud), brokering a deal whereby Jerusalem surrenders, but the inhabitants are able to depart unharmed. Unlike most of the films discussed in this chapter, the roles of the Muslims are played by Arabic actors, with Siddig born in Sudan and Massoud a Syrian. This provides the film with a greater verisimilitude and sense of realism (Lindley, 2007).

Saladin is the great Islamic hero of the Crusades. Victorious in battle at Hattin, he was able to reclaim Jerusalem. He then held that city in the face of the Third Crusade. In achieving this, he has become known throughout history as a medieval nation-building hero, comparable to an Alfred, Charlemagne or El Cid. Furthermore, he is commonly characterised as wise and chivalrous. As a recent Arab historian commented, he was:

> so different from the monarchs of his time, indeed of all times; he was able to remain humble with the humble, even after he had become the most powerful of the powerful. The chroniclers, of course, evoke his courage, his sense of justice, and his zeal for the *jihād*, but through their writings a more touching, more human, image always transpires.

> (Maalouf, 1984: 177–178)

However, what greatly distinguishes Saladin is that such a representation has been widely adopted in the West. The credit for this lies with Sir Walter Scott. As discussed earlier, his novel *The Talisman* (1825) constructed Saladin as a worthy adversary for the crusaders, being equal to – if not greater than – Richard the Lionheart. Later film-makers have drawn heavily on Scott for both the plot of *The Talisman* and for their portrait of Saladin. In the films of the twentieth century, he was played by aristocratic Western actors. These included Ian Keith in *The Crusades* (1935) and Rex Harrison in *King Richard and the Crusaders* (1954). It was only with *Kingdom of Heaven* that he was played by an Arabic actor, and the result was a more pragmatic and nuanced representation.

Knightfall (2017–2019)

Following on from the success of *Vikings* (see Chapter 9), the History Channel produced *Knightfall*. As with *Vikings*, this series weaves a rollicking action-packed story around some basic historical facts, though in this instance, the embroidery was even more pronounced. The core of the narrative is the 1307 destruction of the Knights Templar by King Philip IV of France. The Knights Templar had originally been established in the early twelfth century as a monastic military order to protect pilgrims and had its headquarters at the Temple Mount in Jerusalem. Over time, the Templars became increasingly wealthy and involved in money-lending, and King Philip took advantage of increasing criticism to dissolve the order and thereby cancel his debts. The arrests of the Templars took place on Friday the 13th of October in 1307, and it is popularly believed that this is the origin of Friday the 13th being an unlucky or cursed date.

The action in *Knightfall* starts in 1306 in France. Following the fall of Acre in 1291 – shown in flashbacks – the Templars have partly lost their way. They are still powerful and dream of a new Crusade, but without a presence in Palestine, their role has been eroded. The focus is on Landry (Tom Cullen), an accomplished knight who led the defence of Acre. Now, Landry has grown disillusioned and neglectful of his vows. He has an affair with Queen Joan (Olivia Ross) and this provides the motivation for King Philip (Ed Stoppard) seeking to kill Landry and destroy the Templars. The series is in many ways suggestive of *Star Wars*, with the Templars cast as the Jedi Knights, a once-important military order that has declined and lost relevancy in a changing world. King Philip, who seeks to increase his power and crush all opposition, may be seen as akin to *Star Wars*' Emperor Palpatine. Such connections are even stronger in the second series, in which Mark Hamill, the actor who played Luke Skywalker in the original *Star Wars* trilogy, stars as Talus, who trains the Templars.

Knightfall follows the strong convention in crusader narratives that the enemy is not so much Islam, but rather self-interest within the Christian ranks. Even though he is the Master of the Paris Temple, Landry is self-absorbed and dissolute. The initial role of protecting pilgrims has been lost. The Templars have become focussed on their internal rituals and protecting their accumulated treasure. This trope of the Templars as a powerful secret society flows through recent films focussed on the modern-day search for their legacy, such as *National Treasure* (2004) and *The Da Vinci Code* (2006). King Philip and other lords are presented as having no interest at all in the Crusades. Most powerfully, the series captures the sense that medieval society has lost its way in the fourteenth century. Faith is increasingly questioned as France is beset with disease, heresy, paganism and dissolute and sceptical rulers (Tuchman, 1978).

Robin Hood (2018)

This most recent version of the Robin Hood story follows the convention of the eponymous hero returning from the Crusades. In this case, however, there is a major scene detailing his experiences in Palestine. Robin (Taron Egerton) is part of a patrol into a war-devastated city that is ambushed by Arab troops. The scenes of street fighting with a barely seen enemy draw heavily on modern-day computer games and war films set during the Iraqi Wars. The Arabs are superior in ambush tactics and pick off the crusaders with bows and arrows. The crusaders, for their part, are restricted by the narrow streets and are unable to use mounted knights or even engage in swordplay. In a poorly conceived film, this section regarding the Crusades is probably the best executed.

The Muslim in the West

The latest *Robin Hood* also follows the convention of a lone Muslim journeying to England. Played by Jamie Foxx, he Anglicises his name to John, convinces Robin to become a thief and trains him in the Arab style of street fighting. His rationale is that if they can stop the Sheriff of Nottingham (Ben Mendelsohn) from collecting war taxes, then the crusaders will have to abandon their war. In one of many confusing scenes, the Sheriff warns that the enemy is infiltrating England and engaging in sabotage. Our heroes shake their heads in wonder at such ridiculous claims, and it is a scene that is clearly designed to evoke audience distaste with modern ideologues. However, in this case it is exactly true, for John is engaged in covert operations to destroy the war efforts.

There is a long history of the lone Muslim in cinema. In *The Black Knight* (1954), Sir Palamides (Peter Cushing in blackface) is a Saracen knight at the court of King Arthur (the Knights of the Round Table includes members from many lands). He plots with King Mark of Cornwall (Patrick Troughton) to launch a secret invasion, a common trope in many Cold War medieval movies (see Chapter 5). Adding to the mix is that King Mark is very strongly attracted to Palamides. For modern viewers, it is a strange pair of subversive villains, particularly as both actors would eventually play Doctor Who.

In *The Long Ships* (1964), West Indian actor Sidney Poitier played Aly Mansuh, a Moorish prince who has vowed to find the Lost Bell of Byzantium. He explains that it was made with stolen Saracen gold, and reclaiming it would give increased heart to Muslims to fight against the infidel. To help retrieve the bell, he captures a crew of Vikings. Rather than the cartoon villain of Palamides in *The Black Knight*, Aly Mansuh is portrayed as a complex character, worthy of respect and sympathy. *The 13th Warrior* (1999) took the idea of Arab–Viking interactions even further. Ibn Fahdlan (Spanish actor Antonio Banderas) has been sent on an embassy to the West. He is open and curious, eager to learn as much as he can, and he dreams of writing a book of his travels. He falls in with a group of Vikings in Russia, and gradually admiration and friendship grows. An additional example was Azeem (Morgan Freeman), Robin's Saracen companion in *Robin Hood: Prince of Thieves* (1991). He is portrayed as the epitome of loyalty and common sense, the most worthy of Robin's band.

Westerners as the savage Other

In most instances, the media portrays 'civilised' Western Europeans encountering 'savage' Others. In a small number of cases, however, these perspectives are reversed, and it is the West that is depicted as savage and predatory. Two examples of such revisionism are found in the films *Alexander Nevsky* (1938) and *Braveheart* (1995).

Alexander Nevsky is a Russian epic made during the lead-up to World War II. The eponymous hero is the Prince of Novgorod, who leads the opposition to an invading force of Teutonic Knights. This culminates in victory at the Battle on the Ice, which took place on Lake Peipus on the border of Estonia and Russia in 1242. Made during a period of heightening tension between Nazi Germany and the Soviet Union, the film contrasts a worthy and loyal Russian militia against their opponents in the Teutonic Knights. The latter are depicted as merciless, bloodthirsty and treacherous, clad in monstrous helmets and armour. They are also identified as crusaders bent on conquest and wear cloaks decorated with the crusader insignia of the Cross of St George. In the finale of the battle, the armoured Teutonic Knights fall through the ice and drown, representing that their defeat is due to a combined resistance from the Russian people and the landscape. While a spectacular set-piece, there is no historical evidence for this occurring, and it seems to have been an inspired invention of director Sergei Eisenstein (Ostrowski, 2006).

Braveheart tells the story of William Wallace, who leads the Scots to victory over an invading English army at the Battle of Stirling Bridge in 1297 and is later captured and executed in 1305. Played by Mel Gibson, Wallace is a loyal and heroic leader. Represented as somewhat like Robin Hood (see Chapter 8), Gibson's Wallace is initially reluctant to be involved in opposing the English and only takes up arms after his wife is killed. Outnumbered and lacking the armour of the English knights, the Scots are successful through clever ruses and their determination to defend their home soil from invasion. Leading the invasion of Scotland, Edward I (Patrick McGoohan) is depicted as ruthless and inhuman. The representation of his savagery is reinforced by his decision to treat Wallace as a traitor rather than as a foreign leader, ordering his execution through hanging, drawing and quartering.

Whereas *Alexander Nevsky* is specifically about resistance to a crusade, the invasion in *Braveheart* has no religious element. It is open to argument that Edward I and the English are little different from other cinematic villains seeking power, such as Prince John in the various Robin Hood movies. This may be further reinforced if we view Gibson's Wallace as a generic individualistic hero, fighting back against injustice. This character is common to many of Gibson's films and has universal appeal. There are, however, differences that distinguish *Braveheart* from other historical romances. Edward I is not attempting to usurp power, but rather to conquer another country. As a ruler of a major European state, he is attempting to extend his power by launching an invasion of a peripheral state. A century earlier, this could have been a crusade, but that option is no longer available. Instead, Plantagenet England seeks expansion in Scotland, Ireland and Wales – all regions in which Edward I was active. *Braveheart* constructs Edward I and his supporters as the savage, brutal and inhuman Other, disrupting the settled and relatively peaceful Scottish agrarian society. Over 20 years later, *The Outlaw King* (2018) functioned as a sort of sequel to *Braveheart*, focussing on further resistance under the Scottish king Robert the Bruce. Once again, the representation is of the English as barbaric invaders who are led by an unhinged king in Edward II, and who have set aside all concepts of chivalry.

Tourism on the Muslim–European frontier

The medieval conflict between Muslims and Christians continues to exercise a powerful fascination for tourists. In this section, we consider two examples of cities that were on the medieval Muslim-Christian frontier and as a result attract tourists. These are Córdoba in Spain and Palermo in Sicily. Both were capitals of frontier states, and both first changed hands through Islamic expansion and then were later reconquered by Christian forces. Interestingly, in both cases, tourists are drawn to World Heritage sites that are marked by spectacular architecture, art and design. These heritage gems arose as markers of status and power, being consciously and lavishly constructed to demonstrate the legitimacy and strength of the political states that existed along a shifting frontier zone.

As discussed at the beginning of this chapter, Córdoba was the capital of Islamic Al Andalus in Spain from the eighth through the thirteenth centuries, before being retaken as part of the Spanish *Reconquista*. Accordingly, the city developed as a hybrid of Western and Islamic cultural heritage, providing it with a highly distinctive image. Chief amongst its attractions is the Mosque-Cathedral. As local tourism authorities explained to Duarte Alonso (2015), this 'is the "axle" of the [city's] historic area; there are other historic sites with a significant cultural patrimony located around it, however it would be impossible for them to compete against the Cathedral-Mosque' (p. 27). Rather than competitors, these heritage sites exist in a complementary network, with the iconic Cathedral-Mosque as an anchor point from which tourists gravitate outwards. An alternative way of conceptualising this is to see the Cathedral-Mosque as the destination attraction, which provides the primary motivation for tourists to journey to Córdoba. In their journey through the city towards the Cathedral-Mosque, tourists then encounter other attractions and experiences. This was certainly our experience during fieldwork. As we walked from the railway station to the Cathedral-Mosque, we became immersed in the laneways and cafes of the historic city centre

Figure 10.2 Laneways of Córdoba.

Source: Jennifer Frost.

(Figure 10.2), meandering and taking hours. In this sense, how tourism plays out at Córdoba is very similar to that of other medieval cities throughout Europe.

While the Mosque-Cathedral has long been Córdoba's primary attraction, increasing tourism has led to a wider range of attractions and activities becoming part of the tourist experience. These include the laneways, courtyards, cafes, shops, art, music and festivals. In particular, the Festival de Patios has developed as a tourist-focussed celebration of the distinctive courtyards and laneways of the historic centre (Duarte Alonso, 2015; López-Guzmán and Santa-Cruz, 2017). Further diversification has arisen through the development of a distinctive gastronomic style drawing on the strong Moorish influences and resultant traditional dishes (Sánchez-Canizares and López-Guzmán, 2012).

The Arabs occupied Sicily for approximately 250 years between the ninth and eleventh centuries. They were ousted by a Norman force led by Robert Guiscard, who captured Palermo in 1072. This 'Norman Conquest' paralleled the one that had occurred in England six years earlier, and it is striking that neither invasion has been the subject of any films or television series. The Normans had come to southern Italy as mercenaries drawn to a fractured land and had rapidly built up their power. Most prominent were the sons of Tancred of Hautville, a minor lord on the Cherbourg Peninsula of Normandy. In a similar manner to the sons of Ragnar Lothbrok (see Chapter 9), these land-hungry brothers divided up their conquests, with Robert ruling Apulia – and attempting to conquer Byzantium – and Duke Roger taking charge of Sicily. Robert's son Bohemond would also be one of the four leaders of the First Crusade (Norwich, 2015).

Newly conquered Sicily was a multicultural mix of Arabs, the native Sicilians, who culturally identified as Greeks, and the Normans. To effectively rule this volatile society, the Normans practised tolerance and cultural accommodation. A resultant economic boom attracted traders and craftsmen, further broadening the cosmopolitan nature of Norman Sicily (Norwich, 2015). The richness of this culture was manifested in two magnificent church interiors; commissioned by the Norman rulers and executed by Arab and Greek craftsman skilled in the use of mosaics. The first of these was in the Arab citadel in Palermo, which was refashioned as a Norman palace. Here, the highlight for tourists is the Palatine Chapel (Figure 10.3). The second is the cathedral at Monreale, a short distance inland from Palermo (Figure 10.4). This was built in the late twelfth century by King William II, Roger's great-grandson. Locked in a dispute with the Bishop of Palermo, the king's solution was to create a new diocese beyond the city walls, which he endowed with a larger and grander cathedral, rich in mosaic interiors.

Whilst Hollywood has ignored the Normans in Sicily, travel documentary-makers have found them a rich subject. One worth considering is *Sicily Unpacked* (2012). This features two hosts with differing, though complementary, backgrounds: art historian Andrew Graham-Dixon and chef Giorgio Locatelli. In their previous series, they had focussed on mainland Italy, usually alternating discussions of food with art and architecture. In the case of Sicily, they examined different time periods, with the first episode centred on the medieval interactions between Arabs and Normans.

Figure 10.3 The Palatine Chapel, Palermo.
Source: Warwick Frost.

At Palermo, Graham-Dixon guided Locatelli around the Palatine Chapel. Presenting it as one of the great gems of medieval art, he explains how its development was rooted in the political needs of the Normans. It was commissioned in 1132 by King Roger II, Roger's son, who through an alliance with Pope Anacletus had been granted the Sicilian crown by papal authority. Constructing a magnificent chapel was strategic and affirmed his newly gained royal status, and the art in the chapel reflected his multicultural kingdom. The use of Byzantine mosaics boldly proclaimed that the Normans were the legitimate heirs to the Byzantines who once ruled Sicily. In addition, there were Islamic motifs in the interior decorations, reflecting that Sicily was a cultural melting pot with an important Arab population who were valued and protected (Laing and Frost, 2019).

Following on from this discussion of medieval art heritage, Locatelli hosted a segment examining medieval culinary heritage. He cooked *pasta con le sarde* (pasta with sardines), a dish particularly associated with Palermo. As he prepared the dish, Graham-Dixon asked questions, prompting the chef to explain further how Sicily has culturally diverged from mainland Italy. This is a dish, explained Locatelli, which was strongly influenced by Arab culture. It is accordingly unlike any other pasta dish in Italy and, 'that in the north, around Milan, we would never cook anything like this'. What differentiates pasta con le sarde is the pairing of seafood with sultanas. The inclusion of dried fruit in a savoury dish is common in the Arab world and completely unheard of in Italy. This iconic dish of Palermo, Locatelli concluded, epitomised the heritage of Sicily as being on

Figure 10.4 Monreale.

Source: Warwick Frost.

the Muslim-Christian frontier and reminded us that as well as conflict, there was cultural interaction and adaptation (Laing and Frost, 2019).

Conclusion

The release of *Kingdom of Heaven* in 2005 stimulated a great deal of heated discussion in regard to how the Crusades and historical conflicts between Muslims and Christians should be portrayed in cinema. Though the film's makers intended to provide a nuanced and more sympathetic view of the Islamic 'Other', they also wanted to show that both sides committed atrocities against non-combatants. The result was that the film received criticism on both counts (Lindley, 2007). Given the potential for the Crusades to provoke passionate reactions, it seems that film-makers may now steer well clear of this topic as a major theme. This is despite a wide range of successful films based on modern-day Islamic–Western conflicts, such as *The Hurt Locker* (2008) and *Argo* (2012). This is an unusual situation in that historical films may be seen as taboo, whereas contemporary versions are acceptable. Furthermore, the trend that has emerged has been to focus on the Crusades as a backstory, a conflict briefly represented, from whence the hero returns and which explains their issues and motivations, as in *Knightfall* and various Robin Hood productions.

In terms of heritage tourism, these conflicts underpin a range of attractions and destinations around the periphery of Western Europe. In Scotland, the success of

Braveheart stimulated a conventional brand of film-tourism, particularly attracting tourists to the National Wallace Monument at Stirling. This is, however, not the case with places associated with medieval Muslim-Christian conflicts in southern Europe. While Córdoba is a well-established heritage tourism destination and Palermo is an emerging one, their attraction is in the otherness of their art and architecture and how that has been influenced by their medieval periods of Muslim history. What is missing is any connection to film-tourism, for there have been no cinema productions exploring their history. It is an intriguing situation that while medieval Muslim-Christian conflicts are still highly important in the modern world, their very controversy seems to have militated against direct coverage in film and television dramatic productions in recent times.

References

Aberth, J. (2003) *A knight at the movies: Medieval history on film*, London and New York: Routledge.

Duarte Alonso, A. (2015) 'Far away from sun and beach: Opportunities and challenges for cultural tourism in Córdoba, Spain', *Journal of Heritage Tourism*, *10*(1), 21–37.

Eco, U. (1986) *Faith in fakes*, London: Secker & Warburg.

Eyman, S. (2010) *Empire of dreams: The epic life of Cecil B. DeMille*, New York: Simon & Schuster.

Follett, K. (1989) *The pillars of the Earth*, London: Pan, 2007 reprint.

Goldstein, E. (2011) 'Redeeming holy wisdom: Britain and St. Sophia', in M. Hall (Ed.), *Towards world heritage: International origins of the preservation movement 1870–1930* (pp. 45–62), Farnham, UK and Burlington, VT: Ashgate.

Heston, C. (1995) *In the Arena: The Autobiography*, London: Harper Collins.

Laing, J. and Frost, W. (2019) 'Gastronomic tourism and the media', in S. Dixit (Ed.), *The Routledge handbook of gastronomic tourism* (pp. 516–523), Abingdon, UK and New York: Routledge.

Lindley, A. (2007) 'Once, present and future kings: *Kingdom of Heaven* and the multi-temporality of medieval films', in L. Ramey and T. Pugh (Eds.), *Race, class and gender in 'medieval' films* (pp. 15–29), New York and Basingstoke: Palgrave Macmillan.

Lock, P. (Ed.) (2006) *The Routledge companion to the Crusades*, London: Routledge.

López-Guzmán, T. and Santa-Cruz, F. (2017) 'Visitors' experiences with intangible cultural heritage: A case study from Córdoba, Spain', *Journal of Heritage Tourism*, *12*(4), 410–415.

Maalouf, A. (1984) *The Crusades through Arab eyes*, New York: Schocken.

Monteiro, L. (2011) 'The mezquita of Córdoba is made of more than bricks: Towards a broader definition of the "heritage" protected at UNESCO World Heritage Sites', *Archaeologies*, *7*(2), 312–328.

Nicholson, H. (Ed.), (2005) *Palgrave advances in the Crusades*, Basingstoke, UK: Palgrave Macmillan.

Norwich, J.J. (1988–1991) *Byzantium, 3 volumes*, London: Viking.

Norwich, J.J. (2015) *Sicily: A short history from the ancient Greeks to the Cosa Nostra*, London: John Murray.

Ostrowski, D. (2006) 'Alexander Nevskii's 'battle on the ice': The creation of a legend', *Russian History*, *33*(2–4): 289–312.

Runciman, S. (1951–1954) *A history of the Crusades*, 3 volumes, London: Penguin, 1991 reprint.

Sánchez-Canizares, S. and López-Guzmán, T. (2012) 'Gastronomy as a tourism resource: Profile of the culinary tourist', *Current Issues in Tourism*, *15*(3), 229–245.

Scott, W. (1819) *Ivanhoe*, London: Dent, 1965 reprint.

Scott, W. (1825) *The talisman*, Project Gutenberg reprint 2009, http://www.gutenberg.org/files/1377/1377-h/1377-h.htm, (accessed November 15, 2020).

Stock, L. (2009) '"He's not an ardent suitor, is he, Brother?" Richard the Lionheart's ambiguous sexuality in Cecil B. DeMille's *The Crusades* (1935)', in K. Kelly and T. Pugh (Eds.), *Queer Movie Medievalisms* (pp. 61–78), Farnham and Burlington, VT: Ashgate.

Tuchman, B. (1978) *A distant mirror: The calamitous 14th century*, London: Papermac, 1992 reprint.

Wickham, C. (2017) *Medieval Europe: From the breakup of the Western Roman Empire to the Reformation*, New Haven, CT and London: Yale University Press.

11 Japan and medievalism

The samurai, cinema and cultural appropriation

Introduction

Whilst the medieval period is a Western concept developed to specifically apply to European history, it has also been applied to other geographical regions. Taking a global or 'World History' approach, Bauer (2010) advanced a reinterpretation of the medieval world which juxtaposed developments in Europe with those in China, India, Persia, Japan and Mesoamerica. In specific regional studies outside of Europe, the adjective 'medieval' has been applied to Africa (Fauvelle, 2018; Oliver and Atmore, 2001) and China (Graff, 2002; Hinsch, 2018). Such usage is perhaps provocative, deliberately used to challenge entrenched assumptions and terminology; but it does point to shifting world views of the use and meaning of the term medieval. These reinterpretations also highlight ideas that past societies in Europe, Asia and Africa were more connected to each other in terms of trade and cultural exchange than has previously been accepted. It is also notable that these new applications shift the timeframe of the medieval. For Africa, Oliver and Atmore (2001) focus on the period 1250–1800; whereas for China, it is placed much earlier, with Graff (2002) covering the period 300–900 and Hinsch (2018) considering the third to sixth centuries.

Most notably, the concept of a medieval age outside of Europe has been applied to pre-modern Japan from the twelfth century through to the advent of the Tokugawa Shogunate in 1603 (Bauer, 2010; Bentley and Ziegler, 2000; Keirstead, 2004; Turnbull, 2005). Such an application is underpinned by the Japanese history of this unstable period including competing warlords, feudal nobles, castles, *samurai* (skilled warriors with a strong sense of a cultural code and who may be equated with knights), *ronin* (master-less samurai who we may equate with outlaws or mercenaries) and peasants. This designation of a Japanese medieval period may even be extended into the nineteenth century, stretching up to modernisation and opening up to the West through the Meiji Restoration in 1868.

However, to use the Western term medieval to describe a non-Western history is fraught with problems, and its limitations need to be recognised. As Keirstead explained of Japan:

> It is startling to realize, given the immense popularity the medieval era enjoys today, that no indigenous concept supplies Japan with the idea of a Middle

Ages ... The idea that the years between 1150 and 1600 might comprise a distinct era – a medieval period – is ... not much more than a century old, and ... gained a formal place in Japanese only when historians began to reconceive Japan's past in terms of the succession of eras – ancient, medieval, modern – familiar to European history.

(2004: 5)

Placing Japan into a medieval framework requires some difficult refashioning. Again, as Keirstead highlighted:

The medieval era, by contrast, seems inextricably linked to places and practices that are peculiarly European: the forests of ancient Germany, knights in armor and the strange rituals of the joust; the Gothic architecture of Catholic cathedrals, the fanciful creatures gracing illuminated manuscripts; and the sonorities of Gregorian chant. None of these things is easily transported to other places and times. The particularity of these features of the medieval period suggests that in order to gain a Middle Ages, Japanese history has to be recast in a European mold.

(2004: 6)

Nonetheless, the idea that Japan experienced a medieval period with some similarities to Europe's has entered into popular culture. This chapter explores media representations of Japan as having a medieval history, mainly drawing on Japanese productions that have attracted audiences in the West. These include films (*Seven Samurai* [1954] and *Yojimbo* [1961]) and television (*The Samurai* [1962–1965] and *Monkey* [1978–1981] – a Japanese production based on Chinese mythology). In addition, Western films are considered in *The Last Samurai* (2003) and *47 Ronin* (2013) as well as the appropriation of Japanese samurai culture into Western popular culture through television and games. The application of these media representations to tourism and cultural heritage is considered through a discussion of our fieldwork in Kyoto.

Japan's medieval cast: samurai, ninja and ronin

Between about 1150 and 1603, Japan experienced a period of political instability. The *daimyo* (hereditary feudal lords and their families) became very powerful. Raising great armies, they engaged in internecine warfare and power struggles. While the Emperor was the titular monarch, the *Shogun* (great army commander) was effectively a dictator, though at times even they were little more than a figurehead as various daimyo warlords exercised greater power. Such a situation mirrored that of medieval Western Europe, which was often characterised by violent conflicts as kings and lords struggled to seize and maintain control (Wickham, 2017).

With the rise of warlord armies, a class of warriors known as the *samurai* came to prominence. Samurai literally means 'those who serve' and over time became applied mainly to a Japanese military elite of soldiers (Turnbull, 2005: 7). The popular view was that the samurai were 'proud, individual mounted knights whose goal in life was to serve their lord with unswerving devotion' (Turnbull, 2005: 11). The samurai may be considered to be similar to European knights, for, as Turnbull argued, 'an analogy between samurai and European knights is a helpful way of understanding who these warriors were and what they did' (2005: 8). These similarities are most apparent in three main features of the samurai. First, they wore armour, though this was generally made from small metal scales rather than metal plate. Strikingly, some wore elaborate horned helmets not too dissimilar from the fantasy helmets attributed to Vikings in popular culture (Turnbull, 2005). Second, they served noble warlords and were often based in castles. Originally a simple stockade on a mountain top, over time these castles evolved into huge fortresses. Similar to those in Europe, these dominated the surrounding countryside, were defensive in nature and usually featured a keep as a stronghold of last resort. Third, the samurai followed a code of honour, or *Bushido*, that they saw as distinguishing themselves from ordinary soldiers and regulated how they related to each other, their masters and to the rest of society. While these concepts of chivalry were tied up with the provision of service and loyalty to a master, some samurai became *ronin* – samurai without masters – either through being dismissed from service or their masters being defeated – which forced them to become brigands or mercenaries, with consequent diminution of honour and status. As with European knighthood, the traditions of samurai chivalry and honour were developed over centuries and over time became embedded and inflexible. While defeated by more modern forces at the end of the Japanese medieval period, their traditions continued to influence concepts of honour amongst the military up until the twentieth century (Turnbull, 2005). This defeat by disciplined professional soldiers and the anachronistic survival of exclusive codes of honour into the modern period parallels the situation in Western Europe.

Developing at a similar time were another Japanese military force in the *ninja*. These were often disguised and engaged in covert operations. As a result they were perceived in a contrasting way to the samurai, and there was really no counterpart in medieval Europe. The role of the ninjas involved:

> secret intelligence gathering or assassinations carried out by martial-arts experts … although they were almost invariably despised because of the contrast their ways presented to the samurai code of behaviour. This may be partly due to the fact that many ninja had their origins in the lower social classes, and their secretive and underhand methods were the exact opposite of the ideals of the noble samurai facing squarely on to his enemy.
>
> (Turnbull, 2005: 142)

As occurred with European medieval knights and chivalry, the media has tended towards a highly romanticised view of the samurai. Such representations are not necessarily based on historical interpretations, but rather the storytelling agendas of media creators. The samurai in particular have been constructed as akin to European knights, with, 'filmic emphases on unswerving loyalty, sword worship, and rigidly ethical behaviour [which] all fly in the face of historical evidence'

(Schiff, 2007: 59). In order to examine how the samurai have been depicted, we consider a detailed case study of the most famous of Japanese historical epics in the film *Seven Samurai*.

Seven Samurai (1954)

Directed by Akira Kurosawa, this is a masterpiece that introduced both Japanese cinema and the mythology of the samurai to the rest of the world. It also established many of the tropes and set-pieces of the action genre and stimulated many Western copies, most notably the Western *The Magnificent Seven* (1960 and 2016). Extraordinarily, it was released less than a decade after World War II. As part of the American occupation after the war, major changes to Japanese institutions had been implemented, the military had been disbanded and the media subject to heavy censorship. Kurosawa could have fashioned a surreptitious and insular glorification of Japan's military heritage, but instead he created a film that had universal appeal.

The story is set in 1586, during a time of chaos just before the advent of the Tokugawa era. Central authority has broken down and peasant villages are preyed upon by bands of outlaws. The great period of samurai power is in the past, making this an elegiac vision of the twilight of the samurai. The heroes – the eponymous seven samurai – are masterless ronin, struggling to survive in a fast-changing world, though they still cling to the concepts of a 'timeless world of loyal service and honor' (Schiff, 2007: 60).

Kurosawa took a strongly humanistic view of the samurai and their medieval world (Cowie, 2010). Though they are ferocious and skilful warriors, their future is limited, both personally and as a class. As Kurosawa commented:

> I wanted to say that after everything the peasants were the stronger closely clinging to the earth. Rather, it is the samurai who were weak because they were being blown by the winds of time.
>
> (quoted in Cowie, 2010: 123)

The seven are deliberately portrayed as anachronisms, with little place in a Japan on the edge of shifting from the medieval to the early modern. In a sense, they are possibly reminiscent of Japanese soldiers after World War II, struggling to adapt to changed circumstances. In a world of great instability, they have lost their masters and indeed the lines between the samurai and the bandits they oppose are blurred (Schiff, 2007). Under slightly different circumstances, they could easily be on the same side.

The seven are a group of individuals working for a common cause. The recruitment of each samurai dominates the first part of the film, setting out their individual stories and skills. In some ways, this is comparable to the stories of Robin Hood and how he recruits his band of men. Extended in this case to seven vignettes, the recruitment narrative became much copied in Western caper and action films (Cowie, 2010). Each of the samurai may be viewed as a universal archetype, contrasted with the military discipline of the modern armies that will soon replace the samurai and comparable with other self-defined chivalric elites of Western Europe:

> Each of the samurai has an idiosyncratic personality. They are not the obedient well-drilled foot soldiers … The seven individuals have been cut loose from society, even as they embody the dwindling heroic ideals that in the West might be associated with Camelot and the Knights of the Round Table.
>
> (Cowie, 2010: 126)

Their leader is Kambei (Takashi Shimura). Once he was a famous warrior; now he is an ageing unemployed samurai. Though world-weary, he resolutely clings to a code of honour. He first appears when a crazy man is threatening to kill a young boy. Without hesitation, Kambei volunteers to be the rescuer. To pose as a monk in order to get close, he cuts off his top-knot, the visible marker that he is a samurai. The message is clear: Kambei is ready to make major sacrifices, and following the code of protecting the weak is more important to him than the outward display of his status. The villagers are impressed and ask him to help fight the bandits. Kambei agrees, again choosing to protect the weak. That he will only be paid with food and shelter is meaningless. He wants to live and die as a samurai.

Kambei recruits five samurai. While each has doubts about the meagre pay and the strong likelihood of being killed, they are attracted to the venture by Kambei's authority and reputation. They have all seen better days and are acutely aware that the time of the samurai is coming to an end. Shichirōji (Daisuke Katō) is an old comrade of Kambei and functions as his loyal lieutenant. The taciturn Kyūzō (Seiji Miyaguchi) is a legendary swordsman, of whom all of the other samurai are in awe. Gorōbei (Yoshio Inaba) is a skilled archer. The fourth is Heihachi (Minoru Chiaki), whose strength lies in always being positive and maintaining their morale. The fifth is Katsushirō (Isao Kimura), the son of a wealthy landowner samurai, whose dream is to become a samurai and he convinces the initially reluctant Kambei to allow him to join the group.

Originally, Kurosawa's intention was for the story to be about six samurai. However, he eventually decided that it made a better narrative to include an out-sider, who would give a different perspective. This is Kikuchiyo (Toshiro Mifune). He attempts to pass himself off as a samurai through showing a stolen scroll list-ing his supposed lineage – a similar narrative to William Thatcher (Heath Ledger) in *A Knight's Tale*. He desperately wants to prove himself as a samurai. Most likely the son of a farmer, he has run away from his village and has no place in society. The others dismiss Kikuchiyo as a fraud, pointing to his lack of self-dis-cipline as evidence that he is merely a peasant rather than an aristocratic samurai. Kikuchiyo is the most explosive and dynamic of the group, prone to outbursts of temper, which contrasts sharply with the reserved samurai personas of the others. In the end, they do recognise him as one of them, particularly through his ability to mediate between them and the peasants (Schiff, 2007).

The samurai undertake a mission that could easily be translated into any cul-ture or time period. True to their code of honour, they protect the weak villagers with little prospect of reward. Heavily outnumbered, they rely on their superior martial skills and use various strategies to gain the advantage. This could easily be a film about medieval knights in Europe, gunslingers in the American West, or a platoon of modern soldiers in enemy territory. At the end, the bandits are defeated; though Kambei ruefully notes that it is the villagers who have won, not the samurai. The three surviving samurai leave, as there is no place for them now in the village. Of the four who died, none were bested in their samurai skills. Instead, they were killed by muskets, the new weapon that will soon transform warfare in Japan and leave little room for archaic swordplay.

Further samurai productions

Seven Samurai was an immense hit, and Kurosawa followed this up with *Throne of Blood* (1957). Starring Toshiro Mifune, this was a retelling of William Shakespeare's *Macbeth*, with the setting shifted from Scotland to medieval Japan. *Yojimbo* (1961) was an even bigger success. Toshiro Mifune starred as a ronin who enters a town in which two clans are fighting for control. The mysterious unnamed ronin has no backstory and seems to be out to make money, but it is slowly revealed that he does have a sense of honour. Both factions want to hire him as a *Yojimbo* (bodyguard), but the samurai plays them off against each other. Eventually, both sides are wiped out. Commenting that the town is now better off, the mysterious ronin leaves.

The television series *The Samurai* (1962–1965) followed the adventures of Shintaro (Koichi Ose). In disguise as a wandering ronin, he was actually an agent of the shogun and was on a mission to foil various plots. His chief opponents were the black-clad masked ninja. The series was curiously very popular in Australia, especially with children who had not experienced World War II as their parents had. The concept of ninjas as secret agents was further advanced in the James Bond film *You Only Live Twice* (1967). Its finale of a ninja attack on SPECTRE's secret volcano base firmly established the ninjas as an ambiguous modern-day force in the popular imagination. Another Japanese television series that gained a cult following worldwide was *Monkey* (1978–1981), which was based on a sixteenth-century Chinese story.

In the twenty-first century, samurai films were made with mainly Japanese casts, but with an American star as the lead in order to maximise their box-office appeal to Western audiences. In *The Last Samurai* (2003), Tom Cruise plays Nathan Algren, a disgruntled US cavalry officer in the 1870s. He is recruited as a military advisor as part of the Meiji Restoration, which is battling a samurai rebellion. Algren changes sides and fights with the samurai, but as history cannot be changed, they are ultimately defeated. Interesting parallels are drawn between the samurai and Native Americans, with both characterised as noble warriors who now have no place in the modern world. The historical juxtaposition of the American West and the Meiji Restoration also opened up credible possibilities that samurai warriors could have journeyed to the Wild West. Such ideas were explored in *Red Sun* (1971) – which starred Toshiro Mifune – and *The Warrior's Way* (2010).

The film *47 Ronin* (2013) starred Keanu Reeves as a samurai. Though of part Chinese ancestry, Reeves's occidental features were explained by his character being half Japanese and half English. The film is based on a famous Japanese story, in which a daimyo lord is required to commit *seppuku* (ritual suicide) after assaulting a court official. His samurai entourage are now ronin, and they revenge their master's disgrace by killing the official before carrying out seppuku themselves. The story of the 47 ronin was returned to in *Last Knights* (2015), which transferred it to a mythical medieval world. In this case Clive Owen was the leader of the ronin and Morgan Freeman their master. This was an example of a *colour-blind* production in which the lead actors are from multiple races, the supporting cast are all Japanese and this situation is never acknowledged or explained. Consistent with the modern trend, all three films were made outside of Japan in order to take advantage of financial incentives. *The Last Samurai* was shot in New Zealand – with Mount Taranaki standing in for Mount Fuji – while *47 Ronin* was made in Hungary and *Last Knights* in the Czech Republic.

Reimagining and appropriating medieval Japan

Medieval Japan features an engaging cast of dramatic characters and concepts for film-makers to draw upon. It is not surprising, then, that these have been copied in a range of Western films. This is a striking case of *cultural appropriation*, in which elements of the cultural identity of one culture are taken over and made their own by another culture. Typically, this involves Western culture appropriating iconic features of non-Western groups and raises issues of Western privilege and power. There are also often concerns that profound cultural meanings are lost or diminished through this process. It could also be argued to constitute an example of *intertextuality*, in that one production (text) is influenced by that of another.

The success of *Seven Samurai* brought the samurai and related concepts to the Western world and quickly led to imitation. Kurosawa's epic was remade as *The Magnificent Seven* (1960). The story was shifted to Mexico in the late nineteenth century. Beset by bandits, the villagers cross the border into the USA to recruit a band of gunslingers (including Yul Brynner, Steve McQueen, Charles Bronson and James Coburn). The narrative was very similar, including the recruitment and backstories of the out-of-work gunslingers (see Hannan, 2015 for details). Yul Brynner and Anthony Quinn came up with the idea of turning the *Seven Samurai* into a Western, and producer Walter Mirisch bought the adaptation rights from Toho Studios (Hannan, 2015).

On the other hand, *Yojimbo* was remade as a Western without any negotiation, forcing Kurosawa to successfully sue for damages and credit. This new version was *A Fistful of Dollars* (1964), a 'Spaghetti Western' directed by Sergio Leone and filmed in Spain. The plot of the 'Man with No Name' entering a town of two warring factions and playing them off against each other was almost exactly the same as that of *Yojimbo*.

The idea of modern Western gangsters being presented in terms of the Japanese medieval period first came to the fore in *Le Samurai* (1967). Part of the French New Wave of cinema, it featured Alain Delon as Jef, an underworld hitman being pursued by the police. The title came from director Jean-Pierre Melville's fascination with the samurai. The film begins with an invented quote – ostensibly from the samurai bushido code – that, 'there is no solitude greater than a samurai's, unless perhaps it is that of a tiger in the jungle'. This is Jef's curse; he is alone and can trust nobody. A generation later, the Hollywood production *Ghost Dog: The Way of the Samurai* (1999) followed a similar narrative of a non-Japanese hitman following the samurai code. In a similar vein, *Ronin* (1998) was about four free-lance mercenaries in Europe who are recruited to steal a briefcase (Robert de Niro, Jean Reno, Stellan Skarsgård and Sean Bean). Ageing and conscious that they are expendable, they try to follow a code of honour. At one stage, de Niro and Reno's characters discuss the story of the Japanese ronin, directly comparing themselves to them.

From comparing oneself to a samurai, it became a short step to becoming a samurai. In *Kill Bill Vol. 1* (2003), an American woman known only as the Bride undergoes training to become expert in a range of martial arts, including the use of a samurai sword. In the first season of the Danish–Swedish television series *The Bridge* (2011–2018), a troubled young Danish man is obsessed with training to become a samurai. He is being manipulated by a killer, who convinces him to commit murder with a samurai sword. In *Daybreak* (2019), a pandemic has killed off all the adults in Los Angeles. High school student Wesley (Austin Crute) reacts to this confronting new world by deciding that he will become a samurai and follow the bushido code. This he achieves by simply raiding abandoned houses to find a samurai sword and costume. In all three of these instances, these are Westerners with no connection to Japan who make a decision to become samurai warriors. They could arguably have decided to become medieval knights, but in the modern world of popular culture, appropriating the Japanese image is often viewed as much cooler.

In the late twentieth century, samurai and ninjas became staples of contemporary urban culture. This was particularly due to the increasing popularity of comics and graphic novels, which were sometimes spun off into television and cinema productions. Perhaps the most successful of these was the tongue-in-cheek *Teenage Mutant Ninja Turtles*, originally a comic and then an animated television series from 1987 to 1996. In addition, a wide variety of media productions featured Western characters who had gained skills in martial arts from other Asian countries, including China, Korea and Tibet. In Western youth culture, the imagery of medieval Japan was widely seen as a cool alternative to the mainstream. This was particularly apparent in hairstyle fashions, with the samurai *chonmage* (top-knot) appropriated by hipster males and referred to as the 'samurai bun'.

Japanese appropriation of the medieval

Whilst Western producers have been mining Japanese culture for images and concepts, Japanese film-makers have also similarly looked to the West. Kurosawa, for example, acknowledged that he was greatly influenced by John Ford and his iconic Westerns (Cowie, 2010). For *Throne of Blood*, Kurosawa closely adapted *Macbeth*, shifting the location from Scotland to Japan but still keeping the medieval timeframe and associated imagery. It is, however, in Japanese *anime* that the use of Western and medieval references have been consistently appropriated.

To illustrate this trend, we consider four animated films produced by Studio Ghibli. The first is *Laputa: Castle in the Sky* (1986). Drawing on the commonality of castles to Japan and Europe, the tone was more steampunk than medieval. The concept of a flying castle came from *Gulliver's Travels* by Jonathan Swift, which featured Laputa as a flying island. A mobile castle was repeated in *Howl's Moving Castle* (2004), which was adapted from the 1986 novel of the same name by English author Diana Wynne Jones. *Tales from Earthsea* (2006) was based on the *Earthsea* series, which American novelist Ursula Le Guin had commenced in 1968. This was the most overtly medieval of these productions, with a mythical realm of dragons, wizards, knights and castles. The fourth is *Ponyo* (2008) which was heavily influenced by writer-director Hiyao Miyazaki's visit to the Tate Britain in London, where he was entranced by the painting *Ophelia* (1852) by John Everett Millais, who was one of the artists in the Pre-Raphaelite Brotherhood (see Chapter 2).

Medieval Japan and tourism

We conclude this chapter with a consideration of the linkages between film-tourism and Japan's medieval heritage. Unfortunately, research into Japan's film-tourism is still in its early days. Connections between well-known films, popular culture and particular destinations and sites are apparent (Ng, 2008; Strielkowski, 2017), but much more work needs to be done, particularly on the drivers of film-tourism and the different motivations and behaviours of domestic and international visitors. It is a frustrating situation, given that Japan is such an established and popular tourism destination. In this instance, our aim is to merely explore some of the patterns through a case study of a medieval heritage attraction.

Nijō Castle in Kyoto was visited as part of fieldwork in 2016. This is a World Heritage site, one of 17 in Kyoto. Most of these are temples and shrines, and this is the only castle listed in this cluster. Like many heritage cities around the world, Kyoto is a classic example of *overtourism*, with high numbers of tourists and extreme overcrowding at popular sites. Nijō Castle was no exception, exemplifying the strong interest in Japan's medieval heritage. The castle was constructed in 1603, right at the end of the period associated with the medieval in Japan. At that time, the newly created Tokugawa Shogunate moved the capital to Edo Castle, now the Imperial Palace in Tokyo. The Emperor remained at the old capital of Kyoto and Nijō Castle was built as the Shogun's official residence when in Kyoto. Whereas the Imperial Palace in Kyoto remains closed to the public, Nijō has been open to tourists since 1939.

A number of markers of status and power attract the attention of visitors to Nijō. The first is the *Karamon*, an elaborate ceremonial gateway (Figure 11.1). Its use was reserved for either the Shogun or the Emperor and was a highly visible symbol of the Shogun's authority. It leads into two areas or wards within the

Figure 11.1 The *Karamon* or Ceremonial Gateway to Nijō Castle, Kyoto.
Source: Warwick Frost.

castle, known as the *Ninomaru* (outer) and *Honmaru* (inner). The Ninomaru is dominated by a spectacular wooden palace (Figure 11.2). Much of this structure consists of waiting and reception rooms, designed for visitors seeking an audience with the Shogun and intended to impress such nervous supplicants with the power and the magnificence of the Shogun. These are the most popular areas of the complex, crowded with slowly shuffling tourists taking a glimpse into how government worked in pre-modern Japan. In terms of tourist numbers, this was one of the most crowded of the medieval castles we visited on our fieldwork for this book. The Honmaru is a more utilitarian defensive zone, conforming to conventions of what a castle should look like. Similar to many European castles, it has a moat, strong stone walls and defensive gateways (Figure 11.3). Inside, it contains the remains of a central keep.

International tourists at heritage sites in Japan often fall into two clear demographic segments. The medieval heritage of castles and temples tends to attract older tourists, while younger visitors are drawn more to the modern cultural heritage linked with anime and other popular culture representations, as is found at places like Akihabara in Tokyo (Ng, 2008). Such a divide is not confined to Japan and is also apparent at medieval heritage sites throughout Europe. Where exceptions occur, they are highly influenced by the media, as in the cases of the appropriation of the samurai into global popular culture and the ubiquitous popularity of medieval European princesses (see Chapter 4).

Figure 11.2 The Ninomaru Palace, Nijō Castle, Kyoto.

Source: Warwick Frost.

Figure 11.3 The Moat, Wall and Gate for the Honmaru, Nijō Castle, Kyoto.

Source: Warwick Frost.

Conclusion

Japan provides a fascinating outlier in our examination of the intersection between the media, medieval heritage and tourism. The conventional definition of the medieval confines it to Europe, though there is an increasing tendency to apply it to non-European societies. Japan stands out as having historical elements that are often characterised as medieval. These include castles, feudal lords and samurai warriors (with swords, armour and a code of honour) who are similar to knights. Following on from the success of *Seven Samurai*, the media has popularised this view of pre-modern Japan. Further media productions have reinforced this and introduced ninjas and ronin to the Western world. Some of these productions have been Japanese and some have been Western in origin, leading to a great deal of intertextuality and cultural appropriation. As one of the world's leading tourist destinations, Japan draws visitors seeking to experience its distinctive culture. This heritage tourism includes both its medieval history, as found, for example, at Nijō Castle in Kyoto, and the more general interest in Japan's vibrant popular culture, which does include some medieval elements.

References

Bauer, S. (2010) *The history of the medieval world: From the conversion of Constantine to the First Crusade*, New York: Norton.

Bentley, J. and Ziegler, H. (2000) *Traditions and encounters: A global perspective on the past*, Boston: McGraw Hill.

Cowie, P. (2010) *Akira Kurosawa: Master of cinema*, New York: Rizzoli.

Fauvelle, F.-X. (2018) *The Golden Rhinoceros: Histories of the African Middle Ages*, Princeton, NJ: Princeton University Press.

Graff, D. (2002) *Medieval Chinese warfare 300–900*, London: Routledge.

Hannan, B. (2015) *The making of The Magnificent Seven: Behind the scenes of the pivotal Western*, Jefferson NC: McFarland.

Hinsch, B. (2018) *Women in early medieval China*, Lanham, MD: Rowman and Littlefield.

Keirstead, T. (2004) 'Medieval Japan: Taking the Middle Ages outside Europe', *History Compass*, 2, 1–14.

Ng, B. (2008) 'Hong Kong young people and cultural pilgrimage to Japan: The role of Japanese popular culture in Asian tourism', in J. Cochrane (Ed.), *Asian Tourism: Growth and change* (pp. 183–192), Oxford and Amsterdam: Elsevier.

Oliver, R. and Atmore, A. (2001) *Medieval Africa 1250–1800*, Cambridge: Cambridge University Press.

Schiff, R. (2007) 'Samurai on shifting ground: Negotiating the medieval and the modern in Seven Samurai and Yojimbo', in L. Ramey and T. Pugh (Eds.), *Race, class, and gender in 'medieval' cinema* (pp. 59–72), New York and Basingstoke: Palgrave Macmillan.

Strielkowski, W. (2017) 'Promoting tourism destination through film-induced tourism: The case of Japan', *MARKET/TRŽIŠTE*, 29(2), 193–203.

Turnbull, S. (2005) *Warriors of medieval Japan*, Oxford and New York: Osprey.

Wickham, C. (2017) *Medieval Europe: From the breakup of the Western Roman Empire to the Reformation*, New Haven and London: Yale University Press.

12 Fictional media and heritage from the medieval perspective

Trends, issues and setting a research agenda

Introduction: the battle at Battle

The Battle of Hastings in 1066 is acknowledged as one of the seminal points in English history – with the defeat of the Anglo-Saxon king Harold by William, Duke of Normandy, having long-lasting effects. The Norman conquest led to changes in language and culture as a result of their dispossession of 'almost the entire English aristocracy, replacing them with French families' (Wickham, 2016: 103). The eleventh-century Bayeux Tapestry, nearly 70 metres in length, immortalised the conquest in visual form through embroidery on cloth and still attracts visitors today to the French city of Bayeux, who marvel at the figures. In particular, there is the famous panel showing a figure with an arrow in his eye, which is popularly believed to be Harold, although there is no evidence supporting this form of death for the king.

The council in Hastings has staged an annual commemorative week since 1966, the 900th anniversary of the battle. This has included a re-enactment of the battle each year, apart from 2012, when it was cancelled due to the weather, and in 2013, when a decision was made to take a hiatus to re-grow the grass (BBC, 2014). The re-enactment event is staged on successive days over a weekend and is organised by English Heritage, which looks after the battlefield, visitor centre and the nearby Abbey built by Duke William. We were fortunate enough to visit the re-enactment in 2011, on what was a glorious sunny day, arriving at the town of Battle by train from Hastings. The programme included warm-up skirmishes or melees between groups of re-enactors, culminating in the full re-enactment of the battle in the afternoon. Various announcers tied the activities together, introducing and commentating on the different events to the crowd, which sat behind ropes on the grass. Many of the visitors brought picnics, as we did, and there was a festival atmosphere. A group of re-enactors had created a camp near the battlefield, where visitors could see them cook food, attend to weapons and mend and wash clothes. We watched as 'kids are encouraged to put on helmets and pick up swords and battleaxes' (Frost and Laing, 2013: 104), in a form of living history. English Heritage encourage this, as they are keen for 'spectators to see what life was like in 1066' (Euronews, 2019), beyond the battle itself. We spoke to some fellow attendees, a man and his young son dressed in armour (Figure 12.1), and established that the boy was a fan of the *Merlin* television series, which was very

Figure 12.1 Dressed in Home-Made Armour for the Battle of Hastings.
Source: Warwick Frost.

popular at the time (see Chapters 3 and 4). The battle itself was incredibly visceral, with horses and the sounds of swords clashing and people yelling. The re-
enactor playing Harold pretends to have his eye pierced by an arrow, but we are
told by the event announcer that this is probably an invention. There is a mix of
the imaginary and the authentic in this event, which ends with a minute's silence;
a modern invention which helps to bring us back from the liminal space that has
been created to our normal lives (Frost and Laing, 2013).

For the re-enactors, involvement in the event can be a way to learn about their
medieval past. According to one woman who took part in the living history camp
at Battle in 2018, 'You don't need a formal education to learn about history.
Probably 90% of us are not formally educated but you just pick it up as you go
along' (quoted in Weeks, 2018). Other re-enactors at the 2018 event liked being
in a bubble away from everyday life ('You look around here, there's nothing in
sight that's modern and we enjoy it') or putting themselves in the shoes of people
from another era ('We're trying to be people of a certain place and a certain time')
(both quoted in Weeks, 2018). The attraction for visitors is to see the medieval
world brought alive. Without the colour and movement of the re-enactment event,
visitors to the battlefield at Battle would simply see an open expanse of grass, as
the abbey is the only tangible fabric of the medieval past. The re-enactment com-
plements the vast array of media productions that are available to modern medieval enthusiasts and is an example of heritage tourism that is not influenced by a
particular production but brings into the mix various elements that we are used to
seeing and expect to be present in representations of the medieval.

For this concluding chapter, our aim is to draw together our discussion and highlight nine key trends and issues that have arisen from our examination of the medieval imaginaries provided by the media and heritage tourism. These issues are still playing out in the modern world and offer a research agenda for future studies.

New media and a renewed focus on the medieval

While the medieval has been a feature of fictional media for a very long time, it is noticeable that interest has surged in the early twenty-first century. This is particularly apparent in terms of new media distribution formats, such as streaming and on-demand services. If we take Netflix as an example, at the time of writing it offers the television series *Merlin* (2008–2013), *Vikings* (2013–2021), *The Last Kingdom* (2015 onwards), *The Norsemen* (2016 onwards), *Knightfall* (2017–2019), *Marco Polo* (2014–2016) and *The Letter for the King* (2020). In addition, it is showing the films *Outcast* (2014), *Northmen* (2014), *Dracula Untold* (2014), *Last Knights* (2015), *King Arthur: The Legend of the Sword* (2017), *The Outlaw King* (2018) and *The King* (2019). No other historical period provides this quantity of content on this provider.

This focus on the medieval is likely to be due to two reasons. First, the success of *Games of Thrones* (2011–2019) encouraged imitation, particularly of productions that were of cinema quality with good casts and epic action scenes. Second, the medieval themes of heroes, quests, chivalry, redemption and military conflict seem to have a strong resonance to modern audiences in an uncertain and challenging world. Many of the productions currently on Netflix have common tropes of a medieval hero seeking to prove themself, claim their inheritance and battle against dark forces. Such plots are suggestive of the *Hero's Journey* (Campbell, 1949), which remains highly influential upon film-makers. They also suggest the *outlaw myth* discussed in Chapter 8, in which injustice and corruption forces the hero to operate outside of the law in order to return society to normalcy and safety.

The rapid success of streaming services is an example of *digital disruption* (Skog, Wimelius and Sandberg, 2018), where the quickfire adoption of new technology causes major changes in social behaviours and displaces old patterns and institutions. The rise of streaming has effectively killed off the video rental shop and reduced DVD sales. When we wrote our study of films and tourism in the American West (Frost and Laing, 2015), we relied heavily on watching video rentals. Less than a decade later, we were very conscious that in writing this book, our options for accessing films – particularly older films – had significantly narrowed. It is a very strong likelihood that future audiences will struggle to view older films, for these seem to be unpopular with the new world of streaming providers.

Mouvance or intertextuality

Some narratives come in multiple versions, which, in the case of the medieval period, reflects the *mouvance* or fluidity of the original story (Driver, 2004). The legends of Arthur and Robin Hood have been told many times, with variations in plot, characters and meaning. In crafting new representations, creators take new pathways. A mature star is available – Sean Connery, for example – so why not make Arthur or Robin older? Or, why not take another approach and cast younger actors, as in *King Arthur: Legend of the Sword* (2017) and *Robin Hood* (2018)? How about placing Arthur and Robin Hood in the same novel, as in *The Sword in the Stone* (White, 1938)? Or, remaking the 47 Ronin story outside of its Japanese context, as in *Last Knights* (2015)? The source material can also be changed. It is important to understand whether and how these variations or intertextuality can affect how these medieval narratives continue to be imagined. Do they give life to old tales and attract new audiences? Do they confuse or alienate fans?

When novels are made into films, the variations often stir up controversy. Even though *The Lord of the Rings* film trilogy essentially differed only in minor ways from Tolkien's novels, this divergence generated a great deal of discussion amongst fans on social media. A greater variation came between the *Game of Thrones* television series and the novels on which they were based, with characters and plots omitted from the television show in order to condense the story. A further problem came when author George R.R. Martin fell behind in writing his novels, so that later seasons of the television show had to venture into unwritten territory. Perhaps the greatest gulf occurred when the Dutch novel *The Letter for the King* (Dragt, 1962) was made as a television series in 2020. While the essential story of a teenage squire promising a dying knight to deliver a message was retained, three significant changes were made with the view of creating a narrative that was more appealing to modern audiences. First, rather than simply being brave and honourable, the hero Tiuri was given a more complex backstory of being riddled with doubts and teenage angst. Second, his chief companion was changed from male to female (see Chapter 4 for more on this). Third, magical powers were introduced that were entirely absent from the novel. Again, future studies could consider whether and how this changes the appeal of the narrative and how audiences engage with the multiple versions of the story. Does this make the story less medieval in the eyes of audiences?

The decay factor for media-induced heritage tourism

How long successful media productions will influence heritage tourism is a topic which deserves further research. Two examples illustrate the promise of longevity. The first is *Braveheart* (1995). Taking the little-known tale of William Wallace, Mel Gibson won the Academy Award for Best Picture and stimulated new flows of tourists to Scotland. A quarter of a century on, there appears to be no diminution of interest in Wallace, with the nineteenth-century National Wallace Monument in Stirling being the chief drawcard for tourists. On the occasion of the 20th anniversary of the film in 2015, Ken Thomson of Stirling District Tourism was reported as stating that:

> visitor numbers at the Wallace Monument more than doubled, from about 80,000 a year to 180,000, following the release of the film, and he said its

appeal has proved lasting. 'That's one of the amazing things about Braveheart, because very often film tourism is a fairly short-lived impact. But here we are 20 years later and people are still driven to come here with an interest in Wallace stimulated by the film. We believe at least a million visitors to Stirling have come here as a result of the film'.

(BBC, 2015)

Why, then, were tourists still interested in visiting a site associated with a 20-year-old film? In the same news report, it was argued that it was due to the story's continuing contemporary appeal:

Mr Thomson said the issues addressed in the film still resonate with viewers today. He said: 'So many people identify with Wallace and recognise exactly what he was doing. He wasn't just leading the campaign from a political perspective; he was fighting injustice, discrimination and poverty, he was addressing inequality, and so many people in so many parts of the world can identify with those campaigns, which are still so important today'.

(BBC, 2015)

The second example is the ongoing success of the Hobbiton Movie Set as a tourist attraction in New Zealand. Originally built on farmland for *The Lord of the Rings* trilogy (2001–2003), tourists were often disappointed that much of the set had been cleared after filming. Major changes occurred with the filming of *The Hobbit: An Unexpected Journey* (2012), for which the Hobbiton set was reconstructed and retained afterwards. With an experience now based on a greater array of tangible movie heritage, numbers of visitors increased dramatically. In 2012, the attraction recorded annual visitation of 52,000, whereas in 2018, this had climbed to 640,000 (Walker, 2018).

In contrast, there are instances where a decay factor is evident. While set in medieval Scotland, *Braveheart* was filmed in County Wicklow, Ireland. To leverage tourism off the film's success, a Braveheart Trail was developed. However, when we undertook fieldwork in 2006, trail brochures were no longer available, and there were no plans to print more. As discussed in Chapter 8, Nottingham has launched marketing campaigns with websites and trails to tie in with the release of Robin Hood films, but these have been disestablished within five or so years. Such examples suggest that the upkeep of marketing efforts may be important to maintaining the interest of tourists, and there is a need to guard against notions that film-induced tourism just happens automatically without planning and investment.

Medievalism in a global world

Historically, the medieval has typically been defined as a European concept. However, as discussed in Chapter 11, there has been a trend towards applying it to non-European histories. Furthermore, interest in the medieval period is not just confined to Europeans. As is evident at many of the main medieval heritage sites in Europe, a diverse pool of visitors are attracted from various countries. It is also apparent that media productions set in the medieval period draw fans from all over the world. Medievalism is accordingly a global phenomenon, and that has implications for how it will be constructed and consumed in the future.

The globalisation of the medieval is manifested by the development of medieval attractions outside of Europe. Many of these are in countries which have a European diaspora, such as the USA, Australia, New Zealand and Canada. In these instances, people may see the medieval as connected to their personal heritage, as occurring in 'homelands' from which their families migrated in the past. As such, they remember and value medieval heroes, stories, folklore and traditions as still being important and relevant to them. This process is reinforced by media productions. Examples of such diaspora medieval attractions include replica castles, such as at Disneyland and Disneyworld; Castello Amorosa in California's Napa Valley and Kryal Castle in Ballarat, Australia. In North America, European castles and medieval villages feature in entertainment attractions such as Excalibur Casino in Las Vegas; Medieval Times Dinner Theater and Tournament, Florida; Castle Park, California; Enchanted Forest, Oregon; and Canada's Wonderland near Toronto. To varying levels, these suggest *hyperreality*, blending the real and imaginary in order to provide a fun experience for visitors (Eco, 1986; Emery, 2017). Also of note in these European diasporas are the wide range of medieval and renaissance fairs, medieval re-enactment events and competitions and medieval banquets. These medieval-themed events allow audiences and participants to enter into a world that they have seen on screen or read about (Emery, 2017; Robinson and Clifford, 2012).

There are similar attractions in Asia. These include Ba Na Hills French Village, near Da Nang in Vietnam; the French Village at Riverland in Dubai and the Colmar Tropicale Medieval French Village in the Berjaya Hills of Malaysia. All three are fantasy replica resorts/precincts, offering restaurants and shopping within faux medieval stone buildings. Their representation as French rather than generically European offers a further layer of promised sophistication. They are all aimed primarily at domestic or regional tourism markets, providing the exoticism of French cultural heritage without the expense of long-haul travel. Again, they represent hyperreality and demonstrate the global fascination with the medieval. Future research could tease out the appeal.

Invention and authenticity

In any discussion of representing history, issues of authenticity and anachronism are always to the fore. Cinema and television are often highlighted as the villains for twisting, ignoring and inventing history. Such changes are justified by filmmakers as necessary to improve or condense a story, though this 'playing with history' may lead to dissatisfaction amongst some viewers. The medieval period is particularly open to issues of invention and inauthenticity in terms of media representation. Three examples are worth noting.

The first example concerns the initial television series *Blackadder* (1982–1983). Actor Sir Tony Robinson recalled that he was fearful that its medieval setting would lead to its failure:

> The show took place in the 1480s, during the War of the Roses. But this was problematic. It wasn't like the Tudor or Victorian period which everyone knew at least something about. The War of the Roses were very confusing, a confusion redoubled by the fact that two of our main characters were called King Richard.
>
> (Robinson, 2016: 247)

Compounding this problem, Robinson felt, was the invention of an 'alternative history' plot which writers Richard Curtis and Rowan Atkinson saw as giving the show an edgy feel and would be appreciated by audiences brought up on William Shakespeare's *Richard III*. Robinson felt that this reversal of actual history was confusing, as,

> in our story Richard III … didn't kill the two princes in the Tower as history tells us he did; instead one of the little princes grew up, became Richard IV, and the Tudor succession was delayed by half a century.
>
> (Robinson, 2016: 247)

At the time, it probably did cause confusion amongst audiences, as the concepts of alternative history and worlds were not as well-known and accepted as they are now. The series did not rate as highly as expected, and the BBC approved a second series only after the producers agreed to a much lower budget (Robinson, 2016).

A second example is the book and television series *The Last Kingdom* (discussed in Chapters 3 and 9). These utilised the device of focussing on a fictional character who interacts with real historical people and events. This allows the story to remain true to history, but also contain charismatic heroes, dastardly villains and exciting plots, twists and romances (Ortenberg, 2006). Accordingly, *The Last Kingdom* is the story of a fictional warrior Uhtred (Alexander Dreymon). Born a Saxon but raised by Danes, he reluctantly becomes involved with King Alfred (David Dawson) and his efforts to defeat Viking invasions. This set-up allows for an exploration of the complexity of Alfred's personality, free of the need to cast him as a conventional hero. Both the books and the television series were very successful, and this was in part because they covered historical events and persons about which little was known. For example, historians know that Alfred's daughter Aethelflaed married Ethelred of Mercia and, after he died, ruled as the Lady of Mercia. However, nearly all other details of her life are lost. This allows *The Last Kingdom* to speculate on her character and story, turning Aethelflaed (Milly Brady) into a dynamic heroine (see Chapter 4). Such inventions work in this case because they bring this very sketchy period of medieval history to life without changing the core facts.

A third example occurs with the television series *Knightfall* (2017–2019). This tells of the suppression of the Knights Templars by Philip IV in fourteenth-century France. As with *The Last Kingdom*, a fictional hero – Landry (Tom Cullen) – is set against an array of real historical figures. The interesting conceit of this series concerns the depiction of the deaths of these characters. Historically, it is recorded that Philip (Ed Stoppard), Queen Joan (Olivia Ross) and Pope Boniface VIII (Jim Carter) all died of natural causes, albeit with little specific detail recorded. The invention in *Knightfall* (and we feel this is very effectively done), is that all are murdered as various conspiracies play out, but that is covered up and their deaths ascribed to natural causes.

This common use of invention within historical fiction raises interesting questions of how these are received by audiences. There is clear evidence that fans will accept invention, but to understand to what extent and in which circumstances, more research is required. Did the alternative history approach of *Blackadder* contribute to its having only modest success? Is it safer to follow the approach of inserting a fictional hero amongst real historical characters, and how far can this be pushed? *Knightfall*'s device of covering up violent deaths worked well for us, but it may be less successful if applied to better-known historical narratives. In addition, do such inventions affect how heritage tourism is manifested? We know from the past that some inventions do become accepted as part of the original story. Maid Marian, for example, is a later addition to the Robin Hood stories, while Sir Walter Scott invented the story of Robin Hood splitting an arrow at an archery contest for *Ivanhoe* in 1819. Will some of these modern inventions ultimately become accepted as true? This may lead attraction operators and interpreters to be tempted to engage more successfully with visitors by focussing on the fiction within historical fiction. Perhaps Uhtred will become part of Winchester's heritage, presented to tourists alongside Alfred.

The changing nature of the hero

Film screenwriters have often drawn on Campbell's *Hero's Journey* (Batty, 2011). This may be deliberate or it may be unconscious, given the ubiquity of the hero *monomyth*. Campbell (1949) based his theory on myths and folklore from around the world, arguing that there was a common pattern for hero narratives. Heroes were, Campbell argued, often unwilling to act until some form of *Call to Adventure* required them to embark on a quest, facing many challenges that would test and ultimately transform them. For the creators of fictional media, often drawing on the same myths as Campbell, the concept of a hero's journey provided an appropriate framework for their story. Furthermore, audiences were also conditioned to accept such a narrative structure through previous works. Two examples of this approach are worth noting. First, in *The Sword in the Stone* (White, 1938) and subsequent versions of the King Arthur story, young Arthur is brought up in obscurity not knowing his royal identity. It is only after he travels to London and draws a magical sword from a stone that his destiny is revealed. Second, in *Braveheart* (1995), William Wallace is originally not interested in opposing the English invasion of Scotland and only changes his mind after his wife is murdered.

Utilising a heroic framework for a narrative often led to a simple representation of a worthy hero. There is a crisis, whether it be war or injustice, and this forces a good man to take action. This was very apparent in the chivalric cycle of medieval films of the 1950s (see Chapter 5) and also seen from time to time in more recent productions, such as *A Knight's Tale* (2001), *Kingdom of Heaven* (2005), *Robin Hood* (2018) and *The Outlaw King* (2018). However, the latter four films highlighted a change in how heroes are represented in the modern world. As with earlier narratives, they were unquestionably brave and honourable and they were opposed to unredeemable villains. In addition, there was one further element that mediated their depiction of the hero. This was a strong disillusionment with authority. It was not just the case that they were working to restore law and order after a temporary hiatus – a common trope in the 1950s cycle – but rather that they were confronted with deeply embedded flaws in society that entrenched injustice. This is a common motif in many modern films, playing on fears of conspiracies and corruption, and it is clearly seen as popular amongst filmgoers. How this is manifested in these films varies. In *A Knight's Tale*, it is the crushing omnipotence of a class system; in *Kingdom of Heaven*, it is the ongoing crisis in Palestine. *Robin Hood* focuses on the failings of government and even argues for Brexit, and for *The Outlaw King*, it is imperialism. Accordingly, the heroes in these films fight against these societal issues.

Other common approaches are to focus on a *flawed hero* or *anti-hero*. Flawed heroes abound in *Game of Thrones*, and it is their complexity and human frailties that made them popular with viewers. A good example is Ned Stark (Sean Bean). A fundamentally good man, his call to adventure leads to his doom. Content as the Lord of the North, he is perturbed when his old comrade King Robert requests that he venture to the capital to take up the senior position of Hand to the King. Ned tries to resist, but the king insists that he is needed due to his trustworthiness and honesty. Once at King's Landing, Ned uncovers the truth that Robert is not actually the father of the royal children. He reveals his knowledge of her adultery to Queen Cersei, recommending that she should leave the capital. Instead, Cersei acts. Robert is killed and Ned arrested. The execution of Ned by Cersei's son, King Joffrey, starts a civil war. Ned's good and honourable intentions have been undone by his naivety. A feared warrior, he was not successful at playing the 'Game of Thrones'. He also seemingly has one other flaw. His household contains a bastard son, Jon Snow (Kit Harrington), which is a source of animosity with his wife. Only at the end of the series is it revealed that Jon is actually the grandson of the previous king and has the strongest claim to the throne. Ned made a promise to his dying sister that he would raise her son and keep his identity forever secret, and he dutifully shoulders this burden, never revealing the truth.

The anti-hero came to prominence in films of the 1960s. While motivated by base desires – typically greed and the lust for power – the anti-hero has something that makes them appealing to audiences. They may be opposed to evil villains or just have a charismatic personality. Ragnar Lothbrok (Travis Fimmel) in *Vikings*

(2013–2021) is a good example. While violent, rapacious and ruthless, he is also portrayed as a clever and popular leader who is followed by the other Vikings, generally without question. His invasions of England and France are presented as the natural consequence of his desire to better himself and build a new life, and even his natural curiosity. His character is also appealing in that he has a friendly relationship with Athelstan (George Blagden), a young Anglo-Saxon monk whom he captures and eventually frees.

In all of these instances, heroism is equated with military skill. As Driver and Ray commented, the medieval period, 'grant films license to present extreme forms of masculinity and to justify, even celebrate war' (2004: 9). An alternative approach comes in medieval narratives which have a hero who is generally non-combative and whose leadership and admirable qualities lie in other areas. As noted in Chapter 4, the female heroine is often found in medieval imaginaries, and while some may be warriors, the majority are not and rely instead on their intelligence, wisdom and assertiveness. A range of male heroes also rely on their wit and learning. These include the monk/detective, as represented by Brother Cadfael (Derek Jacobi) in *Cadfael* (1994–1998), based on the book series by Ellis Peters, and Brother William of Baskerville in *The Name of the Rose* (Eco, 1980). A trio of brilliant young architects are the heroes of Ken Follett's *Knightsbridge* trilogy.

At the greatest extreme from the military hero are humble servants. Generally played for laughs, they exhibit humanity and realism while trying to look after their masters and survive in a violent medieval world. Pre-eminent is Baldrick in *Blackadder* (1982–1983). Played by actor Sir Tony Robinson, he recounted a conversation with producer John Lloyd just before they started filming the first series. Lloyd predicted that while the series would be a success due to the popularity of Rowan Atkinson in the title role, 'who will they [the audience] be rooting for? The comedy servant, everybody does' (Robinson, 2016: 246). As the knowing dogsbody who was far more intelligent than his masters, Baldrick indeed became the fan favourite with his quotable punchlines. A similar role of a lowly servant was Jacquard (Christian Clavier) in *Les Visiteurs* (1993). In both instances, the servant character provided a different – even subversive – view of medieval hierarchies from the bottom up. As servants, these characters are almost invisible to their aristocratic masters, but they are able to acutely observe their betters, including their foibles and absurdities. A variation of this trope was Samwise Gamgee (Sean Astin) in *The Lord of the Rings* trilogy. As both a Hobbit and Frodo's servant, he is the humblest member of the Fellowship, but his loyalty, resilience and geniality make him critical to the success of the quest.

The centrality of heroes to medieval imaginaries raises key questions. Does a strong hero narrative play out in cultural heritage tourism and attract visitors to certain places? Research into how media-tourism works wrestles with issues of whether it is the scenery/environment or engagement with the characters/people that appeal to potential tourists (see Frost and Laing, 2015, for a summary of this debate). How relevant and appealing is the old-fashioned straightforward hero, the *white knight* of the past? Are audiences more attracted to a flawed hero, who comes with a complex and psychologically charged backstory? How appealing is the anti-hero, or can that be overdone? Is there demand for heroes that are not military? Finally, do female heroes need to be warriors, or can they have other very different attributes? The success of narratives featuring detective monks, architects and servants suggests that there is a role for heroes that are outsiders, operating and observing medieval society from a perspective that is not the mainstream.

The narrative of everyday life

Just as heroes may be dynamic warriors or ordinary people, there are different perspectives about how medieval times should be represented to contemporary audiences. A common approach has been to focus on narrative history, emphasising pivotal battles, rulers and military leaders. In modern historiography, the tendency has been to move away from this approach, with academic historians often seeing it as old-fashioned and elitist. In popular history, it still tends to dominate, as seen in many paperback biographies and histories of military campaigns. The alternative to narrative history is social history, which focusses on the lives of ordinary people.

In contrast to narrative history, social history dominates amongst academic researchers, where there is an increasing tendency to explore the experiences of previously overlooked and marginalised groups, such as women, the poor and ethnic minorities. Whilst not particularly prominent as a subject for popular historical writers, an exception is the Kingsbridge trilogy by Ken Follett. These novels explore the lives of wool-traders, nuns, priests, quarrymen, tavern workers and itinerant workers on building sites. The last of these display parallels with the precarious work of the modern 'gig economy'. Medieval social history is often at the forefront of documentaries. An example of this approach is seen with *Britain's Most Historic Towns: Medieval Lincoln* (2020), which stresses that ordinary people were usually poor, miserable and underfed, explains how Lincoln's medieval economy was based on wool, touches on twelfth-century climate change and finishes with the onset of the Black Death.

How do these divisions play out for cultural heritage tourism? An immediate issue is that various stakeholders, including academic historians, popular historians, tourism operators, destination marketers, host communities and tourists will have different ideas of what is important and should be focussed upon in terms of heritage interpretation. Such diversity of opinion may be healthy and stimulating, but it may also be confusing for those interpreters who want just one approach (Frost, 2006). It does, however, align with the recent philosophy behind the new museum, which emphasises multiple narratives rather than one overarching master narrative (Arnold-de-Simine, 2013; Cook, 2016; Laing and Frost, 2019).

There is a tendency for interpretation at tangible medieval heritage sites to focus on social history. An example of this is the restored kitchen at Glastonbury Abbey (Figure 12.2). The stewardship of such sites is often invested in public or not-for-profit bodies, which see themselves as having an educative role and are accordingly comfortable with this approach. Indeed, some see themselves as having a mission to explore new directions and will focus on social history topics that

Figure 12.2 Social History at Medieval Heritage Sites: The Kitchens at Glastonbury
       Abbey.

Source: Jennifer Frost.

have previously been ignored or understated, such as the role of medieval women
or minority groups (Dempsey *et al.*, 2020). Through using costumed volunteers
and staff, re-enactments and other activations, life in the medieval period can be
'brought to life' for visitors, as in the living history camp at the Battle of Hastings
(Figure 12.3). However, in other instances, narrative history still prevails. At
Tintagel Castle in Cornwall (Chapter 3), the visitor interpretation provided by
English Heritage is primarily social history, whereas many of the visitors are
drawn to it by its association with King Arthur; creating a notable disconnection
between the expectations and perspectives of the two groups. At Warwick Castle
(Chapter 6), the private operators emphasise narrative history through the story of
Warwick the Kingmaker and the War of the Roses. There is a pressing need for
further research into how such differences are strategically managed and whether
or not effective compromises are possible or desirable.

Eco's medievalisms revisited

In Chapter 1, we detailed a framework set out by Umberto Eco (1986). These
were a series of *medievalisms*, which were ways in which the medieval period
could be understood and utilised in modern culture. In this book, we have applied
them to representations of the medieval provided through heritage tourism and
the media. Whilst developed by Eco over a third of a century ago, we found that

Figure 12.3 Social History at a Re-enactment Event: Costumed Volunteers Dyeing
Clothing at the Battle of Hastings.

Source: Warwick Frost.

they were still widely applicable to recent imaginaries of the medieval. Three in
particular stand out as still in widespread usage. The first is the depiction of the
medieval period as a barbaric age, characterised by fighting and cruelty. Apart
from knights, castles and battles, this is also manifested in tourist attractions
incorporating medieval dungeons and torture museums, which may be characterised as 'dark tourism' (Powell and Iankova, 2016). The second – quite contrast-
ingly – is seeing it as a romantic age, often a setting for the telling of love stories.
The third is the age of 'so-called tradition', which characterises the medieval
period as a time of sorcery and magic. In addition, the medieval is often represented in terms of national identity, allowing the construction of narratives about
national stories and legends. Whilst powerfully used in a number of instances, it
is not as ubiquitous as the other three.

Eco's framework is particularly useful for understanding fictional media.
However, there is further scope for applying it to visitor interpretation at medieval heritage sites. As noted in the previous section, such tourist attractions tend
more towards a social history approach as distinct from the narrative history that
is common in fictional media. This raises interesting possibilities as to how that
interpretation may be structured to better satisfy both visitors and other stakeholders. Are there cases – for instance – in which creators of interpretation are
using Eco's framework? Alternatively, it may be that certain of Eco's medievalisms are being commonly used, while others are not. An example of this might be

that while the media embraces magic and fantasy as part of so-called tradition, heritage operators adopting a social history approach may be far less inclined to go down that path. Warwick Castle has its Merlin display, though this seems a rarity undertaken by a private operator.

A young person's Middle Ages

In reviewing Eco's framework, we have identified an additional common use of the Middle Ages – as a setting for fictional media directed at children and young adults. Further research could explore the appeal of this era for children in greater depth, especially in the face of new technological developments. Many books, films, television series and now video games are based on fairy tales and incorporate magical elements such as dragons and unicorns, as well as princesses, knights and castles. Walt Disney's love of the medieval can be seen in his suite of films based around fairy-tale princesses such as Cinderella and Rapunzel, underpinning many girls' romantic fantasies (Otnes and Pleck, 2003; see Chapter 5). His version of the Arthur legend, *The Sword in the Stone* (1963), follows White in depicting Wart (the young Arthur) as a wide-eyed young boy, always up for fun and adventures and innocent of his true identity. Chapter 3 expands this discussion of the intertextuality of the various Arthur narratives. The popular *Harry Potter* series of books and films is also pertinent here. Ward (2017) notes that these books contain 'plotlines and motifs drawn from medieval narratives and … references to medieval people and places, while the films anachronistically compound the effect of the books, especially through their selection of medieval historical sites as set locations'. Many of these filming locations are Gothic cathedrals such as Gloucester and Durham, examined in Chapter 7.

Others build their narrative to capitalise on the acknowledged interest of younger audiences in the medieval period. In some instances, this builds on interests in dressing up and playing with toy swords (Figure 12.4). A series of contemporary films directed at younger audiences have used gentle humour to frame a medieval plotline. An example is *Ella Enchanted* (2004), a romantic comedy vehicle for Anne Hathaway, about a girl who is cursed by a fairy to always do what she is told, and who eventually marries the handsome Prince (Hugh Dancy). The medieval town of Frell where she lives has its own shopping mall, complete with shops such as Wands R'Us and an escalator that is cranked by hand, while Ella's stepsisters read *Medieval Teen* magazine. Animation has also traded on medieval whimsy, with *Shrek* (2001) based on fairy-tale characters, with the green ogre Shrek (Mike Myers) forced to go on a quest to rescue Princess Fiona (Cameron Diaz), who is imprisoned in a castle guarded by a dragon.

Some of these medievalisms are based on the idea of 'the Middle Ages as a lost time of innocence, which corresponds with a widespread cultural desire to view children themselves as avatars of innocence, but both of these desires for innocence are cultural fantasies' (Pugh and Weisl, 2013: 7). While the popular view of medieval childhood as non-existent or without importance has been criticised by historians such as Hanawalt (1995) and Orme (2003), it is fair to say that life expectancies of the time were short, and many people were put to work at a young

Figure 12.4 Toy Swords for Sale in Tintagel.
Source: Jennifer Frost.

age and considered to be of a marriageable age once they reached puberty. Much of this harsh reality is whitewashed from depictions of young knights and princesses, particularly the Disney variety.

Another medievalism involves the 'coming of age' stories (Pugh and Weisl, 2013), such as the Harry Potter series and *The Letter for the King* (Dragt, 1962; television series 2020). A young boy (or girl) must overcome challenges and dangers to become an adult and achieve their destiny. They are further examples of Campbell's (1949) myth of the hero's journey. In *The Sword in the Stone* (White, 1938), Wart is transformed by Merlin into different animals to teach him what makes a good king; symbolising his ultimate transformation from boy to man.

Some final words

Our aim in writing this book was to explore what we saw as the continuing interest in the medieval in the contemporary world in which we live and to examine in particular how this is influenced by media narratives and the way in which this phenomenon is played out in heritage tourism development. It is a huge topic, and we could only scratch the surface in this book, resulting in many worthy topics being beyond its scope. We tried to emphasise voices that are being heard more strongly in both media and tourism narratives, such as women and the Islamic 'Other', as well as the greater focus on everyday life in the medieval period. While we covered some non-Western places such as Japan, this is predominantly a Western view of the medieval. It is a dynamic period of more than a thousand years. We appreciate its variety and fluidity and recognise that an immense body of ongoing historical work is constantly challenging how we interpret and understand this period.

The nineteenth century saw an explosion of passionate interest in the medieval, fuelled by the work of writers, artists and architects. The twentieth century added the strongly visual influences of cinema and television, and the first decades of the twenty-first century have seen even further advances through the use of computer-generated imagery. While these technical advances have stimulated great interest in bringing historical periods to life, medieval stories and legends are what profoundly engage with audiences and readers, often leading them to further their imaginaries through visiting and experiencing heritage sites and attractions. It is the intersection of the media and heritage tourism that we sought to explore in this book, in order to better understand the cultural phenomenon of heritage tourism.

Part of what we have dealt with in this exploration have been time-honoured and well-known stories. Examples include King Arthur, Robin Hood and knights and chivalry, and these may even be viewed as clichéd markers of the medieval, of which little more remains to be said. Despite this, they are still commonly featured in new media productions and remain the mainstays of heritage tourism attractions. Potentially hackneyed, they can be the subject of fresh approaches as new generations reinterpret them. In addition to this established medieval canon, there are lesser-known perspectives and narratives that from time to time are taken up as a basis for new productions by the media, and we have canvassed some of these in this book, including female and non-Western voices and those of ordinary people. It is these unknown or previously unsung stories that we believe will drive medieval imaginaries into the future.

References

Arnold-de-Simine, S. (2013) *Mediating memory in the museum: Trauma, empathy, nostalgia*, London: Palgrave Macmillan.

Batty, C. (2011) *Movies that move us: Screenwriting and the power of the protagonist's journey*, London: Palgrave Macmillan.

BBC (2014) 'Battle of Hastings re-enactment to be staged after absence', *BBC News*, 1 October, https://www.bbc.com/news/uk-england-sussex-29442839 (accessed January 4, 2021).

BBC (2015) 'Stirling screening marks Braveheart film anniversary', *BBC News*, 3 September, https://www.bbc.com/news/uk-scotland-tayside-central-34127673 (accessed January 4, 2021).

Campbell, J. (1949) *The hero with a thousand faces*, London: Fontana, 1993 reprint.

Cook, M.R. (2016) 'Counter-narratives of slavery in the Deep South: The politics of empathy along and beyond River Road', *Journal of Heritage Tourism*, *11*(3), 290–308.

Dempsey, K., Gilchrist, R., Ashbee, J., Sagrott, S., and Stones, S. (2020). 'Beyond the martial façade: gender, heritage and medieval castles', *International Journal of Heritage Studies*, *26*(4), 352–369.

Dragt, T. (1962) *The letter for the king*, London: Pushkin, 2020 reprint.

Driver, M. (2004) 'What's accuracy got to do with It? Historicity and authenticity in medieval film', in M. Driver and S. Ray (Eds.), *The medieval hero on screen: Representations from Beowulf to Buffy* (pp. 19–37), Jefferson, NC and London: McFarland.

Driver, M. and Ray, S. (2004) 'Preface: Hollywood knights', in M. Driver and S. Ray (Eds.), *The medieval hero on screen: Representations from Beowulf to Buffy* (pp. 5–18), Jefferson, NC and London: McFarland.

Eco, U. (1980) *The name of the rose*, London: Vintage, 2004 reprint.

Eco, U. (1986) *Faith in fakes*, London: Secker & Warburg.

Emery, E. (2017) '*Medieval Times*: Tournaments and jousting in twenty-first-century North America', in G. Ashton (Ed.), *Medieval afterlives in contemporary culture*, London: Bloomsbury.

Euronews (2019) 'Battle of Hastings re-enacted after nearly 1000 years', *Euronews*, 13 October, https://www.euronews.com/2019/10/13/battle-of-hastings-re-enacted-after-nearly-1000-years (accessed December 12, 2020).

Frost, W. (2006) '*Braveheart*-ed *Ned Kelly*: historic films, heritage tourism and destination image', *Tourism Management*, *27*(2), 247–254.

Frost, W. and Laing, J. (2013) *Commemorative events: Memory, identities, conflicts*, London and New York: Routledge.

Frost, W. and Laing, J. (2015) *Imagining the American West through films and travel*, London and New York: Routledge.

Hanawalt, B. (1995) *Growing up in medieval London: The experience of childhood in history*, New York: Oxford University Press.

Laing, J.H. and Frost, W. (2019) 'Presenting narratives of empathy through dark commemorative exhibitions during the Centenary of World War One', *Tourism Management*, *74*, 190–199.

Orme, N. (2003) *Medieval children*, New Haven, CT: Yale University Press.

Ortenberg, V. (2006) *In search of the Holy Grail: The quest for the Middle Ages*, London and New York: Hambledon Continuum.

Powell, R. and Iankova, K. (2016) 'Dark London: Dimensions and characteristics of dark tourism supply in the UK capital', *Anatolia, 27*(3), 339–351.

Pugh, T. and Weisl, A. (2013) *Medievalisms: Making the past in the present*, London and New York: Routledge.

Robinson, R.N. and Clifford, C. (2012) 'Authenticity and festival foodservice experiences', *Annals of Tourism Research, 39*(2), 571–600.

Robinson, T. (2016) *No cunning plan: My story*, London: Sidgewick & Jackson.

Skog, D., Wimelius, H., and Sandberg, J. (2018). 'Digital disruption', *Business & Information Systems Engineering, 60*(5), 431–437.

Walker, R. (2018) 'Hobbiton marks two decades stronger than ever', *Waikato Business News*, 4 October, http://wbn.co.nz/2018/10/04/hobbiton-marks-two-decades-stronger-than-ever/ (accessed January 5, 2021).

Ward, R. (2017) Harry Potter and medievalism. In G. Ashton (Ed.), *Medieval afterlives in contemporary culture*, London: Bloomsbury.

Weeks, J. (2018) 'Battle of Hastings revisited: Hundreds re-enact conflict of 1066', *The Guardian Picture Essay*, 16 October, https://www.theguardian.com/artanddesign/2018/oct/16/battle-of-hastings-revisited-reenact-1066 (accessed December 5, 2020).

White, T.H. (1938) *The sword in the stone*, London: Harper Voyager, published in *The Once and Future King* omnibus 2015.

Wickham, C. (2016) *Medieval Europe. From the breakup of the Western Roman Empire to the Reformation*, New Haven, CT and London: Yale University Press.

Filmography

Cinema

Title	Year	Director
Robin Hood	1922	Allan Dwan
The Crusades	1935	Cecil B. De Mille
Snow White and the Seven Dwarfs	1937	David Hand
The Adventures of Robin Hood	1938	Michael Curtiz
Alexander Nevsky	1938	Sergei Eisenstein and Dmitriy Vasilev
Dawn Patrol	1938	Edmund Goulding
Henry V	1944	Laurence Olivier
Cinderella	1950	Clyde Geronimi, Wifred Jackson and Hamilton Luske
Ivanhoe	1952	Richard Thorpe
Knights of the Round Table	1953	Richard Thorpe
The Black Knight	1954	Tay Garnett
King Richard and the Crusaders	1954	David Butler
Prince Valiant	1954	Henry Hathaway
Seven Samurai	1954	Akira Kurosawa
The Court Jester	1955	Melvin Frank and Norman Panama
Lady Godiva of Coventry	1955	Arthur Lubin
The Seventh Seal	1957	Ingmar Bergman
Throne of Blood	1957	Akira Kurosawa
Robin Hood Daffy	1958	Chuck Jones
The Vikings	1958	Richard Fleischer
Sleeping Beauty	1959	Clyde Geronimi
The Magnificent Seven	1960	John Sturges
El Cid	1961	Anthony Mann
Yojimbo	1961	Akira Kurosawa
The Sword in the Stone	1963	Wolfgang Reitherman
Becket	1964	Peter Glenville
A Fistful of Dollars	1964	Sergio Leone
The Long Ships	1964	Jack Cardiff
The War Lord	1965	Franklin Schaffner
Le Samurai	1967	Jean-Pierre Melville
You Only Live Twice	1967	Lewis Gilbert
The Lion in Winter	1968	Anthony Harvey

(Continued)

Title	Year	Director
Red Sun	1971	Terence Young
Monty Python and the Holy Grail	1975	Terry Jones and Terry Gilliam
Robin and Marian	1976	Richard Lester
The Norseman	1978	Charles B. Pierce
Excalibur	1981	John Boorman
Laputa: Castle in the Sky	1986	Hiyao Miyazaki
The Name of the Rose	1986	Jean-Jacques Annaud
The Princess Bride	1987	Rob Reiner
Henry V	1989	Kenneth Branagh
The Little Mermaid	1989	Ron Clements and John Musker
Beauty and the Beast	1991	Gary Trousdale and Kirk Wise
Robin Hood: Prince of Thieves	1991	Kevin Reynolds
Robin Hood	1991	John Irwin
Aladdin	1992	Ron Clements and John Musker
Les Visiteurs	1993	Jean-Marie Poiré
Braveheart	1995	Mel Gibson
First Knight	1995	Jerry Zucker
Pocahontas	1995	Mike Gabriel and Erik Goldberg
Ever After: A Cinderella Story	1998	Andy Tennant
Mulan	1998	Tony Bancroft and Barry Cook
Ronin	1998	John Frankenheimer
Ghost Dog: The Way of the Samurai	1999	Jim Jarmusch
The 13th Warrior	1999	John McTiernan and Michael Crichton
A Knight's Tale	2001	Brian Helgeland
Harry Potter and the Philosopher's Stone	2001	Chris Columbus
The Lord of the Rings: The Fellowship of the Ring	2001	Peter Jackson
Shrek	2001	Andrew Adamson and Vicki Jenson
Harry Potter and the Chamber of Secrets	2002	Chris Columbus
Kill Bill Vol. 1	2003	Quentin Tarantino
The Last Samurai	2003	Edward Zwick
The Lord of the Rings: Return of the King	2003	Peter Jackson
Ella Enchanted	2004	Tommy O'Haver
Howl's Moving Castle	2004	Hiyao Miyazaki
King Arthur	2004	Antoine Fuqua
National Treasure	2004	Jon Turteltaub
Kingdom of Heaven	2005	Ridley Scott
The Da Vinci Code	2006	Ron Howard
Tales from Earthsea	2006	Goro Miyazaki
Enchanted	2007	Kevin Lima
The Hurt Locker	2008	Kathryn Bigelow
Ponyo	2008	Hiyao Miyazaki
The Princess and the Frog	2009	Ron Clements and John Musker
The Young Victoria	2009	Jean-Marc Vallée

(Continued)

Title	Year	Director
Robin Hood	2010	Ridley Scott
Tangled	2010	Nathan Greno and Byron Howard
The Warrior's Way	2010	Sngmoo Lee
Argo	2012	Ben Affleck
Brave	2012	Mark Andrews, Brenda Chapman and Steve Purcell
The Hobbit: An Unexpected Journey	2012	Peter Jackson
47 Ronin	2013	Carl Rinsch
Frozen	2013	Chris Buck and Jennifer Lee
Dracula Untold	2014	Gary Shore
Maleficent	2014	Robert Stromberg
Northmen	2014	Claudio Fäh
Outcast	2014	Nicholas Powell
Last Knights	2015	Kazuaki Kiriya
The Magnificent Seven	2016	Antoine Fuqua
Moana	2016	Ron Clements and John Musker
Beauty and the Beast	2017	Bill Condon
King Arthur: Legend of the Sword	2017	Guy Ritchie
Thor: Ragnarok	2017	Taika Waititi
Avengers: Infinity War	2018	Anthony and Joe Russo
The Outlaw King	2018	David Mackenzie
Robin Hood	2018	Otto Bathurst
Frozen II	2019	Chris Buck and Jennifer Lee
The Kid Who Would Be King	2019	Joe Cornish
The King	2019	David Michôd
Hood: A Legend Reborn	In production	Adam Collins

Television

Title	Year	Creator
Robin Hood	1953	BBC
The Adventures of Robin Hood	1955–1960	ITV (UK)
The Samurai	1962–1965	Shinichi Nishimura
Doctor Who	1963 onwards	BBC
Monkey	1978–1981	Nippon TV
Antiques Roadshow	1979 onwards	BBC
Blackadder	1982–1983	BBC and Channel 7 (Australia)
Robin of Sherwood	1984–1986	Harlech Television
Teenage Mutant Ninja Turtles	1987–1996	Kevin Eastman, Peter Laird, David Wise and Fred Wolf
Seinfeld	1989–1998	Larry David and Jerry Seinfeld
Cadfael	1994–1998	Central Television
Friends	1994–2004	David Crane and Marta Kauffman
The Choir	1995	BBC
Band of Brothers	2001	Dreamworks
Mists of Avalon	2001	Uli Edil (Director)
The Lion in Winter	2003	Andrei Konchalovsky (Director)

(Continued)

Title	Year	Creator
Robin Hood	2006–2009	BBC
The Big Bang Theory	2007–2019	Chuck Lorre and Bill Prady
Merlin	2008–2013	Johnny Capps, Julian Jones, Jake Michie and Julian Murphy
Desperate Romantics	2009	BBC
Horrible Histories	2009 onwards	Lion Entertainments
The Pillars of the Earth	2010	Sergio Mimica-Gezzan (Director)
Sherlock	2010–2017	Mark Gatiss and Steven Moffat
The War of the Roses: A Time Team Special	2011	Jeremy Cross
Game of Thrones	2011–2019	David Benioff and D.B. Weiss
The Hollow Crown	2012–2016	Neal Street Productions
Sicily Unpacked	2012	BBC
World Without End	2012	Michael Caton-Jones (Director)
Richard III: The King in the Car Park	2013	Louise Osmond
Vikings	2013–2021	Michael Hirst
Marco Polo	2014–2016	John Fusco
The Last Kingdom	2015 onwards	Carnival Film & Television
Wolf Hall	2015	BBC
Norsemen	2016 onwards	Jon Iver Helgaker and Jonas Torgersen
Victoria	2016–2019	Daisy Goodwin
Knightfall	2017–2019	Don Handfield and Richard Rayner
Britain's Most Historic Towns: Viking York	2018	presenter Alice Roberts
Daybreak	2019	Aron Eli Coleite
The Name of the Rose	2019	Giacomo Battiato
Robbie Hood	2019	Ludo Studio
Britain's Most Historic Towns: Medieval Lincoln	2020	Alice Roberts (presenter)
The Letter for the King	2020	William Davies

Index

Note: Page numbers in *italics* refer to figure; page numbers in **bold** refer to table.

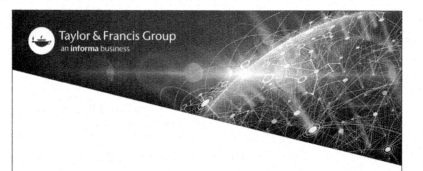